BOOKS BY ANN AND LARRY WALKER

The Pleasures of the Canary Islands

The Best of California

Tapas

Tequila: The Book

A Season in Spain

TO THE HEART OF SPAIN

Food and Wine Adventures Beyond the Pyrenees

ANN AND LARRY WALKER

BERKELEY HILLS BOOKS
BERKELEY, CALIFORNIA

PUBLISHED BY
BERKELEY HILLS BOOKS
P.O. BOX 9877, BERKELEY
CALIFORNIA 94709

COVER DESIGN AND MAP BY LISA SCHULZ/ELYSIUM, SAN FRANCISCO

COVER PHOTOGRAPH: SHEEP CHEESE MAKER
IDIAZABAL, BASQUE COUNTRY
PHOTOGRAPH BY PIERRE HUSSENOT/AGENCE TOP

MANUFACTURED IN THE UNITED STATES OF AMERICA

PUBLISHER'S CATALOGING IN PUBLICATION
(PREPARED BY QUALITY BOOKS INC.)
WALKER, ANN, 1944-
TO THE HEART OF SPAIN: FOOD AND WINE ADVENTURES
BEYOND THE PYRENEES/ANN AND LARRY WALKER.
P.   CM.
INCLUDES BIBLIOGRAPHICAL REFERENCES AND INDEX.
PREASSIGNED LCCN: 96-86239
ISBN 0-9653774-0-7

I. SPAIN—DESCRIPTION AND TRAVEL. 2. COOKERY, SPANISH.
3. COOKERY—SPAIN. 4. WINE AND WINEMAKING—SPAIN.
I. WALKER, LARRY, 1936- II. TITLE

DP43.2.W35 1997   914.604'83
QBI96-40272

To our sons—David, Jude and Morgan—
who have always been ready
with knife, fork and wine glass.

Table of Contents

Acknowledgments

The history of this book goes back several years, including an earlier incarnation as *A Season in Spain*, from which much of this book has been adapted. Our deepest thanks go to Martha Casselman, our former literary agent, who was willing to take on a nontraditional food book; to José Pons, one of the first to introduce us to the pleasures of the Spanish table; to Marimar Torres, whose two books, *The Spanish Table* and *The Catalan Country Kitchen* are milestones in the development of Spanish cuisine; and to our good friend Ron Scherl, who helped with planning of the book.

Our thanks go especially to all those bartenders, waiters, cooks and friends in Spain who were there to patiently answer our thousands of questions and point the way to the next step on the journey.

¡Viva España!

Preface

To the Heart of Spain is not quite a cookbook or a wine book, nor is it a travel guide. It is, instead, a little of all three, with a smattering of history and culture to boot. For those of you who want recipes, you will find them. For those of you curious about wine, you will, we hope, come away with a better understanding of the range and exceptional quality of Spanish wines. For those of you who want to know where to stay and where to eat, you will find stories of our adventures in favorite places.

What this book is really about is Spain. Spanish days and Spanish nights. Spain is unknown territory to many otherwise experienced travelers. Even though the pace has quickened a bit, Spain is not to be taken at full gallop, not to be rushed, either at the table or elsewhere. An example: rarely in Spain—except in Madrid and Barcelona, which are being internationalized to a degree—does one see people eating while walking down the sidewalk. Even American-style fast food establishments have had to adapt to Spanish attitudes, radically changing their industrial, do-it-fast-and-get-it-over-with approach. McDonald's and Pizza Hut have added more seating space, and taken on more the ambiance of cafés. They stay open later at night, serve more coffee and pastries, and often have mini-tapas bars.

It is a pace and style of life that many fear is being swallowed up as Spain moves rapidly into a newly integrated Europe. And it is true that Spanish industry has become more efficient, the Spanish businessman more aware of that dreadful scrip, 'time is money,' that is paid out in solemn misery all over the post-industrial world. Regular visitors to Spain can see changes almost from month to month as the country pushes more confidently into modern Europe.

No one can expect Spain to stand still just so it can offer charming, quaint vistas to tourists. It has been the 'Mexico of Europe'—a playground for the more affluent—for far too long. But post-Franco, it seems at times too intent on becoming the 'Florida of Europe.'

There are a number of encouraging signs, however, that Spain—as always—will remain Spain, even while learning to hustle a bit. At best, many Spaniards have found a way to fit the hustle into a traditional, more graceful style of life.

One of the great attractions of Spain for the modern traveler is the feeling that something a little out of the ordinary might happen at any time. This is because Spain is not quite Europe, not quite Africa, but altogether something else. In Spain, the unexpected is only a step or two away. Life often takes a slightly bizarre, almost surrealistic twist, as if you were living on the extended set of a high budget film noir.

We wish you a good journey.

Ann and Larry Walker

TO THE HEART OF SPAIN

A Zigzag History

Donde menos se piensa salta la liebre.
Where one least expects it, the hare leaps up.
—Spanish proverb

We landed in Paris in April with light snow falling. From there we traveled to Bordeaux, researching wine and food stories for magazines. The weather steadily worsened. In Bordeaux it alternated between sleet, hail, rain, thunder and lightning, with brief periods of pale sunshine. We promised ourselves that when our work in France was over, we would reward ourselves with a few days in Spain.

Although the almond trees were in flower, it was snowing when we crossed the border at Puigcerda, after a harrowing drive up the mountain pass in heavy snow in a rented Renault without chains. Sheer craziness. The road dropped rapidly beyond the frontier and in a few miles we were in sunshine. We stopped at a truck driver's café, perhaps ten kilometers into Spain.

At once we felt at home. The counter man encouraged our rusty Spanish. He made no fuss about accepting our French francs. (You can imagine what the French reaction would have been had we offered pesetas, even a few kilometers north.) We drank hearty red wine with slices of cured Valencia ham, rough bread and olives.

One of the truck drivers came over to ask if we had driven over the pass? Was it still snowing? He had no chains, should he wait? Others joined the conversation with advice, concern, a little friendly bantering that became more friendly as we persisted with our Spanish.

Very soon, someone brought another bottle of wine. Our benefactor had a cousin who worked in San Francisco. Would we take his cousin's name and address, and call him when we returned to California? Perhaps buy his cousin a small brandy? Yes, yes, we could do all that.

After weeks with the very proper, very correct, but never very friendly Bordelaise, it was wonderful. It was Spain. The wine was cheap and good. The food was abundant and tasty. The sun was shining.

One is accustomed to thinking of history as a linear affair, a stepping stone series of dates leading in an orderly, reasonable fashion directly to now. It's best to shed that attitude when considering the history of Spain. It's a zigzag, a mosaic of time and people moving sideways, inside-out and sometimes backwards like a rabbit in a field. Sometimes, again rabbit-like, it seems to come to a stop, to be frozen midcourse.

In Spain, perhaps more than anywhere in Europe, the geography of the land has played a major role in political and cultural history. It has certainly played a role in what people put in their cooking pots.

Spain is a bewildering patchwork of mountain ranges dominated by huge rock outcroppings. With the exception of the Ebro and the Guadalquivir, the rivers are short and often dry. Alexander Dumas and Washington Irving have both left us accounts of their disappointment at the size and water volume—or lack of it—of Spanish rivers. Yet, to the Moors, Spain was a land of rivers. Coming from the deserts of North Africa and the Middle East, even short, scrawny rivers that often run dry must have been impressive to them. The mountain ranges and lack of navigable rivers have made communications difficult and, no doubt, played a major role in Spain's lack of national unity.

One enters Spanish cultural history about fourteen thousand years ago in Basque country, at the cave of Altamira with its remarkable animal paintings. There are other cave paintings scattered throughout northern Spain. Haunting pieces of Spain's distant past. The Basques themselves may be the descendants of cave dwellers from the Pyrenees. Their origin and language remain a mystery. People still live in caves in Spain. Gypsies have been living for centuries in caves in the hills around Granada. In fact, there is a flourishing subculture there, with bars and music, cafés and craft shops.

The first historical people in Spain were the Iberians, a desert-dwelling tribal folk from North Africa, who settled southern and central Spain in slow waves of migration, starting perhaps as early as 3000 BC and continuing until the sixth century BC. These are the people who gave their name to the entire peninsula. The word Iber is believed to be based on their word for river, and the River Ebro is probably the northern limit of Iberian occupation. The center of Iberian culture was apparently around Valencia, on the Mediterranean coast.

Early writers were impressed by the Iberian talent for war. The early Roman writer, Pompeius Trogus wrote that the Iberians 'prefer war to ease and, should they lack foes without, seek them within. Rather than betray a secret they will often die under torment, setting a silent reserve before life itself. Active of body, restless of spirit, they commonly set more store by their horses and fighting accouterment than by the blood of their kin.'

The Phoenicians were active in Spain as early as the twelfth century BC, calling in at Valencia to trade with the Ibers. They also founded the cities of Cádiz and Málaga in southern Spain. The Phoenicians were after the silver and gold of Spanish mines, and Spain may be the semi-legendary Biblical land of Tarshish, so rich with mineral wealth that Phoenician trading ships were said to return with anchors of silver.

A few centuries later, Celts from northern Europe began crossing the Pyrenees, often mingling with the Ibers in a cultural mix called Celtiberians. The Celts themselves are a bit of a mystery, appearing out of northern and central Europe, worshipping strange gods, including a kind of beer-swilling backwoods Dionysus. The Celtic influence remains dominant in Galicia and Asturias.

In considering the history of the Mediterranean, the Greeks always turn up sooner or later. Beginning about the seventh century BC, Greek trading posts were established in the Balearic Islands and along the southeast coast, in competition with the Phoenicians. Then came the Carthaginians. Carthage, under the leadership of Hamilcar Barca, seized most of Andalusia and the Valencian coastal area north to Barcelona in the lull following the First Punic War with Rome—which Carthage lost. The city of Barcelona was named after Barca. He also established Carthago Nova, today's Cartagena, as the capital of Spain. It was his son, Hannibal, who led an army, using elephants as a kind of armored division, over the Pyrenees, the Alps, and into Italy where he won every battle but lost the war, and his elephants as well.

✦✧✦

As can be seen, it is remarkable how tangled early Spanish history is. It is even more remarkable that it stays that way right up to the day before yesterday. Everything has seemed to happen at the same time, with different groups of people arriving from all directions, sometimes trading with each other, sometimes killing each other.

Even the various names given Spain and the Peninsula are difficult to sort out. The name Iberia has stuck pretty well, but the Greeks called Spain *Hesperia,* meaning something like 'land of the setting sun.' The Carthaginians called it *Ispania,* from *span,* their word for rabbit, so *Ispania* means 'land of the rabbits.' When the Romans came in the third century BC, they drove out the Carthaginians, but kept the name *Hispania,* which has evolved into the modern *España.*

There are rabbits shown on early Iberian coins, and some variation on rabbit stew is one of the main and often most tasty dishes of the Spanish countryside. Considering also that the erratic course of Spanish history could serve as a kind of ideograph of a rabbit running, *España* does seem an appropriate name.

There are scoffers who say that *España* is actually a Basque word meaning frontier or boundary. Since no one knows anything for sure about the origins of the Basque or their language, it is easy enough to make that statement. But since there was no written Basque language until about the tenth century, their claim to the naming of Spain is weak.

Virginia Woolf—not noted as a Spanish scholar but strong on language—offers perhaps the strongest evidence for the rabbit theory in her book, *Flush,* a biography of Elizabeth Barrett Browning's cocker spaniel. Woolf wrote, 'Many million years ago the country which is now called Spain seethed uneasily in the ferment of creation. Ages passed; vegetation appeared; where there is vegetation the law of Nature has decreed that there shall be rabbits; where there are rabbits, Providence has ordained there shall be dogs.' And if the dogs chase spans, or rabbits, they could be called Spaniels. And the Spaniel is, of course, of Spanish origin.

✦✧✦

The Romans, whose appreciation for rabbit is apparent in Apicius' first century cookbook, *De Re Coquinaria,* began their conquest of Spain even as Hannibal and his elephant brigade were still in Italy. In 209 BC the chief Carthaginian base, Cartagena, fell to Rome, and in 205 BC the last Carthaginians were driven from Spain. The Roman conquest of the peninsula was virtually completed in 133 BC with the fall of the Celtiberian city of Numantia, north of Madrid, although there were still holdouts in the mountains until the time of Augustus almost a century later. The *Pax Romana* lasted in Spain for five centuries, with legions settled in for a good bit of serious road building, bridge construction and general civilizing.

The Phoenicians had been interested primarily in the rich deposits of gold, silver, copper and iron that were found throughout the peninsula. The Greeks were not above taking an interest in silver and gold, but the Greeks also turned to agriculture. Olives, olive oil, wheat and wine, along with wax, honey, fish and wool, were all exported from Greek settlements. Spanish olive oil was recognized then as now as being of superior quality. So when the Romans arrived, they found a thriving agricultural trading economy, with connections all around the Mediterranean. And the center of that agricultural economy was—and to a large degree still is—the olive.

It is probably impossible for us to fully understand the importance of the olive in the ancient Mediterranean world. We are more accustomed to thinking of the olive as a green or black decorative flourish on the appetizer plate. Olive oil is more central to our kitchens, but still used by many people as simply one of several virtually interchangeable cooking oils.

To the Greeks and other Mediterranean people, however, the olive was central. Waverly Root notes in *Food*, 'It has thus, over a period of five thousand years or more, shaped the cuisines of the Middle East, Greece, Italy, Spain and southern France as we know them today and as they are likely to remain.'

The goddess Athene is said to have brought the olive tree to Greece at the time of the founding of the capital city. Athene struck the ground with her spear and an olive tree sprang up. The grateful Greeks named the city Athens in her honor. (Athene would be an excellent candidate for anyone's kitchen goddess. According to the poet Robert Graves, she invented the earthenware pot, an essential element in the Spanish kitchen.)

The olive tree itself is not native to Spain. The cultivation of the olive appears to have spread from the eastern Mediterranean, where it had been cultivated since Neolithic times. Egypt, Syria, Palestine and even Crete have been offered as the original home of the olive. No doubt it was brought into cultivation many times in many places. The olive gradually became widespread enough to enter into commerce by 2500 BC, when Egyptian records show olive oil being imported from Crete.

For anyone who has driven for hours through the olive groves of Andalusia in the south of Spain, it is difficult to believe that the tree hasn't always been a part of the Spanish landscape. But it was introduced to Spain relatively late, about the fourth or fifth century BC, by the Carthaginians and Greeks.

Like the olive, wheat was grown everywhere in the Mediterranean. It was probably the first crop planted by man, perhaps about ten thousand years ago on the upper Tigris. There is evidence of wheat in Spain from Mesolithic sites, although it is impossible to know whether it was wild or cultivated. Spring-ripening wheat is perfectly adaptable to the often erratic and always sparse rainfall of much of Spain, since the little rain that does fall comes in late winter and spring, just when it is most needed. We have seen vestiges of ancient terraced wheat fields in Catalonia, once an important wheat exporting area.

✦〜✦

One can think of Mediterranean agriculture as a triad. If the olive and wheat are two parts of the triad, the grape is the third. The history of the vine is obscure. Or at least the principal wine-producing vines, *vitis vinifera*. Various forms of vine grow almost everywhere in the world, but few make wine worth bothering about. It is *vinifera* that gives us Cabernet Sauvignon, Chardonnay and the other varietals we think of as wine grapes.

Generally, the home area of *vinifera* is thought to be somewhere between the Black Sea and the Caspian Sea. There were grapes in Spain in Neolithic times, but it is uncertain if they were *vinifera*. It is difficult enough to sort out just what vines one is dealing with in modern Spain, much less 15,000 years ago. What is certain is that by the eighth or ninth century BC, the Phoenicians were trading in wine from Spain. A few centuries later, the Greeks brought the Malvasia grape, a *vinifera* variety, and planted it extensively along the Mediterranean coast, south of Tarragona. By the time of the Romans, Malvasia was grown through much of Spain.

There is no way to know, of course, what these early wines tasted like. But there are plenty of written records about winemaking, which was well established in the Middle East and parts of China by 3000 BC. There is an ancient Chinese text dated 2285 BC which tells of a man being punished for blending grape wine and rice wine. The Egyptians were the first, as far as we know, to vintage date wine and to designate wine from selected vineyards. An Egyptian wine label from the time of Ramses III in the twelfth century BC reads, 'In the year thirty, good wine from the well-irrigated terrain of the temple of Ramses II in Per-amon. The chief of the wine-dressers, Tutmes.' Like most wine writing today, that tells us quite a bit about the wine but not what it tastes like.

The wines of the classical Mediterranean world are described by contemporaries as very sweet and very aromatic. Probably they were sweet because the grapes used for winemaking were naturally high in sugar at maturity. Also, many wines would have fair amounts of residual sugar remaining after fermentation because the inefficient wild yeasts would die or go dormant before converting all the sugar to alcohol.

Oxygen is the enemy of wine. In fact, a modern California winemaker has described his job as knowing when to intervene to keep fermented grape juice from turning to vinegar, as it will given too much exposure to oxygen. Ancient winemakers had no way of completely sealing a vessel to prevent oxygen from reaching wine—at least no way inexpensive enough to use for mass-produced wines—so many strange things were added to wine to keep oxygen out.

The Greeks sealed wine amphoras with resin plugs, for example, and actually developed a tasted for resined wines, which they drink to this day. The Romans and others floated olive oil on top of wine. Infusions of various herbs were also added to wine to mask vinegary flavors. For a time, it was the fashion in Rome to smoke wines. Open wine containers were placed in the chimneys or smoke holes of houses to give the wine a smoky flavor and preserve it. We may be better off not knowing just what these wines did taste like.

The Greeks early on associated the spread of the vine with the spread of civilization. Dionysus, the Greek god of wine, was much more than the drunken lout the Romans made him as Bacchus. The stories surrounding Dionysus from early Greek tradition identify him as the builder of libraries and the founder of cities all across the Middle East and into India.

The god of wine also had his dark side, which Miguel Torres captures well in *Wines and Vineyards of Spain*. 'The Greeks had explored the field of human psychology and created two gods, representing the poles of human life. Apollo, the god of light, was cold, temperate and intellectual, and his code of conduct, inscribed in the temple at Delphi, could be summarized as: "Know thyself and do nothing to excess." His counterpart, Dionysus, was the god of the subconscious, of instinct, impulse and intoxication, and so came to be known as the god of wine, for it is wine that sets men free from cold reason and bares the inner being, or, as the Romans said, *In vino veritas*.'

The Romans vastly extended the vineyards of Spain. Although wine had been made and traded in Rioja since the time of the Phoenicians, the Romans improved the region's vineyards, planting new varieties brought from Italy, as they did everywhere in Spain. The Romans also brought Christianity and with it the institution of the Catholic Church, one of the strongest influences—for better or for worse—on the Spanish character. The Christian experience was vastly different in Spain than it was anywhere else in the world because of the long centuries of warfare against the Moors.

The entire experience of the Christian Reconquest is very difficult for us to imagine today. Perhaps the nearest we can come to understanding it would be to imagine that the nineteenth century Indian wars in North America had lasted eight centuries, and that they had been fought against an often superior foe professing a hated religion. But even that act of imagination falls short in a number of ways. The Reconquest was a war against an invader; the ground fought over was regarded as Christian and sacred, not new territory to be exploited.

Let's backtrack for a second and remember that between the Romans and the Moors stood the barbarians. Beginning in the early years of the fifth century AD, three different Germanic tribes—the Suevi, the Vandals and the Alans—swept into Spain from the north. But the long-range impact of the barbarian tribes on Spain is slight. Their impact on food and wine is nonexistent, so we will banish them from history's kitchen and get right to the Moors.

It is the Moorish occupation that makes Spanish cuisine so completely different from that of the other former Roman provinces of the
western Mediterranean. For although Spanish food is firmly rooted in
that broader Mediterranean cuisine, it has been bent into curious patterns and delicious detours by the Moors. The development of a first-
rate cuisine can take place only in a fairly stable political and social
situation, which the Moors achieved over much of Spain for centuries.

It is impossible to overestimate the impact of the Arab kitchen on
the cuisine of Spain, and through that, the food of the entire western
Mediterranean basin. As one small example, there is *frumenty*. *Larousse
Gastronomique*, which many cooks have used, for good or ill, as the standard encyclopedia of the kitchen, describes *frumenty* as a 'very old country dish, consisting of a porridge or gruel made from wheat boiled with
milk, then sweetened and spiced. Originating in Touraine, it is mentioned as a dessert in *La Menagier de Paris* (1383), being made with milk
in which almonds have been boiled to give flavor.'The use of almonds is
a dead giveaway that we are dealing with an Arab dish, one that did not
originate in Touraine, but either in Spain or North Africa.

Although the term 'Moors' is used as if the invaders were all one
people, they were actually even more disparate than the Germanic tribes
that briefly replaced the Romans in Spain. The invading army was com-
posed of Arabs, Syrians, Egyptians and North Africans, but the unify-
ing force was the Arab language and religion. And an almost sensual
love of food. The Arabs brought the heavy, aromatic spices of the Mideast and the Far East: cinnamon, cloves, nutmeg, and other goodies that
the rest of Europe would not see in any quantity for centuries. They
brought cumin seeds and almonds. They brought the art of drying fruits
of all sorts. They brought the bitter orange. Arab traders brought sugar
cane and rhubarb, quinces, apples and quails, pomegranates and figs.
Saffron and rice.

↜↝

Rice as a cooking ingredient originated somewhere in southeast
Asia probably no later than 3000 BC. One school of modern food
scholarship points to Thailand, while another school opts for China.
Alexander the Great found rice growing in India, and while it is some-

times mentioned by classical writers, there is no evidence at all that it was ever grown in Europe until the Moors brought it to Andalusia and Valencia in the eighth century.

There occurred then one of those moments in the history of food when all the right materials were in the right place at the right time. Rice, saffron and abundant seafood. From those three elements came the best known of all Spanish dishes, *paella.* The dish itself originated around Valencia, a Catalan speaking area. The name comes from the Catalan word for a skillet or cooking pan, *paellera.*

Saffron had been known to the Romans. It was widely cultivated in the eastern Mediterranean and had been an important element of Phoenician trade. Although it grew wild in Italy, Rome imported saffron from Greece. Its use in Europe died out after Rome fell. In classical times, its chief uses had been as a dye, as a perfume and in certain rituals and ceremonies. When the Arabs brought it to Spain as a kitchen herb, it was regarded as an entirely new condiment.

It takes between seventy and eighty thousand saffron flowers to make one pound of saffron. Given that the preparation of saffron is so labor intensive—and skilled labor at that—the production of culinary saffron is limited to those societies willing to divert more than a normal amount of labor, and therefore money, to the kitchen. Then as now, saffron is sold in small containers, by the ounce, in the south of France and in Spain. And a little goes a long way.

Just where and when rice and saffron were first combined is impossible to say. *Paella* may have had an ancestor somewhere in the Middle East even before the Arabs arrived in Spain. The other legendary Mediterranean dish that combines rice and saffron, *Risotto alla milanese,* is first mentioned in the year 1574, certainly several centuries after the creation of *paella.*

There are various herbs that can cast a yellow glow over a dish—safflower and turmeric come immediately to mind—but none has quite the privileged place in the kitchen that saffron has. Its role in *bouillabaisse,* as well as in *risotto,* must go back to the Moors in Spain. There is simply no other source for a culinary use of saffron in Europe.

But whatever culinary treasures the Arabs brought to Spain, and through Spain to other points in Europe, the Christians were not impressed. The Reconquest of the Spanish peninsula began in 722, at the battle of Covadonga deep in Basque country, within a few years of the initial Moorish invasion. Very soon, Christian armies emerged from the Pyrenees to begin the long march south. The eight-hundred-year war of Reconquest began.

The frontier was always a patchwork of conflicting alliances. A Christian king might well be allied with a Moorish prince against other Moors. Or a Moor might fight beside Christians against other Moors. The Reconquest followed a back-and-forth rhythm, with momentum always coming from the north. So the incredible Byzantine zigzag of Spanish history continued, with rabbits popping up everywhere.

It is interesting to speculate about the history of Spain, and indeed, of all Europe, if the Moors had pressed their advantage and advanced into the mountains to wipe out the tiny pockets of Christian resistance rather than falling back and giving the petty Christian kings a chance to regroup and strike back. We might have an Arab Spain today. Consider the impact that would have made on the history of Europe and the New World. For a brief time in the eighth century it was a real possibility.

By the mid-fifteenth century, the balance had tilted to the Christians. It had been moving their way for some time. Spain was finally united under Ferdinand and Isabella with the conquest of Granada in 1492. This last Arab stronghold fell on the 2nd of January of that year. Four months later, their Christian majesties issued a proclamation expelling the Jews from Spain.

On balance, the Moors were always more tolerant of Jews than Christians were, perhaps because they respected the intellectual achievements of many Jewish scholars, or because they felt the Jews offered no threat to their power. But the Christians felt otherwise. There had been frequent sporadic outbreaks of Christian intolerance of the Jews. There was an infamous outbreak against the Jews in Seville in 1391 on Ash Wednesday, when the Jewish quarter of the city was burned and hundreds of Jews were killed. What began as a local riot spread to other parts of Andalusia and then into Castile. In the end, thousands of Jews were killed and tens of thousands were forced to convert to Christianity. Although the Jews left strong cultural marks on the history of Spain, they had little influence in the kitchen and the wine cellar.

The same is true of the Gypsies, another wandering, often persecuted people who first reached Spain only a few decades before the Jews were expelled. No one knows for sure where the Gypsies came from. Perhaps they were fleeing Tamerlane, who invaded India in 1398. If so, they made their way fairly rapidly across the Middle East and North Africa, reaching Spain by 1440 at the latest.

Modern Spaniards simply consider the Gypsies to be leftovers of the Moors, and in most of Spain they are held in great contempt. In Barcelona, however, where money is the great equalizer and where there are wealthy Gypsies, they have to some extent entered the mainstream of Spanish life. To foreigners, who may be forgiven for being a bit more romantic about Spain than the residents themselves, the Gypsies carry on part of the spirit of Spain.

✧

Historical astrologers should take a close look at the year 1492 in Spain. The Moors were driven out, the Jews were expelled and the New World was discovered. And from the modest kitchens of the Indians of South and North America, we may round out our Spanish kitchen. The list of foods brought from the Americas is long. Yet, it isn't just the number of foods that is impressive, but the key role that plants such as the tomato were to play in post-Columbian European cuisine.

The Italians were the first to realize the full potential of the tomato, which most likely entered Italy through Naples. Naples came under Spanish rule in 1522, just about the right time for the plant to have arrived from Peru or Mexico. It was present in both countries, though not as widely cultivated as potatoes, beans or squash, which the Spanish also took to Europe.

Of all the foods brought from the New World, the potato is the one the Spanish most readily welcomed into the kitchen. The first potato encountered in the Americas was the sweet potato, noted by Columbus on his first voyage. What early writers called the Virginia potato, and what we curiously call the Irish potato, was cultivated only in the high mountain valleys of the Andes in South America. It was cultivated in Peru as early as 3000 BC.

The Virginia potato was given its name by English and French writers, who were under the impression that Sir Walter Raleigh was the first to bring the potato to Europe. This impression, according to Waverly Root, came about because in 1586, Raleigh provisioned his ships at

Cartagena in South America and took potatoes from there to Virginia.

Spanish tradition has it that Pedro de Cieza de León first brought potatoes to Europe, and that they were planted in the Hospital de la Sangre in Seville as early as 1539. They were immediately recognized as a cheap and filling food for the poor, for soldiers, and doubtless for prisoners.

In a curious historical parallel, potato farming became a specialty in Galicia, the most Celtic area of Spain, foreshadowing the dominance of the potato on the table of those other Celts, the Irish, a few centuries later. From Galicia, potatoes were shipped to Genoa, and Italy was apparently the second country in Europe to cultivate the plant.

The potato is far from the image most have of modern Spanish food, but in fact, it is present in just about every bar in Spain, usually in the form of a *tortilla* or *Patatas bravas*. In the Spanish countryside, the potato is found on almost any plate in ordinary restaurants. It will often be nestled beside some form of the haricot bean, another Spanish import from the Americas.

The name haricot is said to be based on the Aztec word, *ayacotl,* but the conquistadors found them throughout the New World. As with the tomato, the Italians took to them most rapidly. They were a great favorite of the Medicis, who received them as a gift from Pope Clement VII in 1528, who in turn had received them from an unnamed Spaniard from Mexico. The haricot became so popular in Tuscany that other Italians still call the Tuscans *mangiafagioli* or bean eaters. And it was the New World haricot that was the Tuscan favorite, since *fagioli* refers directly to the New World bean, not the fava bean of Europe.

Chocolate was another great find that the Spanish brought back from America. Columbus sent cacao beans to Spain from Nicaragua in 1502, but no one knew quite what to do with them. In 1519, Cortez learned how the Aztecs made and used chocolate. Aztec chocolate was thick, almost a paste, and was often referred to as a soup, most likely the forerunner of today's *molé* sauces. Spain tried to keep the method of preparation a secret and was successful for a time, until Jews who had been expelled from Spain settled in France and the word was out.

The French scorned chocolate in the beginning. The city of Bayonne would not allow chocolate to be made within the city limits. The French attitude had changed considerably by 1846 when Alexander Dumas wrote *From Paris to Cádiz*. Dumas described his first taste of Spanish chocolate:

'A servant entered bearing a tray upon which were arranged five thimble-sized cups full of a thick black fluid, five glasses of clear water, and a little basket containing small sticks of bread, pink and white.

From our earliest days we had heard of the wonderful chocolate one gets in Spain, and we hardly dared raise the cups to our lips, lest this impression should vanish like so many other illusions of childhood. But no! The chocolate was excellent. Unfortunately there was only just enough to taste.'

The New World foods introduced by the Spanish to the European kitchen, including chilies, squashes, corn, potatoes and more, shine far more brightly that all the gold and silver the conquistadors brought back to Spain.

The gold is gone, the potatoes remain.

✦

Across a hot, dusty plaza in a small Andalusian town, a swarm of children erupt from a shadowed street. They are perhaps five or six years old. A few of them have tattered cloths wrapped around their heads. They are in the lead, weaving and twisting, trying to outrun a much larger group of children. The larger group, many waving sticks like swords, are shouting 'Moros! Moros! Mata moros!'

'Moors! Moors! Kill the Moors!'

And soon they do. In a noisy, jumbled battle that swirls around the table where I sit enjoying coffee and brandy. In the sparse shade of an ancient olive tree, they gleefully reenact eight hundred years of Spanish history.

Kill the Moors!

As the battle sweeps on across the plaza, what Moors are not sprawled and giggling dead on the stones, are taken prisoner and marched away up a twisting street in the direction of the church—either to submit to instant baptism or summary execution on the church steps.

I feel a tinge of sympathy for the minority and remember that in my cowboy and Indian days in mid-America, I was usually the one who stuck the feather of a crow in my hair and ambushed the wagon train making its way across the backyard.

As the Rabbit Runs

While following food and wine routes across Spain, we will also be exploring its regions. Geographical features have kept the separate parts of Spain largely isolated until very recently. Added to the geographical isolation are ancient and modern political and linguistic differences that have created a fierce regional pride. As we move through each of these regions, we'll look in detail at the wines and food, but perhaps a hasty overview—as the rabbit runs—might be in order.

We begin in Andalusia in southern Spain, where the Moorish influence is the strongest. Here, a hasty traveler will find the Spain of Hollywood, of Gypsy dancers and handsome men and women on horseback. It is the Spain that probably comes nearest to the media image of Spain with its bullfights, the white towns, towering castles and fountain-filled, tiled, Moorish fantasy palaces. Oddly enough, it's all true. The Andaluz is romantic, is often filled with the sound of Gypsy guitars and the sight of beautiful horses. It is a picture postcard, but it is also one of Spain's poorest regions. The sons and daughters of Andaluz families can often be found in Madrid or Barcelona, working in shops or factories. But they take Andalusia with them.

The only region in Spain poorer than Andalusia is Extremadura, the land of the conquistadors. It's a harsh, unforgiving land of jagged mountain ranges and high meadows, filled with cork trees and ubiquitous menacing storks, lying between Madrid and the Portuguese border. An ancient battlefield, fought over for centuries by Christians and Moors, there is a certain lean grimness about it that can be off-putting to the casual visitor. Although not a popular tourist destination (indeed, one of the least visited areas of Spain) for some, there is a strange fascination about Extremadura. It is the mystic center of the *Hispanidad,* that pan-Hispanic movement which links Spain with Central and South America. This stark stork and sheep country invites one to view life under the eye of eternity.

La Mancha, the heart of the great central plateau of Spain, has the same brooding intensity as Extremadura, but is somewhat easier. Life is lived not quite so near the bone. Its climate can be as harsh as Extremadura's, but there is the occasional flash of Andaluz gaiety, laughter in the teeth of despair. It is difficult to travel in La Mancha and not think of Don Quixote, of past glories. Nothing wrong with that at all. It's a fairly pleasant occupation, perhaps while sitting in a rare patch of shade in a small pueblo plaza, having a glass of the area's light red wine with a plate of olives and a slice of the famed *manchego* cheese.

La Mancha can be puzzling, hard to get a handle on. It seems all cattle, sheep and vines. A flat landscape fitfully punctuated by bits of village, then, suddenly, one looks up and there is Toledo, maybe wrapped in cloud as El Greco painted it, or maybe just gleaming in sunlight. Toledo—about which more later on—is in some ways the spiritual heart of La Mancha as La Mancha is the spiritual heart of Spain. Toledo has, in common with Florence, that rare urban ability to absorb uncounted tourists, yet literally rise above it all. For all its difficulties, torrid summers and freezing winters, La Mancha repays a closer look.

In some ways, the northern regions of Rioja and Navarre seem an extension of La Mancha. The high plains and long dry valleys, however, gradually give way to the rocky outlying riders of the Pyrenees. Crossing the Río Ebro, we run right out of Moorish country. Although the Arabs occasionally raided north of the Ebro, they never really had a firm grip on this part of Spain. Rioja and Navarre are European Spain, or at least seem to be. But dig a little deeper, wander out into the little hill towns outside Pamplona or the countryside around the great winemaking center of Logroño, and you may fetch up in the Middle Ages.

One of the great pilgrim routes of the Middle Ages, the Camino de Santiago de Compostela, runs through northern Rioja and one may still walk it today. We sometimes think of the small towns of Rioja as time machines, even if of somewhat limited scope. This concept is especially strong at table, where the traditional country fare must not have changed since the tenth or eleventh century. Also, in Rioja, one meets the Basques for the first time, people who take food with playful seriousness.

For a closer look at these fascinating people and their cuisine, we must cross the Pyrenees into Basque country. There are two major Basque provinces, País Vasco with the cities of Bilbao and San Sebastián, and Santander, with its major city of the same name. If there was the occasional vestige of Moorish influence remaining in Rioja and Navarre, it is gone entirely here on the beaches of the Atlantic.

In a certain sense, indeed, we would argue that when you cross the watershed of the Pyrenees, you leave Spain. On the south slope, with a few exceptions, the rivers flow toward the Mediterranean, on the north toward the Atlantic. The climate changes abruptly. One could be in Wales or Ireland, it's that green—and damp. There is also, we believe, a subtle change in the people. They truly become more European, a bit more abrupt. Clocks suddenly become important. There are street signs everywhere and taxis whenever needed.

Recrossing the Pyrenees, skirting too close to the border of France for one who is a Francophobe, you nip across the northern bit of Navarre, a land of pine forests, mountains and clear trout streams that could be Colorado (except the truck stops have better food) and make a stop in Aragon. You are truly back in Spain. The Spain of castles and gaunt knights on horseback, their eyes fixed on a heavenly Virgin. You are also back in a drier land, a jumble of mountains and high plains, climbing into the Pyrenees. The plains below look like west Texas or eastern New Mexico, with scattered mesas rising abruptly, often topped with ancient Arab watchtowers. The Aragonese city of Zaragoza on the Río Ebro is one of the underrated treasures of Spain, a modern city with all the pleasing diversions of a city, yet small enough for a brisk walkaround, with outstanding restaurants and tapas bars. More later on Zaragoza.

Beyond Aragon lies Catalonia and the city of Barcelona. Catalonia is a complex region, not only culturally and gastronomically, but geographically. From the dramatic beaches of the Costa Brava, to the high mountain passes in the north, to the rugged interior mountains that divide Catalonia from Aragon and the Levante, Catalonia is an incredibly diverse land. And that diversity is reflected in its people, its food and drink. We sometimes get impatient with Catalans, accusing them of not really being Spanish. They are, of course, delighted by that, and cite centuries of history when Catalonia was one of the major Mediterranean powers.

From the visitor's point-of-view, one great virtue of Catalonia is its marvelous cities. Barcelona is simply one of the most exciting cities in the world. The ancient Roman capital of Tarragona has managed to keep the past alive without making a museum of it. Lérida is a surprisingly cosmopolitan agricultural center with one of the best restaurants in Europe hiding unexpectedly in an old mansion near the rail station.

The small towns and villages of Catalonia can hold one for days, peeling away layer after layer of pleasure. Yet Catalonia in the end is not for the traveler who expects 'Spain' in the travel poster sense of Andalusia. Catalonia is industrial; it bustles and it rarely looks back, or even sideways. The Catalans believe they have everything they need.

Turning back to the south, you follow the ancient Mediterranean coast into the 'garden of Spain': Valencia, Alicante and Murcia, known collectively as the Levante. This is the land of orange groves, of big red wines and *paella*. Valencia itself is a Catalan-speaking area, but, unlike Catalonia proper, the Arabs have left their mark there on food, on architecture and on the pace of life.

Below Valencia, the coast curves in a gentle arc towards Africa. The Balearic Islands are just out of sight out there in the Mediterranean, and beyond them Sicily and Crete. One begins to look east and south. Europe is a cold dream somewhere in the north. In Alicante and Murcia, life begins to take on the pace of Andalusia, which borders Murcia to the west. Clocks have oddly disappeared. You find bars with barrels of sherry lined up, ready for tapping by barmen who keep your score by chalk marks on the wooden bar top. You have come full circle, and the grapes are heavy on the vine.

✦〜✦

You may get the impression while reading this book that the Spanish eat a great deal. That is not strictly true. They do spend a lot of time eating, but don't eat a lot. Once a young Spaniard of seventeen came to visit us in the States. After a few days we asked him what his impression of America was to that point.

He replied at once, 'There are so many fat people.'

His point was well taken. There are very few fat people in Spain, even though the Spanish put in a lot of time at the table. It begins with a light breakfast in the morning, perhaps a roll, coffee, or chocolate, often taken standing at a bar.

For field workers, there will be a mid-morning break for a substantial snack. In the city, most workers will take only a coffee break before lunch, which typically isn't until one-thirty or two o'clock in the afternoon. Lunch is the most substantial meal of the day, both in the amount of food served and in the length of time—often one and a half or two hours. There has been a ripple of movement in Spain to have shorter 'American-style' lunches, but it hasn't made much headway.

The typical lunch break is from one o'clock until four or even five o'clock. Stores and shops are closed; offices are either closed or on skeleton staff. Business resumes from four or five, until seven or eight in the evening, followed by tapas and dinner at ten or eleven o'clock. If dinner is at home, it is very light, perhaps no more than an extended tapas or a bowl of soup and bread. If eating out, dinner will be a more elaborate affair of several courses lasting until well past midnight.

Andalusia

Andalusia is one of Spain's largest regions. Covering over two million acres, it is roughly the size of Portugal and stretches across the southern tier of Spain from the Atlantic Ocean to the Mediterranean Sea. In the north, Andalusia reaches the plateau of La Mancha, and in the south extends to Gibraltar, where one can catch a tantalizing glimpse of Africa. Throughout, it is crossed and recrossed by mountain ranges, including the huge massif of the Sierra Nevada, the highest mountain range in Spain.

Andalusia can be unbearably hot in the summer. Some of the highest temperatures ever recorded have been reached in Seville. In summer, follow the Spanish lead and take your walkabouts in the morning. Summer nights can also be warm, although more tolerable. Winter temperatures are moderate, with light rainfall along the coast. It can be quite cold in the mountains, with brief snowstorms, but generally sweater weather prevails.

Andalusia was the site of the ancient, almost legendary kingdom of Tartessos, centered around modern day Seville. It was the gold and silver of Tartessos that first attracted the Phoenicians and Greeks to Spain. Already by the ninth century BC, Phoenicians were shipping wine from Cádiz. The Phoenician town of Xera is most likely Jerez de la Frontera, capital of the sherry district today.

After passing through the hands of Carthaginians, Romans and Vandals, Andalusia fell to the Moors in the famous battle of Guadalete, near Jerez, in 711. Moorish influence is reflected everywhere in Andalusia—in the architecture and certainly in the cuisine. Despite strictures in the Koran against alcohol, vineyards thrived under the Moors, and the ancient trade with England in wine began as early as the fourteenth century during Moorish rule. Although the Moors themselves were forbidden wine, they had no objection to Christians living in their territories making it for their own use or even selling it. In either case, the Moors collected the taxes and let the Christians deal with their own God in the matter of alcohol.

Today, Andalusia is one of Spain's sixteen autonomous regions, governed by the Junta de Andalucía. However the individual provinces within Andalusia are also strongly independent, which reflects the political picture for all of Spain.

Almost everything you could want, as a cook or as an eater, can be found in Andalusia. The seafood and shellfish are excellent and widely available. There are olives, avocados, citrus, nuts, fresh berries and vegetables of all sorts in every season. Parts of Andalusia, such as Huelva near the frontier with Portugal, grow three crops of garden produce annually and export fresh vegetables to northern Europe throughout the year.

There is lamb, goat, excellent beef and, of course, rabbit and partridge, which are now raised commercially. Wild game—venison, pigeon, partridge and boar—also plays an important part at the Andalusian table.

The Andalusian kitchen has roots in both Mediterranean and Moorish cuisine. Depending on where you are, you could get the impression that Andalusian cooking is fairly light and delicate. If you believe that, you've been in Jerez. In the mountains outside the major cities, you'll find heartier peasant cooking—stews of lamb, rabbit, or fowl. And hams are everywhere, especially the famed Jabugo hams from the mountains north of Huelva, near the border of Extremadura.

In an odd way, the very abundance of fresh seafood, fruit and vegetables has kept Andalusian cuisine from developing the complexity one expects of a major cuisine. This abundance has encouraged a simple, uncomplicated cooking dismissed by some as lacking 'weight.' This is slowly changing, however, as Andalusian chefs learn to preserve the freshness of their raw ingredients while creating more complex dishes. To this point, the Catalan and Basque cuisines of the north have been Spain's major entries in the international food sweepstakes. But as Andalusian chefs gain confidence in using the area's riches in more creative ways, the regional cuisine is gaining strength.

The Moorish flavor is more prominent in Andalusian cooking than in any other regional cuisine of Spain. There is also a strong Sephardic influence. But whatever their background, Andalusian dishes invariably give the appearance of simplicity. In some parts of Spain, particularly Catalonia, they will tell you that there is no such thing as Andalusian cuisine—just as they will tell you that all Andalusians are lazy and are quite content to live in caves. Spanish regionalism runs deep.

One reason that people in the north of Spain dismiss Andalusian cooking so readily is that it appears deceptively casual. One thinks of the 'simple dishes,' which the Andalusians call *fritos variados*, consisting of fried seafood or boiled shellfish. But there is a baroque complexity of spices and flavorings even for these simple dishes.

Chefs such as José María Solano at the Alboronia in Puerta Santa María, a few miles from Jerez, have taken Andalusian fare and developed a spectacular regional cuisine that deserves to take its place among the best of Europe. Compare two dishes prepared by Solano. On one of our visits we were served an appetizer of tiny brined anchovies on sliced grilled baguettes, with a little virgin olive oil drizzled on top. It was delicious simply because the ingredients—fish, bread and olive oil— were fresh and first-rate.

One of the entrées was a beautifully presented dish of *Pimientos de pequillo rellenos de chipirones en su tinta*, red peppers stuffed with squid. The red peppers were each about twice the size of a large man's thumb. Each contained three *chipirones*, which are very tiny squid, not available in the United States. Each tiny squid was stuffed with its own tentacles and finely diced ham. This was served on a white plate, with a bit of rice in *tinta*, squid ink, and it looked as wonderful as it tasted. Basic ingredients were used to fashion a sophisticated dish.

✠

Andalusia is the heartland of the tapa, that delicious morsel that defines a way of life as much as a culinary style. 'Doing tapas' bears a passing similarity to the American practice of bar hopping. Bar hopping, however, implies a commitment to drinking that is absent from the tapas scene.

Tapas, although usually accompanied by wine, are more about talking and eating than about drinking. The wine elevates the conversation and helps hold the friends and food together, but the primary purpose of tapas is to talk to friends, share gossip, perhaps discuss the latest follies of the politicians. Tapas are part of the communal life of the *pueblo* at the personal level. The concept of tapas also involves that very Spanish social art form, the ability to 'hang out.' The Spanish are experts at hanging out, lingering for hours over a few cups of coffee or glasses of sherry.

Of course, the food is important. The quality and variety of food is so important to the Spanish generally that it is said they spend a higher percentage of their disposable income on food than any other industrial nation. It is not because the cost of food is higher in Spain than it is in France, Canada or Australia, but because the Spanish expect better food and a greater variety of it.

A serious evening of tapas will start at perhaps 7 PM, a few hours after the end of lunch. One ordinarily follows an established route, beginning at the 'local,' but moving on to several different tapas bars before dinner. The choice of where to go will depend on where friends will be found and what special tapa is offered. Some tapas bars gain a reputation for a particular offering and you would visit them just for that. Others are known for a wider selection and are the kind of place you can settle in for the evening if you wish.

Tapas can be just about anything edible, but writ small. At their simplest, the tapa can be a plate of olives or a few slices of ham, a slice of cheese, a few fried squid or grilled prawns. They can also be as elaborate as the cook's imagination and resources.

There is no real agreement about when or where the term first came into use. *Tapa* means a cover or a lid. The story goes that in the old roadside inns in the south of Spain, the innkeeper would have glasses of wine ready to sell to travelers while horses were being changed. This was often a split-second affair—one team unhitched, while the other was quickly put to the yoke. The innkeeper would rush the wine to the carriage in a kind of primitive takeout arrangement. What with all the dust, flies and other unmentionable debris swirling around the courtyard, innkeepers, so it's said, began covering the wine glass with a thin slice of bread. Thus a *tapa* or cover. As competition increased, innkeepers began putting a slice of ham or cheese on the bread as an inducement to the hungry traveler to take a few minutes longer and order another glass of wine.

In many bars today, basic tapas are still free. In fact, you can get curious looks from a bartender if you decline the offer of a plate of olives. Especially is this true in the countryside, or in the more traditional bars of Madrid or Seville, where it is rare for anyone to drink without a bite of something.

Like flamenco, the friendly pursuit of tapas has spread from the south all across Spain. Tapas bars can now be found in San Sebastián, in Catalonia, in Valencia, everywhere in fact. In Barcelona, the tapas bar is combined with that delightful Catalan institution, the *xampanyería*. There, instead of sherry, one can sample glasses of *cava* with the tapas.

In Andalusia, Seville is especially famous for its tapas, and one can wander endlessly through the streets of the old quarter near the cathedral, sampling a bit of this and a bit of that. In most of Seville's tapas bars, the tab is still kept with chalk marks on the surface of the bar, or sometimes just kept in the barman's head.

Each part of Seville has its own characteristic tapas bars with special dishes just a little different from the place a block away. There are countless tapas bars in the old Santa Cruz quarter near the Alcázar, the cathedral and the Giralda, that fantastic Arab tower which gazes calmly across the Plaza del Triunfo at the Alcázar. At some of the larger establishments, there will be two bars, one serving kitchen tapas, which require preparation and are served warm, and a smaller bar serving premade, cold tapas. The best sherry can generally be found at the smaller bar, probably because customers go there to concentrate on the wine, the food being secondary.

Some typical Seville tapas include *pringa*, a stew of vegetables, pork, salt pork and sausage. When the stew is well cooked, the meats are taken out and shredded, then stuffed into partially cooked rolls. The rolls are then baked. *Espinacas con garbanzos* is a refried chick pea and spinach tapa, garnished with a paste made of garlic, fried bread, vinegar and salt. It is sometimes served with a dash of paprika. *Pavias* are strips of salt cod that have been well soaked, dipped in a batter of flour, saffron, baking soda, salt and hot water, then fried in olive oil until crisp. There are two different snail tapas: *caracoles* and *cabrillas*. The *caracoles* are very small, while *cabrillas* are somewhat larger. Both are cooked in sauce with various spices. A dipping sauce called *Mojo picón* is typical of Seville. It is slightly *picante*, and can be used for dipping almost anything. It is especially good with grilled pork. It is made of oregano, cumin, garlic, vinegar, water, salt, cayenne, pimento, onions and garlic.

Grazelema. A picture postcard white town in the mountains on the seldom-traveled backroad between Arcos de la Frontera and Ronda, deep in Andalusia's Lorca country. Early morning coffee, with just a splash of brandy, at the parador in Arcos, sitting on the terrace watching the hawks drift down the deep canyon below. We will push on later for a late lunch, planned for Ronda, but delayed because of the sighting of a goddess in Grazelema.

We were in the plaza, where we had stopped for a glass and a tapa and found, unexpectedly, the Fiesta del Carmen in full rout. The saint, a wooden statue, half life-size, beautifully dressed, her coiled black hair freshly painted, had taken her annual outing, by donkey cart, to the edge of town just to the first fields, then back through the main plaza to the church. There was the usual wild Spanish confusion of horses, children, guitar players, dogs and fireworks.

But in a small island of stillness, walking only yards behind the saint herself, was a woman dressed all in white. Her hair was braided high on her head and from the braided coils long stalks of wheat and other grains spilled out. There were flowers woven into the hem of her dress and across her breast. Here was a goddess more familiar with the streets of Grazelema than the Christian upstart in the cart.

After the sainted Carmen entered the church, the corn goddess turned away to a nearby bar, El Postigo, where we joined her for sherry and a few bites of loma manteca, a Spanish country dish that simply will not translate into the modern American kitchen. Think of sheep intestines and lard. Think no further.

As the corn goddess sipped her sherry, we exchanged news of the day with one of her acolytes, a wiry man who could have passed for a none-too-threatening bandit. He identified himself as a 'pig-sticker' who traveled all about Andalusia and into Extremadura during the butchering season. Ordering the loma manteca was his idea.

After another half bottle of fino, he joined two friends at the bar, leaving the goddess to explain that he was an 'hombre loco.' The three men at the bar stood in a semi-circle, involved in a quiet conversation. Without warning, one of the men—the oldest, with many gaps in his teeth—began singing, singing the harsh, full throated deep song of the south of Spain.

The words pushed and twisted from his body, throat muscles taut and straining. The man across from him answered in song, syllables repeated, each word drawn-out and stretched seemingly to the breaking point, the harsh tones rising and falling like an ancient prayer. Then the third man came in and the trio began trading phrases, pushing and tugging at the rhythm.

One was utterly unprepared. This had to be the beginning of poetry, this unrehearsed ritual of vocal give-and-take. Around the bar, people continued to eat and drink, to order wine and talk to their friends, but the tone was quiet, with many glances in the trio's direction. While the men were still singing, a sevillana band began playing in the plaza outside. The amplified music broke into El Postigo, jarring, unwelcome, like a fingernail drawn across a blackboard. The three singers—only moments before a weather-worn frieze on an ancient vase—returned to their wine and their loma manteca. *The corn goddess got up, walked into the night and was seen no more.*

✦

'A good sherris sack hath a twofold operation in it. It ascends me into the brain; dries me there all the foolish and dull and crudy vapors which environ it; makes it apprehensive, quick, forgetive, full of nimble, fiery and delectable shapes; which delivered o'er to the voice, the tongue, which is the birth, becomes excellent wit. The second property of your excellent sherris is the warming of the blood. . . . If I had a thousand sons, the first human principle I would teach them should be to forswear thin potations and to addict themselves to sherris sack.'

—Sir John Falstaff, *Henry IV, Part Two,*
William Shakespeare

Sir John flourished near the end of the sixteenth century, but sherry is still the best known wine of Andalusia, certainly Andalusia's most important contribution to the international wine market. You can include Montilla and Málaga wines here too; neither is quite the same as sherry, but both are made in a similar fashion.

There are also excellent local table wines all over Andalusia. First-rate wines are produced from grape varieties surprising to find in a region known for hot weather. One unexpectedly encounters Riesling, Cabernet Sauvignon, even Pinot Noir, growing at Andalusia's higher altitudes. There is, for example, a flourishing table wine industry around Arcos de la Frontera a few miles east of Jerez de la Frontera. Started by French winemakers who settled in Spain around the time of the French-Algerian war, it is planted mainly to French varietals.

But sherry is the signature wine of Andalusia. Americans may stand in need of some basic lessons in sherry. Somehow, we have learned only part of the equation—the sweet part.

There are really only two kinds of sherry—*fino* and *oloroso*. Everything else is simply a variation within these categories. The light and dry *finos* are the most refreshing wines in the world. A nutty aroma mingles with slight scents of damp, cool earth. There is something green, almost vegetal in the nose of a good *fino* sherry, reminiscent of a garden on a hot afternoon. *Fino* also gives an impression of coolness on the palate, followed by the tangy, spicy surprise of a finish that lingers for nearly a minute. It's a wine of great complexity that goes well with a number of foods. A well-made sweet sherry—all variations on *oloroso*—is a magnificent dessert wine, subtle and complex with a greater range of flavors than any other dessert wine.

To understand the wine in the glass, it is necessary to understand how it is made. And the 'how' of sherry is quite different from the 'how' of table wine. There are two key elements in understanding sherry. First, the fermentation and aging process, which is quite different from the process for table wines. Second, the blending process. One of the most helpful explanations of how sherry is made was sketched in chalk one morning on the side of a stainless steel tank by José Ignacio Domecq Jr. of the famed sherry family, in a cool bodega in Jerez.

After grapes destined for sherry are picked and crushed, their juice undergoes rapid fermentation in a stainless steel tank, exactly like the one Domecq used as a chalk board. Fermentation takes about six weeks and is where the mystery at the heart of sherry begins, a mystery even now in an era of scientific winemaking. It centers on the yeast bloom called *flor.*

Flor, flower in Spanish, is a thin white film of yeast cells that grows across the surface of sherry as it ferments. It develops in small yellowish patches that gradually grow and spread, so that within three to four weeks they have covered the whole surface of the wine in the sherry butt. This first and strongest bloom lasts about six months.

The growth of *flor* on sherry is not fully understood, although much has been learned in recent years. It is apparently related to a wild strain of saccharomyces, the yeast that is associated with winemaking all over the world. Because the *flor* bloom occurs spontaneously, it is obviously a wild yeast strain. Despite many efforts by winemakers in California,

Australia and elsewhere, no one has been able to reproduce it. In fact, *flor* taken from Spain to California mutates in a few generations and becomes an entirely different yeast, if it survives at all.

The basic process by which table wines are aged is pretty much the same all over the world, with local variations based on technical skill and inclination. Sherry is something else altogether. Unlike other wines, sherry is stored in partially filled barrels, in the presence of oxygen. For other wines, oxygen is regarded as the enemy because it will, in short order, turn wine into vinegar. If God were the winemaker, all grape juice would end up as vinegar.

Although sherry is intentionally oxidized, the *flor* furnishes protection. Unlike more common winemaking yeasts that eat sugar and turn it into alcohol, *flor* eats oxygen, thus protecting the wine from excessive damage. There are always a few butts that do begin turning into vinegar. These are rushed from the sherry storage area of the bodega to the vinegar house—and very good vinegar they make, too.

In the past, the *flor* played a role in the selection of the kind of sherry each butt would produce—*fino* or *oloroso*. The process of selection would begin when the cellar foreman checked the newly fermented butts of wine. Those with a strong growth of *flor* were likely to be finished as *finos*; those with little or no *flor* would likely become *olorosos* or, in rare cases, a *palo cortado*. The *palo cortado* is a sherry that produces no *flor*. It shares the flavor characteristics of an *oloroso*, but has an aroma as penetrating as *fino*.

This system of letting nature take its course is—for better or worse—no longer followed. Now, in most cases, the difference is simply that *fino* is made from free-run juice (that is, the grapes are crushed, but not pressed) and the *oloroso* made from the first and second pressings.

At the end of fermentation, sherry is dry, whether *fino* or *oloroso*. In the case of *olorosos*, brandy is then added. This stops the growth of *flor*, since no yeast can live if the alcohol content is above 16.4 percent. The addition of brandy, at least in the beginning, gives *olorosos* a rounded feeling in the mouth. As *oloroso* ages, it will becomes truly mouth-filling and complex, with a very long finish.

Olorosos are also sweetened at this point by the addition of the juice of Moscatel or Pedro Ximénez grapes. How much sweet juice is added determines the sweetness of the final product. Some sweet sherries are of very high quality and are among the oldest wines in the world. Others, especially the almost generic cream sherries, are made from lower-quality wines, heavily sweetened to mask the wretchedness of the wine.

An *amontillado*, a kind of *fino* sherry, is left in the cask to deepen in color. It takes on some of the character of an *oloroso* due to longer aging and oxidation, but retains much of the fresh quality of *fino* in the aroma. In its natural state *amontillado* is always dry, but it too is often sweetened for the export market.

Manzanilla, also a kind of *fino*, is made only at Sanlúcar de Barrameda. It is made exactly like *fino* and, interestingly, if a young *manzanilla* is taken to Jerez to mature, it will acquire the character of a *fino*. On the palate, *manzanilla* differs from other *finos* in having a faintly bitter, almost salty taste. In color, it is usually lighter and the alcohol content is somewhat lower. A fresh *manzanilla* with a plate of simple fried fish in a beach front restaurant at Sanlúcar is one of life's great delights. There are some traditionalists who claim that the peculiar tangy flavor of *manzanilla* is a result of the sea air at Sanlúcar. Anything is possible. It could though, also be a peculiarity of the *flor* at Sanlúcar.

Once the future of the sherry has been determined, the new wine is moved into the bodegas. Here, we well and truly enter the cathedral, the holy of holies for sherry, and are introduced to the rituals and mysteries of the *solera*.

Let us begin with the bodega itself. From the outside most of them look more utilitarian than sacred, more like a well-constructed storage building. Since the total sherry inventory hovers between 180 and 200 million gallons of wine, and that concentrated in the hands of a dozen major houses in Jerez and Sanlúcar, the storage space has to be enormous. Each sherry butt contains roughly 500 gallons of wine, so space is needed for about 400 thousand casks of sherry. And that does not even take into account the brandy casks, which probably equal the sherry casks in number.

Once inside, the comparison to a cathedral is unavoidable. Bodegas have high ceilings and high windows, usually of stained glass. Not much seems to be happening. But that arcane process known as the *solera* system is humming quietly along.

On a small, nameless hill on the outskirts of Jerez is the Domecq bodega called *La Mezquita*, or The Mosque. It is roughly modeled on the great mosque in Córdoba. Standing among the forty thousand butts of sherry and brandy at Domecq's Mezquita, one sees the great pillars recede in all directions, creating a seeming maze reflected in geometric patterns across the high whitewashed walls and ceiling.

The patterns are interrupted only by draperies of a fine mold that, in older bodegas, such as Domecq's El Molino a few kilometers away, covers walls, ceilings and barrels. The Spanish leave the mold alone, on the supposition that it favors the growth of *flor.*

The *solera* blending system was established in Jerez in the nineteenth century, partly in an effort to attain a more uniform quality of wine. The system involves stacking long tiers of casks filled with wine. Casks holding the oldest wine are on the ground. Resting upon them are a sequence of tiers known as *criaderas.* Each *criadera* is made up of casks holding wine younger than the tier immediately below. The tier just above the oldest, or bottom tier, is the first *criadera,* followed by the second, third and so on. The number of *criaderas* varies with different producers, but since the minimum aging period is three years, three *criaderas* are commonly used.

What happens is fairly simple and, again, it varies somewhat from producer to producer. For a common *fino,* a maximum of one-third of the wine in the bottom or oldest tier of the *criadera* would be drawn out and bottled. Then, from each *criadera,* one-third of the wine is drawn off—very carefully so as to disturb the *flor* as little as possible—and added to the *criadera* immediately below. At the top *criadera,* in turn, a one-third quantity of new wine is added. In actual practice, a little wine is drawn off for bottling four or five times a year. The total for the year adds up to about a third of a barrel, or less.

Keep in mind that freshness is essential for the enjoyment of *fino.* Even though it is fortified at bottling to between 15.5 and 17 percent alcohol, *fino,* unlike other fortified wines such as port or *oloroso,* fades quickly after opening and within twenty-four hours will have lost much of its charm and flavor. The bitter quality of the wine becomes predominant and it can be downright unpleasant. If you do not intend to finish a bottle of *fino* within a day, it is better to buy half-bottles.

In fact, *fino* begins to change and coarsen as soon as it is removed from the solera and bottled. Shippers are beginning to date *fino* bottles. Look for the date of bottling on the paper foil around the cork.

❧

The vineyards near Jerez de la Frontera, the heart of the sherry triangle, are as dazzling white as the famed 'white towns' of the Andalusian coast a few kilometers away. Long ago the area was covered by a shallow sea, which has left the soil about forty percent chalk. A walk through the vineyards may turn up ancient sea shells that don't look a great deal different from those that will turn up on your plate at lunch. You might even flush a partridge, if you're lucky, which will be dinner. Whatever you have for lunch or dinner, it's a safe bet that the wine will be sherry.

That vast sweep of vineyards to the north and east of Jerez is generally considered the most important—in both size and quality—of the sherry district. Of the forty-six thousand total acres of grapes in the area, about thirty thousand are in the Jerez district. The view from the Domecq vineyards, which lie in the center of the area, looks downward toward the coast and Sanlúcar, and consists of row after row of vines, soft green waves breaking over the dazzling white soil.

Over ninety-five per cent of the vines are planted to the Palomino grape, although only two hundred years ago there were hundreds of grape varieties grown near Jerez. No doubt many dated back to classical times. As late as the 1870s there were about forty varieties under cultivation, but by the end of the nineteenth century the Palomino had become dominant.

Moscatel and the Pedro Ximénez grapes were once much more important in the blending of sherry than at present. Now they account for less than five percent of planted vineyards. The Moscatel is an early ripening grape that produces a wine mostly used to sweeten other sherries, although it makes an excellent dessert wine on its own. In the United States, Lustau imports a delicious Moscatel that improves with bottle age. (It is fantastic poured over raisin ice cream!)

Pedro Ximénez makes an intensely sweet dessert wine, although it is rarely bottled as such. Most of the wine made from Pedro Ximénez goes into blending and into brandies. There is a legend connected with the name involving a German soldier named Pieter Siemenez who was in the army of Charles V (Charles I of Spain). The story goes that the soldier brought a vine cutting with him from the banks of the Rhine— though that seems a rather odd bit of baggage for a sixteenth century soldier to be carrying around. This has led some to infer that the Pedro Ximénez is actually a Riesling.

The Pedro Ximénez and the Moscatel are picked earlier than the Palomino and are still dried on grass mats before crushing, spread out beneath the sun. This raisins the grapes, intensifying the sweetness as the water content is reduced.

✦◡✦

The beach was a circus. A swirling palate of colors, a pageant of beautiful horses, beautiful women and handsome men. It was race week at Sanlúcar de Barrameda, the oldest horse race in all of Europe. Beyond the sands of the beach at Sanlúcar, beyond the misty sunset glimmer of the Guadalquivir, the pale green of the Parque Doñana hung in the darkening sky. It was the last race of the day. Men in tuxedos with white cummerbunds danced on the sand with barefoot women in gowns that cost hundreds of thousands of pesetas, pearls likes kisses on dark necks. The steady beat of a rock band echoed from down the beach where tall blondes of indefinite sex, part of that northern horde that each August washes up on the beaches of Spain, danced topless.

The racing horses flash across the sand, nearing the finish line. A somber man, dressed in black, has positioned his white horse like an icon just beyond the racing horses. A small girl, no more than three or four, dressed all in white with a red sash at her waist and red ribbons in her hair, sits solemnly on the saddle before him. The beautiful, pale young woman next to me says he is one of the judges. What does he judge? She doesn't know. Perhaps riding form, perhaps the winners or losers, perhaps the dancing that will come later. Somehow, he has simply wandered in toward the end of the last race of the day.

At the finish of the race, all is confusion. From where we sit it is impossible to tell who won, nor is there anyone nearby who knows. At some point, some time, it will matter. Here and now it doesn't. A caterer in black and white does a 'hey, presto' routine with a gleaming white cloth on the table set in the sand below us. Plates of local shrimp, squid, fried fish, lobster, heaping fruit platters, crowd the tabletop. Gleaming glasses of chilled manzanilla sherry reflect the last light from the sun. Someone lights the candles that line the table. The scene is repeated dozens of times down the beach.

The somber man and the young girl have joined us. Now he is laughing, exchanging toasts with our host. The young girl, his daughter, sits on his lap, smiling shyly, chewing on a huge prawn, red ribbons hanging loose down her neck. He is not a rich man. He has a very small vineyard but for generations his family have been judges in the races at Sanlúcar. If he has no sons he expects his daughter to be a judge one day, so she is in training.

No, he doesn't know who won. He must consult with the other judges. What other judges? He makes a vague motion toward further down the beach. They are there, somewhere in the dusk, or perhaps they are up on the street watching the Gypsies from the hill towns to the east, toward Granada and Ronda, dance the puro flamenco. They will get together later.

'You see,' said the young woman who had spoken earlier, 'if the judges announced the winner now, it would spoil the night for the others. Tomorrow is soon enough for that sorrow.' Yes, we understood.

The judge smiled at me and raised his glass. I raised mine. We drank to the most beautiful women, the finest horses and the best wine in the world. That night, we were all winners.

✢✢✢

The harvest begins, unofficially, near the end of August or early September. A fierce Andalusia summer sun reflects off the white soil, investing the grapes with that warm intensity that so delighted Sir John Falstaff and thousands of other cold-climate creatures before and since.

Centuries later, the English continue to rely on sherry as a warming, friendly drink. It still appeals, as Gerald Asher wrote in his thoughtful book of essays, *On Wine*, to 'those who lived in the shires of the south and west of England and on the wide flat farms of East Anglia, a region where I spent my entire childhood without ever once feeling warm. . . . An invitation to 'come over for a glass of sherry' promises a relaxed communion of friends, comfortable shoes, an old sweater. . . .'

The story is told in Jerez that the chief impulse behind Sir Francis Drake's daring sixteenth century raid on the port of Sanlúcar was simply to take home enough sherry to keep Queen Elizabeth in good spirits. In fact, there was a marked increase in the sherry trade following Drake's raid, when he seized 2,900 pipes of sherry. (A pipe was a traditional measure of wine—usually sherry, port, or madeira—little in use now. The amount varied, but contained roughly 130-140 gallons.)

Depending on when the actual picking of the grapes begins, the harvest celebration is held the first or second weekend in September, with the *Fiesta de la Vendimia*. The celebration usually outlasts the weekend and continues well into the week, with bull fights, flamenco and the dancing of the *sevillana*, a beautiful and very old dance with a more controlled grace than the fiery flamenco.

The *sevillana* is based on court dances of the eighteenth century, probably originating hundreds of years before in La Mancha-Castile. This rhythmic dance in 6/8 time was known as a *seguidilla manchega* at court, and was one of several castanet dances. It was adopted with such gusto by the citizens of Seville—where it remains a popular street dance—that it now bears the name of that Andalusian city.

The dance takes many forms. Traditionally, the dancers were accompanied by one or two guitars and by singers extolling the virtues of a particular woman, or bull, or the wonders of the city of Seville. The modern dance has become more energetic. There are often *mariachi*-like brass bands, pianos, conga drums, or even a full symphony orchestra. The lyrics have proven just as adaptable.

Whatever the lyrics or the instruments, the dance consists basically of a sequence of four usually brief songs, or *coplas*. Each will have the same tempo, which can range from slow to very, very fast, and the same melody but with different lyrics.

There is really no traditional costume for the *sevillana*. People wear whatever makes them look or feel good, and dancers in period-costume can be found sharing the floor with punk-rockers and barefoot Gypsies. Whatever the dress, it is a graceful affair with lots of upper-body movement, which seems to be more important than just where you put your feet. It has something of the feel of the free-form rock dancing of the 1960s, in that it seems possible, at least after a few glasses of sherry, to participate, even if you haven't the slightest idea of where your partner is leading you. You can only hope for the best.

During the festival, there are countless parades, but the one that matters most is the one featuring the festival queen, a title that is taken very seriously in Jerez. It's a toss-up whether the horses, the women, or the men are more beautiful, perhaps it depends on one's individual inclinations or the luck of the season. The festivities start early in the morning, virtually stepping on the heels of the eating, drinking and dancing of the night before. But given enough Spanish coffee, one can begin to function. Don't imagine that there will be time for a siesta later—not during festival week.

By perhaps 10 AM, the streets of Jerez are filled. Follow the crowds as they move toward the Plaza de Toros and the town center. The bullfight, the *corrida*, is the first great event of the day. It begins at five in the afternoon and bullfights always start on time. Even if the king is expected and he is late, the bull will not wait. The bull would not have waited for Ernest Hemingway.

The bullfights at Jerez are generally among the best in Spain, but during the harvest festival they are outstanding. Most of the fighting bulls of Spain come from the area around Jerez, so the local fans know a good bull, and the best bullfighters come from where the bulls are good. Before and after the bullfight, the bars around the Plaza de Toros are crowded with *jerezanos*, drinking sherry, eating tapas, carrying on the endless conversations that beguile the Spanish hours.

The main set piece of the wine festival is the blessing of the grapes on the steps of the sixteenth-century Collegiate Church of San Salvador by the Bishop of Cádiz. The harvest queen, accompanied by swirling clouds of maids of honor dressed in white with blue silk scarves, dumps a basket of grapes into an old press where barefoot civic dignitaries and various important folk (all with *Don* preceding their name) ritually stomp them. Then huge clouds of white doves are released and the harvest has officially begun, as all the church bells in the city are set to ringing. The juice from this blessed stomping is put in a wooden cask and taken to that year's bodega of choice on the traditional donkey cart. Each year, the first cask is dedicated to a different country or city outside of Spain. During the following year, envoys from Jerez may take samples of the cask to officials in the honored city.

There is also a nonstop flamenco festival which is not as rewarding as it might be. Since flamenco has become so popular, many of the shows are tourist affairs where the dancers hardly work up a sweat. But once in a while, lightning strikes. It is necessary to be in the right place at the right time, as we were one morning about 3 AM in a small bar near the bull ring in Jerez. It seemed that the very long day was about to end with the prospect of a few hours sleep. Suddenly, the doors burst open and a Gypsy troupe entered. These were not the costumed marvels one sees in special stage shows put on for the tourists in Seville or Madrid. Someone said they had just come into town from El Bosque, a small mountain village in the Sierra de la Ronda east of Jerez.

There was an instant revival of flagging spirits. The barman set up a long row of half-bottles of *fino* and the dancing began. Puro flamenco is an ancient art. Some say it goes back to the Greeks and is related to sacred dance of pre-classical times. In this version of history, elements were added to the dance by the Moors and it was brought to perfection by the Gypsies. It is said that the Gypsies did not invent flamenco, either the dance or the 'deep song' that accompanies it, but there is no hard evidence one way or the other.

In *puro* flamenco, the guitar often follows the lead of the dancer. It all begins in silence. The dancer, or dancers, stand dead still, looking at nothing, usually not acknowledging the shouts or applause from the audience. That night, the music began when a tall, rather fierce looking Gypsy woman raised her arms, castanets clicking. As the guitar rhythm cut in, her feet began driving at the floor, not moving from the space, and we were off for three hours of music, interrupted only by short breaks for *fino* and food for the dancers. At dawn, a grizzled old bare-foot Gypsy man, who had been playing the guitar practically nonstop for three hours, passed through the crowd, hat in hand. It was soon filled to overflowing with pesetas.

We went off for a few hours' sleep before the festival continued. It is a very good thing that grapes are not one of the crops that attain three harvests a year in Andalusia. Mere humans could not endure such exhaustion—or so much fun.

After witnessing a few of these performances, one begins to day-dream of finding a small space to practice a few flamenco steps of one's own. The important thing is to stomp your feet really hard, as if trying to drown out the guitar music. Having just listened to a taped performance of a live flamenco festival, a friend said it sounded like a lot of people wearing wooden shoes moving boxes around upstairs, after first taking up the carpet.

After all that stomping, you should be ready for a snack. There is a wonderful workingman's tapas bar in Jerez, just off the Plaza de Arenal, called Bar Juanito. Almost every inch of wall space is filled with pictures of bulls and bullfighters or other famous people (Frank Sinatra, Ava Gardner, Ernest Hemingway) posing with bullfighters. The tables spill out into the narrow street, mercifully closed to cars. Everywhere there are children, darting in and out, whole tides of them, washing from one side of the narrow street to the other, clustering briefly around a family table where they quickly snatch a bite or two of food, a glass of juice or cola.

The dishes at Bar Juanito are not refined. They have that intense, gutsy quality that make tapas such a delight to the taste buds. There is a kind of stew called *guisado de atún*, tuna with peas, based on a *sofrito* of peas, onions, parsley and garlic, which is utterly delicious. We have also enjoyed one of the best stuffed squid dishes we've ever had here. The squid is stuffed with bread, its own tentacles, veal, parsley and onions. Bar Juanito also has an absolutely fresh *fino* that is the perfect complement to these dishes.

✦✦✦

We were meeting our sherry master, José Ignacio Domecq Jr., at his favorite beach front restaurant in Sanlúcar. José Ignacio is the technical director of Pedro Domecq, the oldest of the major sherry houses. It was actually founded by an Irishman, Patrick Murphy, who came to Spain and started in the wine business in 1730. The Domecq family married into the business in the late eighteenth century. The Domecqs have since played a major role in Jerez, taking the lead in innovations in the winery and the vineyard. Along the way the family has established a worldwide wine and brandy empire, with huge interests in South America and Mexico.

Our simple lunch lasted about three hours, during which only sherry was poured. Even though much of the fare was local catch of the day and so cannot be precisely duplicated in most of the rest of the world, the general approach to eating can be followed anywhere.

The restaurant that Domecq intended we go to was closed for remodeling. He shrugged and said it didn't really matter. They were all good. Our window table at Mirador Doñana overlooked the beach and, as the name suggests, looked out on the Parque Nacional de Doñana wildlife refuge across the broad, shallow estuary of the Río Guadalquivir.

Domecq, who had hunted and fished the Doñana from childhood, gave us an excellent table-side tour. Doñana is the delta of the Gaudalquivir, the 'big river' of the Moors. It is the major stopover in Europe for birds migrating from northern Europe to Africa and back. There are also 125 species of bird that breed in the Doñana, including seventeen varieties of duck, as well as twenty-eight species of mammal, including the Spanish lynx, found nowhere else in southern Europe.

The area was set aside as a royal hunting preserve by the kings of

Castile in the thirteenth century. A few centuries later, Doña Ana de Silva y Mendoza, a duchess of Medina Sidonia, built a retreat there and the region became known as Doñana. The national park was created in 1969. It is a huge area, but actually only a besieged remnant of the coastal marsh, a vast open area that has been slowly drained and converted to farmlands, except for the refuge of Doñana.

Domecq sipped at a glass of *manzanilla* and gazed rather dourly across the river toward Doñana. He remembered the days before it was a park, when hunting was allowed. 'We would go in with horses and wagons and set up camp for days, even weeks at a time, going across and back by boat, for there were no roads then into the Doñana.' He felt, on the whole, that the Doñana had been better cared for when it was in private hands. Surprisingly enough, many conservationists agree with him.

As part of the agreement to establish the park, sections of the old hunting areas to the north were converted to co-op rice fields. Pesticides from those fields have now entered the ground water system of Doñana, creating problems for breeding birds and threatening the entire ecosystem of the park. There is also no buffer zone to protect the park's boundaries from urban sprawl, and lynxes have been run over by cars on adjoining highways. Cats and dogs have entered the park from nearby towns to play havoc with many of the ground-nesting marine birds. Domecq feels that the Spanish government gave away too much to establish the park, and that the ban on hunting has encouraged an explosion in the wild boar and deer population that threatens the ecological balance.

But as the food started to arrive, Domecq set aside his pessimistic mood. The first nibbles were baroque-looking sea snails, tightly-spiraled, perhaps two inches long, served barely steamed in their shell. We had first made the acquaintance of these snails, or their cousins, at a *xampanyería* in Barcelona where they were served as a tapa. It was necessary to dig into the little beasts with a toothpick, or use the pointed tip of a shell to pry out the snail. The opening in the bottom of the shell was plugged fairly tight by what must have been the snail's foot. Once that muscular plug was breached, there was a tiny, tasty morsel of flesh, about big enough to fill a good-sized cavity in a rear molar.

The delights just kept coming and it was a typical *jerezano* feast: calamari roe, lightly fried whole baby sole, lobster and rockfish, all accompanied by sherry. There was *manzanilla* until the fish arrived, then *fino*.

The element that tied the meal together was the salsa: peppers, onions, capers, celery and tomatoes. Domecq, an accomplished cook, remarked that he doesn't use celery in his salsa. His insistence on his own recipe for salsa is typical of Andalusian cooks, and helps explain why no two dishes are ever the same. *Gazpacho*, for instance, probably Andalusia's best known culinary export after sherry, has as many versions as there are cooks.

The lunch ended with one of the most popular desserts in Spain—a tall glass of slightly chilled, freshly squeezed orange juice. The juice is served with sugar on the side. Well, and there was a glass or two of old *oloroso* sherry. And then espresso. And we all agreed that a drop of Domecq brandy would be excessive. Agreed and then ordered a round.

Outside of the sherry district, the food of Andalusia takes on a country richness and intensity of flavor. We remember in particular a long lunch in the Hotel Juanito in Baeza, in the hills above Granada, deep in the heart of Andalusian olive country.

It is an incredible experience to drive for hours through nothing but olive groves, with endless tree rows marching up the mountains and down the valleys. It is agro-monoculture gone mad. No matter how fast one drives, at the next turn of the road there are more olive trees. Suddenly one is very glad of the sun shining, very glad there are many hours of daylight before darkness falls on this forest of trees. Olive trees go back so far in European culture that surely they have gathered the ghosts of long-dead civilizations in their roots. These ancient trees have absorbed so many generations of life that they appear at certain times to take on an existence beyond the merely vegetable.

One could look up statistics—the millions of gallons of olive oil exported each year, the billions of pesetas that grow out of these millions of trees. But mere numbers fade beside the essence and idea of the olive tree itself, so characteristic of the Mediterranean experience, so basic to the entire Mediterranean kitchen. The first-century Roman Pliny the Elder wrote, 'Except the vine, there is no plant which bears a fruit of as great importance as the olive.'

Sometimes, far up a hillside, there is a glimpse of the ruins of a castle (the Moors and Christians fought over this territory for generations), or perhaps an oddly modern looking farm house, besieged by olive trees, sunlight glinting off the television antenna. The small towns and villages turn up like misplaced stage sets in the center of the groves, with real paved streets, banks, schools, churches, women gossiping on doorsteps, children playing, old men leading donkeys. It is hard to imagine that they do anything besides watch the olives grow, pick the olives, crush the olives. It gets almost scary after a while. We were glad finally to pull into the courtyard of Hotel Juanito, where we had been promised authentic Andalusian country fare.

The parting words of our Valencia host were still ringing in our ears: 'You'll find nothing fit to eat in Andalusia outside of the cities. Don't even bother. Drive straight through to Córdoba.' The outward appearance of the Hotel Juanito did nothing to quiet our misgivings. It was away from the main part of town, across a dusty graveled street from a seedy-looking garage. A faded looking building of three or four stories, remarkable only for its obscurity. It could have been anything— an office building, an apartment building, even a once-grand private residence, now somewhat come down in the world. But in Spain, perhaps more than anywhere else, one doesn't judge the contents by the wrapper. Inside the hotel one entered another world, leaving the shabby exterior miles away, and perhaps centuries behind.

The town of Baeza itself, ringed by olive groves, is on the way, more or less, from nowhere to elsewhere, a few miles from the headwaters of the Guadalquivir in the foothills of the Sierra de Segura. There is little to recommend it except the Hotel Juanito.

We were late for lunch, but the staff took pains to make us feel welcome. Not for the first time, we wondered where the standard image of the dour, unfriendly Spaniard originated. It is true that the typical Spaniard can be a bit reserved, but there is nothing unfriendly in that reserve, only the desire to give the stranger a chance to respond, to show his or her own nature. When it became clear that we had made a rather long detour to have lunch at Juanito and that we were very interested in the local food and wine, our welcome was even warmer.

The owner/chef suggested a series of dishes, each showing off some unique aspect of the local cuisine. And there were local wines to match the dishes. The only one we had heard of was a Valdepeñas red wine, La Invincible, from one of the large co-ops, which was quite good. There were many other wines on the list from Valdepeñas, in southern La Mancha. We were not that far, after all, from the area, home of some of Spain's better inexpensive wines.

The most unusual wine on the Hotel Juanito list was a Marqués de la Sierra, a white wine from the mountains above Córdoba, roughly one hundred kilometers to the west. We learned later that it was a Riesling. Riesling, a cool climate grape, had been brought to the area in the sixteenth century and adapted well to the higher elevations in Andalusia. The wine had a characteristic Riesling complexity combined with a slightly oxidized, sherry-like quality. Although it was vintage dated, we suspect it was made by the *solera* method, which would account for the oxidation.

The food itself was sensational, ranging from local freshwater fish, through partridge, rabbit and venison, and ending in a glorious selection of fresh local fruits and cheese. We ate and drank through the afternoon and would have willingly gone on into the evening. We checked with the desk and no rooms were available. Probably just as well. We might be there yet.

Every meal is a drama. It can be a very short, poorly constructed one-act, a kind of fast-food frenzy, or it can be classic theater. Hotel Juanito was classic theater. That would mean very little if there were not Hotel Juanitos all over Spain, many of them having appeared in the last decade or two.

While it is difficult to say exactly what has touched off this renaissance of the Spanish kitchen, it is everywhere, from Barcelona and San Sebastián in the north to the wilds of Andalusia. Perhaps part of it is the overall feeling of freedom that swept Spain after Franco's death. In the beginning, this was rather tentative and took a few false starts. But as the political system moved steadily toward democracy, the Spanish have become more confident—in the fields of film, literature and the visual arts, and in the kitchen. Young chefs of Spain, no matter what region, have kept the best of the past, while borrowing from other regions of Spain and other national cuisines. There is the same sense of excitement in the better Spanish restaurants today that there was in California restaurants of the mid-70s, that wonderful sense of being present at a momentous beginning.

At the end of the meal at Hotel Juanito, just as we thought we were finished, the waiter served tiny glasses of a cherry *aguardiente* made by the house. It is not an uncommon thing anywhere in Spain for the house to present its own *aguardiente*, or fruit brandy. It suits the Spanish practice of never presenting anyone with a bill until the last possible moment. So long, you see, as you have not offered money, you are a guest. The service, the food, is willingly given as a host to a guest. Consideration of the bottom line disturbs this relationship.

Alexander Dumas commented upon this very Spanish trait in his travel memoir *From Paris to Cádiz*, published in 1846. Dumas describes his search for breakfast on his first hungry morning in Spain. After a long hunt, he and his companions managed to secure chocolate and bread. Not a lot of chocolate and bread, Dumas points out, but what there was, was very good. Then the time came for settling up:

'When we wished to pay, our guide stopped us with a gesture, took a peseta from his pocket and placed it on the edge of a chest. *'Vaya usted con Dios,'* he murmured with a gracious bow of farewell. The proprietor, without even glancing to see whether he had been correctly paid, took his cigar from his lips long enough to reply, *'Vaya usted con Dios.'*"

La Mancha

Properly speaking, La Mancha is part of New Castile, that picture-puzzle piece of Spain that fits snugly around Madrid, extending south of the Spanish capital to Andalusia, east to Valencia, and fading into Extremadura in the bleak, mountainous west. Politically, the region includes the provinces of Madrid, Albacete, Cuenca, Ciudad Real, Guadalajara and Toledo. The area is the very hub of the Spanish peninsula and contains two major cities, Madrid and Toledo.

Geographically, La Mancha is a high plain that tilts toward the south, called the Meseta. The average altitude is around 1700 feet. There are mountain ranges all around the borders, which has much to do with La Mancha's lack of rain; no matter what direction the rain is coming from, mountains intercept it.

This is a vast no-man's-land dotted with castles and watchtowers that commemorate the centuries of conflict between Christian and Muslim. This zone of conflict was ruled over by several military orders, owing little allegiance to any prince, only to the sword. It is a vast sheep-grazing territory, where herds were kept on the move much of the time seeking fresh pasture. One can still find traces of old sheep walks in the mountains that ring the plains of La Mancha.

Areas of La Mancha seem to function almost as a museum—cities like Toledo, filled with Roman, Vizigothic, Arab and Mudejar art. You can also find street corner con-artists selling cheap tin swords for the cost of a good meal, to bewildered tourists who haven't yet considered how in the world they are going to get past airport security with a forty-two inch sword.

But La Mancha is actually a state of mind, an invention of Cervantes, contemporary of Shakespeare and creator of Don Quixote. One must understand Don Quixote to understand Spain. Cervantes captured the bizarre spirit of the Iberian Peninsula—or most of it—in that one book, so often quoted, so little read. Quixote was a man of great heart, great courage, great generosity, with an understanding of nothing in this life, but a perfect conception of an ideal, interior life. His love, his pride, his honor, knew no limits. When he enjoyed, he enjoyed immensely, with no thought of the next hour, let alone tomorrow; when he suffered, his suffering knew no depths and was inconsolable.

His companion, Sancho Panza, was his mirror image. He was not intelligent, but cunning; he could not read, but he understood the world; he was cynical, yet totally trusting once his confidence was won. He was willing to compromise to avoid a fight; his honor was flexible. He began thinking about where he would find supper before his breakfast was done. Put them together and, to a large extent, you have Spain. And La Mancha is the heart of Spain.

✦✧✦

La Mancha is a harsh land, but with a greater abundance of food than may be apparent at first sight. Sheep and goat herds abound. There are enough wheat fields to give Kansas a run for its money, plenty of olive trees and plenty of vines, sprawling across the ground rather than tied up in neat, orderly rows as one is accustomed to seeing them elsewhere.

Most guidebooks give little attention to the cuisine of La Mancha. Yet even deep in the countryside, there is marvelous food to be had here. It is simple food, perhaps the simplest in Spain. Even in the far reaches of Navarre and Aragon, contemporary chefs are experimenting with basic peasant fare under the influence of French, Catalan or Basque cuisine. But this is not always a good thing. You can be far better off with unadulterated country cooking, which you will find at its most pure in the kitchens of La Mancha.

Vegetables of all sorts run riot here, especially vine-ripened tomatoes, peppers, beans and herbs. Root vegetables are also excellent, as are eggplant and squashes. Perhaps the most famous product of La Mancha is *Crocus sativus*, saffron. The center of the saffron trade is the town of Consuegra, on the C400, about seventy kilometers south of Toledo.

Game—rabbits, pheasant, partridge and wild boar—is often found on the tables of La Mancha, along with excellent domestic lamb, goat, pig and chicken. Rice dishes are common. And of course, everywhere and always, olives.

La Mancha produces delicious bread, often made from locally-grown wheat. Few things are better than a fresh loaf of *pan pueblo*, especially accompanied by some fresh *manchego*, a sheep cheese and one of the most famous in Spain. *Manchego* comes in three styles, *fresco*, which is aged for about sixty days; the cured, or *curado*, aged for thirteen weeks; and a dried version called *añejo*, or aged, which is matured for at least seven months. The hard version can be grated like parmesan or eaten out of hand.

The food of La Mancha is the soul food of Spain. For the true garlic soups, for the most typical of the *cocidos*, the culinary pilgrim must travel here. Take the dish called *galianos*, or sometimes—confusingly—*gazpachos*. (The final 's' distinguishes it from the cold *gazpacho* of Andalusia.) This started life centuries ago as a shepherd's dish and was most likely brought to Spain from North Africa by the Moors. In the traditional version, partridge and rabbit is fried with sliced onion, garlic, saffron, cinnamon, rosemary and thyme, flavored with wine and thickened with *torta*, a flat, unleavened bread baked on a stone. Another *torta* is used as a dipping tool and in medieval times the galianos was eaten directly from the pot. In the modern *manchego* kitchen, chicken and pigeon are often substituted for the game and *torta* is rarely made these days.

A similar stew is called *tojunto* or *todo junto*, 'all together', since the varied ingredients—meat, rabbit, or chicken and vegetables—are all put to cook at the same time. *Pisto manchego*, the vegetable stew that is found all over Spain, is a long-standing feature of the table in La Mancha. The modern version uses New World vegetables—tomatoes, peppers and squash—but the dish is based on the *alboronia* of the Moors and was originally no doubt an eggplant dish.

The best *churros* we've had in Spain were in La Mancha at the Plaza de Zocodover, the social center of Toledo, a bit uphill from the cathedral. *Churros*, fried dough in twisted loops, resemble light, elegant doughnuts and are one of the delights of street life in Spain. They are cooked quickly in a pot of boiling fat over a wood fire, usually on a street corner or in a plaza. You can buy whatever length you want, or purchase some for take-away on willow hoops, again in various sizes.

Early in the morning, crowds of children will be gathered around the *churros* maker, buying hoops of the freshly fried treats to take home for the family breakfast—*churros* and chocolate. Enough *churros* for four or five people can be bought for fifty or sixty pesetas, about fifty cents. If there was a fiesta the night before, the *churros* maker might sleep at the stand, because he or she will have been there until the end of the party. At two or three o'clock in the morning, it is a marvelous treat to have a small *churro* and a cup of thick chocolate, perhaps with a touch of anise or brandy.

✦

Wine grapes are the third most important agricultural product in La Mancha, after wheat and olives. La Mancha's vines cover a vast amount of territory and in most years account for about forty percent of Spain's total grape production, sometimes as much as half if the harvest has been short in the north.

Of that production, a large percentage gets distilled into brandy to feed the *soleras* of Jerez. Much of it is also distilled into industrial alcohol and a considerable amount ends up as vinegar. Recently, an increasing proportion has gone into the production of grape concentrate, which is sold all over the world to fortify the weak wines of colder areas. Much of the concentrate is sold to the United Kingdom for use in 'British' wines and for use by home winemakers. La Mancha has long been the supplier of inexpensive bulk wines to the rest of Spain, and is also responsible for a good many gallons of Spanish plonk that end up on London dinner tables where the budget is too modest for an unclassified Bordeaux.

But the area is moving toward higher quality with modern winemaking techniques; there is experimentation with plantings of international varietals such as Pinot Noir, Cabernet Sauvignon and Chardonnay. Until the past few years, we wouldn't have given Chardonnay much of a chance, but now, having seen Chardonnay flourish in some of the hotter areas of California, we think that La Mancha may be on to a good thing.

✦

The dedicated wine lover should visit La Mancha at harvest. The harvest festivals here are not as grandiose as those in Jerez or Rioja. But maybe for that reason one understands a little more intimately the mystery of the grape. There are entire towns that reek of wine during the harvest.

It should also be a mandatory part of the experience of La Mancha to endure the late summer heat; to at least go and stand in the vineyard while the stooped men and women move slowly down the sprawling rows of vines, under that hot blue sky. The heat is baking. After a short time it becomes necessary to concentrate on normally unconscious actions such as placing one foot before the other. There is a deliberateness to the progress of the harvesters through the rows of vines that is almost painful to watch. We have yet to see a mechanical harvester in La Mancha, although there are experimental vineyards near Valdepeñas designed to handle them.

The vineyards look much as they must have looked five or twenty centuries ago: a sprawling mass of vines, pruned low to the ground and bent even lower at harvest under the load of grapes. Work goes on from first light to dark, with a long lunch break during the intense heat of early afternoon, when nothing with any option is moving in La Mancha. There may be hotter places in Spain during the harvest than La Mancha (Seville comes to mind), but it is surely the hottest place where anyone is picking grapes.

We once walked a vineyard near Valdepeñas at eight in the morning. The heat was already beating down from above and radiating back up from the earth. The grapes still felt cool to the touch, nestled under the heavy vine canopy that is allowed to develop in La Mancha for that very purpose. There is little effort to bring in cool grapes, however. Because of the slow system of handpicking and the heat that develops in the grapes during trucking to the winery, grapes often arrive with fermentation well underway, especially at the bottom of the picking boxes.

❧

Climbing from the flat heat of the vineyards toward the towers of Toledo, you finally enter a breathable zone below the walls of the city, which is instantly familiar from El Greco's famous painting.

Architecturally and gastronomically, the city is a feast. It has only one serious drawback and that is its fame. During the winter months, Toledo is beset by visitors; but in late summer, when the grapes are being harvested on the plains below, the city fairly swarms with tourists. It is easy to understand why. One could spend a month in Toledo and barely scratch the surface. It would take a lifetime to know the city well. (It is amusing that the Michelin Guide suggests one day for the main sights of Toledo. It takes that long to have lunch and book a table for dinner.)

Unlike some other heavily-touristed areas, the eating in Toledo comes close to matching its sights. There are some typical local dishes, like *Brocheta de ternera y butifarra*, skewers of veal and sausages cooked in a wine sauce; *Sopa de almendras*, a hot milk and marzipan soup with almonds; and, one of Toledo's most famous dishes, *Codornices a la toledana*, braised quail served with vegetables. Naturally Toledo has its own variation of *menestra*, the vegetable stew found everywhere. It's called *Panaché de verduras* and is made with salt pork.

Standard in Toledo tapas bars, which are famous throughout Spain for the variety and quality of their dishes, are tiny sandwiches called *pulgas*, 'little fleas' in the local dialect. These are bite-sized treats of ham, cheese, or perhaps anchovy—anything, in fact, that can be put between two bits of bread.

One can wander for days in the twisting, spiraling streets below the Zocodover, taking a snack here, a morsel there. Perhaps you will decide to stop for a time to listen to a *Tuna*, a band of musicians playing traditional music, often in medieval costume, always with a small collection of *Tuna* groupies, astonishingly beautiful young women given to breaking into brief dances or snatches of song. The music of the *Tuna* is very danceable, based on the rhythm of the *Sevillanas*. Soon there will be general dancing in the streets, led by the *Tuna* ensembles.

+~+

The culture and history of Toledo is rich and complex. For centuries, it was among the leading cities of Europe, where the cultural threads of Christian, pagan, Jewish and Moorish thought were woven together in tolerance and mutual appreciation, each tradition enriching the other.

Surrounded on three sides by the Río Tajo, Toledo began as an easily-defended Iberian hill-fort. The Vizigoths made Toledo their capital in 554, and Hispano-Romans, Goths and Jews lived peaceably together. Here the Vizigothic chief Recared was converted to Christianity, establishing a policy of religious tolerance that did not change even upon the arrival of the Moors, in 712. The city was recaptured by Christians in 1085 under Alfonso VII, who had himself crowned 'Emperor of all the Christian and Moorish kingdoms of Spain,' a title more hopeful than authentic. At any rate, the climate of tolerance continued until 1355, when the brutal suppression of Jewish culture began. This culminated in the expulsion of the Jews from all of Spain in 1492, which proved a commercial and cultural disaster.

During the preceding six centuries, however, while most of Western Europe was mired in dark barbarism, Toledo burned with a bright light. The best scholars from the Mediterranean world gathered at its universities and royal courts. The light can still be glimpsed today, shining in obscure corners of churches, illuminating a painting or a decorated wall down a side-alley. There is so much to see in Toledo that it is one of the few cities where a standard tourist guide is essential. (One of the most complete is the Toledo volume in the Passport Travel Series to Spain, published in cooperation with the National Tourist Board of Spain.)

The only guide you will need to the food is your nose. One evening, following a tip from friends, we set out to find the restaurant Hierbabuena, meaning 'good herb.' We had been unable to find the street Calle de Cristo de Luz, on a map. The desk clerk at our hotel said it was somewhere 'below the cathedral.' That was not a very helpful tip, but we had plenty of time before our 10 PM reservation and it couldn't be more than six blocks away. The usual expedient of resorting to taxis wouldn't work, since autos are not allowed in the old quarter of Toledo.

But we set off merrily soon after 8 PM, planning a few tapas stops on the way and a check of our rented car, the faithful *Bota* Patrol, parked illegally in an obscure plaza off the Zocodover. We visited three tapas bars, always asking directions to the Hierbabuena and the Calle Cristo de Luz. We seemed to be getting closer and were encouraged halfway through the search by actually finding our car unticketed and untowed, wedged in among several dozen other illegally parked cars.

It is impossible for someone who has never experienced it to understand the maze of streets that is Toledo. To call them streets, even by Spanish standards, is to distort the meaning of the word. Even alleys would be too grand a term. Many of them are mere passageways, hardly wide enough for two people to walk side by side, and the streets of Toledo are crowded. You must squeeze past, careful not to knock pots of blooming geraniums off the window-ledges.

Suddenly, without warning or apparent reason, you turn a corner and the narrow alley, poorly lit at the far end, is empty; or perhaps there is only a single figure standing in a doorway halfway down the street. You hesitate, but you have been informed at the last bar that this is a shortcut to Calle Cristo de Luz that will save many minutes of walking. And minutes have become critical since you stayed rather too long listening to the last *Tuna* band. But there is that suspicious person loitering, perhaps with ill intent, and the alley is dark and deserted. Never mind. This is Spain, not New York City or East Oakland. Onward.

The threatening figure is an old lady in black, sitting peacefully on her doorstep, smoking a cigarette. She wishes us a good evening and assures us that Calle Cristo de Luz is straight ahead and to the left. Well, a bit to the left, then straight again, then to the left.

'Where are you going on Cristo de Luz?'

'The Restaurant Hierbabuena.'

'Ah, yes, I know it. One moment, please.'

She steps back into her house and reappears a moment later with a shawl over her head.

'Come, I will show you.'

'But no, *señora*, you mustn't do that.'

She waves her hand. 'It is nothing, I was thinking of going out for a small walk before bed anyway. It will do me good to stir my bones a bit.'

There is no stopping her. We set off briskly down the alleyway, while she apologizes because the street light burned out weeks ago and the authorities had not replaced it. So much for our dark, suspicious alley. Within a few minutes we are at the door of Hierbabuena and our gracious guide is off for her brief walk.

We had been directed to Hierbabuena by friends in Madrid who had assured us that it was one of the best new restaurants in Spain, with a young chef/owner who was doing very exciting work in the kitchen. We were forty-five minutes late, however, and there were no tables left. The headwaiter was polite but firm at first, becoming less polite and firmer still as we insisted that we must have one. At last we reached a compromise after pulling the old 'we are important journalists from California' routine. I don't think he believed us, but recognized that we had to save face, a very Spanish frame of mind. We were seated grandly if rather grudgingly at a table set up in the reception area, on direct display alongside a large pot of flowers.

Hierbabuena is in a magnificent setting. The building was declared a national monument in 1870. Its exact age is unknown, but before 1870 it had belonged to a painter. The design is Mozarabic, tastefully restored where necessary but otherwise left alone. The present owner believes it may have been a stable at one time because there is a long horse trough in the back, now the centerpiece of a small patio.

All in all, we felt rather resplendent and were prepared for a wonderful feast. And so it proved, right from the opening flourish: a scalloped, hollowed-out zucchini, with a sugar cube soaked in brandy placed inside and ignited at the table. The entire dinner was like that—fireworks from start to finish.

Highlights included *Crepe de puerros y gambas*, a folded crepe with bechamel, sautéed leeks and prawns; grilled bread topped with avocado and anchovy cream and sprinkled with toasted cumin seeds—a very Moorish touch; a cold poached bonita with anchovy mayonnaise; and *Brocheta de ternera y butifarra a la salsa de tomillo*, skewers of veal and butifarra sausage marinated in a wine, thyme, oregano and lemon sage sauce.

The anchovy and avocado on grilled bread, topped with cumin, illustrates what can be achieved by experimenting with traditional ingredients. It is a simple enough idea, yet the combination of flavors is unique. Grilled bread is, of course, as old as Mediterranean cooking and grilled bread with anchovy is hardly new; grilled bread with anchovy and tomato has been done, certainly. But the combination of anchovy and avocado was a master stroke. To top that with a North African seasoning, cumin, was the crowning inspiration.

The veal and *butifarra* skewers relied on traditional Spanish ingredients, but combined them in a novel and flavorful way. The sauce and the presentation on skewers is very *manchego*, but the use of northern meats, veal and *butifarra*, gave the dish a new dimension.

As we were having a final espresso and brandy, a young man with an Alsatian at heel came in. He heard us speaking English and asked what we were doing seated in such an unusual location. After we explained, he told us that he was from London but had been living in Toledo over a year, teaching English and scraping by with his dog, Geoffrey. He came in every night at closing time to pick up scraps for Geoff.

'It is such a fantastic city, I can't leave,' he said. 'I was supposed to be here for one semester to research a thesis on Judaism in medieval Spain. But I need years. Do you know how remarkable this city was? For centuries, three cultures usually at war with one another lived here in peace. I simply can't learn enough about it.'

We bought him a cognac so that we could all toast Toledo together, to the light there that never dims.

The basic table of La Mancha crosses borders, resulting in a blurring of boundaries, some culinary twilight zones. Such is Torrecaballeros, a small village northwest of Madrid. Outside La Mancha, cartographers would say, but well within La Mancha when seen from the kitchen.

Torrecaballeros was a pit stop, a quick dash to use the facilities into what seemed to be the only bar in town. Of course, it was our duty and only polite to sample a glass of the local wine. But the smells coming from the dim interior behind the bar stopped us in our tracks. With our two traveling companions, we ordered a local rosé and had a closer look. The establishment was called El Horno de la Aldeguela. An imposing plaque on the wall informed us that it had been founded in 1899 by a Cuban war hero named Zacarias Gilsanz.

The bar itself seemed ordinary enough, with two windows looking out into a nondescript side yard. There was an attractive wooden bar only about eight feet long, a couple of small tables near the back and one narrow door.

By following our noses, we discovered that the wonderful smells were coming from the door, which serviced a dining room. We peeked inside. It was about 1 PM, Sunday afternoon. Too early for lunch, so the small dining room was empty, except for a table of waiters and waitresses lunching in advance of the crowd. There were about six or eight of them, which seemed a lot for such a small place. Then, we noticed another door which opened into another much larger dining room and a stairway leading up to yet another dining room. The space before us was dominated by a huge brick oven built into an exterior wall so it could be fired from outside. We had found the *horno*, the oven, *de la Aldeguela*.

There was one man working by the oven, building and shaping a wood fire. The oven was roughly six feet by eight feet by three feet, lined with brick with a brick slab floor. This was an oven big enough to roast whole sheep in, which was exactly the intention. The cook worked within a three-sided partition, the fourth side being the oven. Stacked all around him were lamb carcasses. He was surrounded by three huge counters, one an enormous chopping block, the other two serving counters.

There was already lamb roasting, which is what had led our noses to the source. Back in the bar, we conferred briefly with our stomachs and our schedule. It didn't take us long to decide. I asked the waiter what time lunch would be served. The first seating, he told us, was at 2:30, and if we wanted the lamb, we should let him know right away as there were only a few portions left. That seemed odd, since the place was empty, but we reserved ourselves a quarter of a lamb, enough for the four of us, and settled down with a pitcher of the excellent rosé.

Within fifteen minutes, the place began filling up. I took a look outside. In the parking lot, there were cars arriving from Madrid, Segovia and a few Toledo plates as well. By 2:30, there wasn't a vacant table in the house.

Our quarter of lamb was served with baked potatoes with *allioli* on the side, as an American restaurant would serve sour cream or butter. Before the lamb was served, there was a richly flavored garlic soup, *sopa de ajo*, made in the usual way, except that the soup stock had been made using smoked meat. After the soup came roasted red peppers, whole grilled cloves of garlic and sliced onions. For dessert there was a *tarta de segoviana*.

It was all perfect country food. The lamb was seasoned only with what the Spanish call 'mountain herbs'—rosemary, sage and thyme—and that sparingly. But the lamb itself was like the essence of lamb. It was Plato's ideal lamb, each bite a revelation. It was perfectly cooked even though the oven man was working at speed. He used a long wooden paddle, not unlike the kind used by pizza makers but with a longer handle, to slide the various cuts of lamb back and forth. After a quick check, he would reposition the lamb in a hotter or cooler part of the oven.

There were quarters, halves and whole lambs, which he moved in and out of the oven like he was shuffling cards. Using the paddle as a serving board, he would pass half a lamb over the counter to one waiter and in the same motion turn back to the oven, slide out a quarter and pass it over the opposite counter to another waiter, never missing a beat. The potatoes and grilled vegetables came from the same oven too, an endless cornucopia dished out with the lamb.

It is impossible to give a recipe for the lamb. You must go there on a weekend or a holiday—it's the only time El Horno de la Aldeguela is open. In the winter, when there is skiing in the nearby Sierra de Guadarrama, it may be necessary to book a table weeks ahead for the second lunch seating at 5 PM.

We discovered there were two similar *hornos* in Torrecaballeros and, in fact, there are hornos all over Castile and León, where one will find excellent garlic soup, grilled vegetables and lamb. The Aldeguela just happens to be the one we chanced upon. And it is not unusual to find cars from Madrid and the urban centers parked outside, for these country restaurants are well known, each with its following among city folk.

One is getting very close in these country places to the roots of Spanish food—simple food of first-rate quality, prepared in such a way as to highlight the inherent taste of the food. The most successful chefs have elaborated on that idea to create the modern Spanish cuisine.

Rioja and Navarre

Much of modern Rioja was part of the kingdom of Old Castile, an area that swept from Madrid to the Bay of Biscay. It also includes parts of ancient Navarre, and it makes good culinary and enological sense to consider the two regions together. Rioja and Navarre cover an area that extends from the high plains south of the Río Ebro to the Basque territory at the foothills of the Pyrenees, then turns abruptly east into the high mountains bordering France. The Pyrenees dominate the northern fringe of Rioja and most of Navarre, with valleys running mainly north-south between fold after fold of mountain range.

The climate is described as continental, which seems to mean that it gets the worst of everything, from bitter winter cold with snow and ice in the mountains, to stifling heat in the summer, especially in the flatlands of Baja Rioja, where the Río Ebro often becomes a tired, muddy trickle by summer's end.

Rioja was well known to the Romans as a wine-producing area, with trading ships from the Mediterranean sailing up the Ebro to Logroño, Haro and other inland ports. The whole area was the scene of heavy fighting between the Moors and Christians in the eighth, ninth and tenth centuries. Eventually the Moors were expelled and much of the Christian Reconquest of Spain was guided thereafter from Navarre and Rioja.

One of the most famous medieval pilgrimage routes, the Camino de Santiago de Compostela, began in Spain at Roncesvalles on the French border and ran through Navarre and Rioja towards its destination in Galicia. It is difficult for us to grasp, at this remove in time and attitude from the late Middle Ages, just how important this pilgrimage was.

The legend of Santiago—St. James—the patron saint of Spain, first came to light during the reign of the Christian King Alfonso II of Asturias (791-842). There had always been a dim tradition in the north that St. James had preached the gospel in Spain. After his missionary work, the legend goes, he returned to the Holy Land and was executed by Herod Agrippa in AD 44. His followers then returned his body to Spain by sea in a marble sarcophagus.

The first of St. James' many miracles took place before he ever got back to Spain. The boat carrying his remains was off the coast of Portugal when the saint saved the life of a man who had been swept out to sea on a horse. Rider and horse emerged from the sea covered with scallop shells. The scallop shell became the saint's symbol and became so well known that the shell, or a jeweled replica, was often worn in France and England as an indication that one had made the pilgrimage to Santiago. In Paris one can still see stone scallops carved above doorways of the homes of people who had made the journey.

St. James, it is said, was buried near the present town of Santiago and then seems to have been largely forgotten—until he was needed, that is. In 813 Alfonso II received word that the tomb of St. James had been revealed by the presence of a bright star which stood overhead. In case the light show wasn't enough, a chorus of angels was also on hand. The saint was found in time to lead Christians in an important battle against the Moors and the battle-cry, 'Santiago y cierra España' (St. James and close in Spain), was sounded. The cry was raised again and again as the Christians slowly forced the Moors southward.

The saint's tomb became known as the Field of the Star and Alfonso ordered a church built on the spot. In time, a town grew up around the site, which was called Santiago de Compostela, St. James of the Star Field. The original church became a cathedral and, in time, the goal of one of western Europe's major pilgrimages.

It wasn't the Spanish, though, who promoted the pilgrimage, but the French Benedictine monks of Cluny, who established monasteries along the route and helped spread the fame of Santiago de Compostela. For centuries it rivaled Rome and Jerusalem as a goal for pilgrims. The monks had realized that Santiago could provide a rallying point for the struggle against the Moors, which was taking place in Spain and in the Middle East.

All this history does lead us back to the table, for where there were inns, there were also kitchens and wine barrels. St. James, as we shall see, came to play an important role at the tables of Rioja and Navarre as well as on the battlefield.

✛〰✛

Rioja and Navarre are meat and potatoes country. The emphasis is on straightforward hearty dishes, with shades of the more sophisticated

Basque cuisine in the north. It is odd that, although the French have influenced Rioja winemaking, there is very little French influence in the kitchen. Taken as a whole, Rioja's food is basic country fare, but as elsewhere in Spain, it is country fare based on fine and fresh ingredients.

We have been very happy at table in Rioja and Navarre, but there are surprisingly few recipes to show for many hours of lovely eating. Rioja fare is perfect for summertime at the barbecue. It is not food that requires a great deal of concentration and leaves plenty of time for the wine and plenty of time for friends and lovers. It leaves time for life.

There are beans of all sorts, which figure prominently in a number of dishes. Bushels of local hot and sweet peppers overflow the counters at every market in the summer; in the winter they are replaced by dried peppers and by fresh supplies imported from Huelva in Andalusia or from the Canary Islands. Leave room for potatoes; they appear daily at table in one form or another.

There is trout from the rivers, often still alive at the market or in a restaurant tank. The region, like everywhere in Spain, is rich in hams and sausages, both dried and fresh. Lamb in season and mutton all year long round out the butcher's market, with a smattering of beef and goat. Rabbit, quail and partridge are raised domestically, but also hunted, especially as you move north into the mountains. There is also deer, wild boar, ducks and geese in season.

✦∿✦

The wines of Rioja represent the world's last great wine bargains. There are world-class red wines at astonishing prices, fresh fruity reds and delicious rosés from Navarre that enliven the simplest meals. The great Rioja red wines have tremendous ageability and would make an excellent foundation for anyone's wine cellar.

There have been vineyards in Rioja since pre-Roman times. The Romans replanted the area's vineyards with vines from Italy, and exported wine not only to other parts of Spain, but also down the River Ebro to the Mediterranean and on to Italy. At Funes in Navarre are the remains of a large Roman winery from the first century AD which, judging from the size of the fermentation vats, produced perhaps thirty thousand gallons of wine a year, roughly the equivalent of a mid-sized California winery in the Napa Valley, such as Cakebread Cellars. Another major winemaking center in Rioja was Cenicero, a town where the Roman legions cremated their dead. In a rather grotesque linguistic development, *cenicero* means ashtray in modern Spanish.

Winemaking declined somewhat under the Moors, although as in other parts of Spain, the Moors didn't ban winemaking by any means. They had no problem with Christians making wine and selling it to one another, or trading it to other areas. And while abstinence may have been the ideal of true Moslems, like men and women everywhere they doubtless fell short of that ideal on occasion and Mecca was far away.

As the Moors retreated before Christian armies, wine assumed greater importance in Rioja. The renaissance of winemaking in the area began in monasteries at San Millán de Suso, San Millán de Yuso and Valvanera, in the hills that lined the pilgrim route to Santiago. As the pilgrimage became more important, wine to ease the labor of the road became more important also.

Inevitably, French merchants joined the monks of Cluny and pilgrims from all over Europe traveling the road to Santiago. And some believe that a more important French immigrant arrived around the same time—the Pinot Noir grape—imported by the French to replace Spain's wild, high-growing, low-yielding, hillside vines. In Rioja, the grape is now called Tempranillo.

This is a controversial idea with the Spanish, who are reluctant to cite a French origin for anything they put on their table, let alone the Tempranillo. But it is a possibility nonetheless. It is difficult to verify botanically as Pinot Noir mutates more dramatically than any other wine grape. One can imagine the changes the grape would undergo moving from the cool, sometimes harsh growing conditions of Burgundy, to the warmer, steadier climate of Rioja.

On the palate, Tempranillo-based wines of Rioja do show a marked resemblance to Pinot Noir. At their best, they have the same silky, velvety character and the lush forward fruitiness that one always hopes for in a Burgundy, but achieves only in rare years. There is also an earthy, mushroomy quality common to both varietals.

In contrast to the harder, more closed wines of Bordeaux, which are based on Cabernet Sauvignon and related grapes, Rioja wines have a quite different sensuous, feminine quality. This is in spite of over one hundred years of effort by expatriate French winemakers to sculpt a

Bordeaux-style wine in Rioja; first from Tempranillo, then by the planting of Cabernet Sauvignon—planting now forbidden for the most part
in Rioja.

Rioja was an important source of wine to supply the New World,
and vineyards expanded rapidly during the sixteenth and seventeenth
centuries. The wine trade grew to such importance that in 1790, the
Royal Society of Harvesters of the Rioja was formed for the purpose of
growing better grapes, making better wine and finding new markets—
things Rioja is still busily engaged in, especially finding new markets.

✦❧✦

Seven major grape varieties are approved to be grown in Rioja. For
white wine and rosé, there are Viura, Malvasia and Garnacha Blanca; of
these, Viura is the most common, with about twenty percent of the
vineyards. White wines of Rioja are made almost entirely from the Viura
while the Garnacha Blanca is used in rosés.

There has been a tremendous change in the white wines and rosés
of Rioja in the past decade. It didn't take the producers there long to see
the success Miguel Torres Jr. of Bodegas Torres had in Catalonia with
his fresh, fruity white wines like Viña Sol. Torres, French-trained and
with a great interest in Californian winemaking techniques, began making white wines using cold fermentation and stainless steel, avoiding
barrel aging or giving only a light smack of oak. His wines emphasize
the fruitiness of the grape and are designed for immediate drinking
pleasure.

For centuries, Spanish white wines had been made in much the
same way that the reds were—hot fermentation, several years in oak
casks. The results were tired, often oxidized white wines with no hint of
fruit, bogged down in oak flavors. They had a following in Spain, but
no place else.

When Torres put his Viña Sol on the market in the 1970s, skeptics
said it would never succeed. The Spanish, it was popularly supposed,
would not take to a light, fruity white wine and it would never get
anywhere on the world market, since the expectation was that Spanish
white wines would be oxidized and oaky. In the event, Viña Sol was an
immense success, not only in the Spanish market, but internationally as
well. The Rioja winemakers, as well as the larger co-op wineries of

Valencia and La Mancha, quickly followed Torres' suit. Within ten years a revolution had taken place in Spanish white wines.

✦❀✦

In the last few years a major controversy has raged in Rioja concerning just what is a 'traditional' Rioja wine—and we are speaking here mostly of red wine—and what is to be done about the 'new style' Riojas. There are two parts to the debate. Part one is involved with grape variety and concerns what many believe to be the unfortunate use of Cabernet Sauvignon in the production of Rioja. Part two involves production techniques, including the use of winemaking methods that have changed the focus of the wine, making it altogether more fruit driven.

First things first. There are five grape varieties approved for red wine production in Rioja: Tempranillo, Garnacha, Graciano, Mazuelo and Viura. There is a quibble on Cabernet Sauvignon, which is allowed in experimental plantings or, in a few cases, grandfathered in with special dispensations.

The blending of Viura, a white wine grape, into red Rioja surprises some Americans, but adding white wine to a red is common practice in Italy and southern France, as well as Spain and Portugal. White grapes, picked young, add acidity and 'bite' to the wine.

Tempranillo is easily the most widely planted, with something approaching fifty percent of Rioja's vineyards given to it. Tempranillo by itself produces a fairly fruity, sometimes low-acid wine, often rather light in color, which can be quite good. The Garnacha pushes the alcohol higher and gives added strength to the wine flavors. Mazuelo adds tannin and acidity, and Graciano can add an elegant, perfumy element to the nose.

Not only can Rioja wine be a blend of up to five varieties of grape, but it is also a blend of vineyards and regions within Rioja. There is some movement toward estate-bottled wines, but not a great deal. That's because about eighty percent of the grapes grown in Rioja still come from small farms of less than an acre of vines. And that single acre may be a jumble of varieties. Many Rioja growers take on grapes as a sideline, tending a few rows, following the same vineyard practices as their fathers and grandfathers.

So when wineries like Conde de Valdemar and Berberana start major experiments with Cabernet Sauvignon, or putting out a one hundred percent varietal Tempranillo, there are those who claim that the traditional wines of Rioja are in danger.

What tradition are they talking about? The pre-Roman or Roman tradition? How about the traditional Rioja wines of the Middle Ages, when thousands of pilgrims annually trekked past the bodega door on their way to Santiago de Compostela? Vines then were grown climbing trees or on pergolas. Certainly not that tradition.

What is regarded today as traditional in Rioja is barely a century old and is largely the creation of French vintners, fleeing phylloxera in the vineyards of Bordeaux in the 1860s. (Phylloxera eventually got to Rioja, but by then, growers had learned to graft the vines onto phylloxera-resistant rootstock.) No doubt a great deal of undocumented Cabernet Sauvignon was introduced into Rioja during that period. And a great deal no doubt remains, no matter what the official statistics report.

The second part of the controversy deals with production methods. 'Traditional' Rioja is normally fermented quickly at high temperatures. No temperature-controlled stainless steel vats, thank you. It then receives long aging in barrels or large casks, usually of American oak, that may be kept in use for several decades. This process works to create a balance and palate richness that goes beyond fruit and addresses the possibility of long aging and uniformity.

Aging classifications of Rioja red wines work out like this:

- *Sin Crianza*—A young wine in its first or second year with less than a year in wood, often with no time at all in wood.
- *Crianza*—Must have at least one year in barrel and one year in bottle before release.
- *Reserva*—Must have three years in a combination of barrel and bottle, of which at least one year must be in barrel.
- *Gran Reserva*—Must have five years in barrel or bottle, of which at least two years must be in barrel.

In practice, the more traditional producers age wines in the *Reserva* and *Gran Reserva* class much longer in barrel than the minimum regulations require.

Full disclosure here. We are aghast at the internalization of wines.

Chardonnay that tastes the same whether it is made in California, the south of France, Chile, Argentina, Australia or Bulgaria is detestable, a commodity, like breakfast cereal. If a wine doesn't speak to a particular place and time, then to hell with it.

On the other hand, some of the changes taking place in Rioja can be seen as natural steps in the evolution of Rioja style, an evolution which has been going on for several thousand years. One could look at the history of any major wine growing region and trace such evolution in varietal use and winemaking style.

We would argue that Cabernet Sauvignon should have a limited role, if any, in Rioja. One of the most innovative of Rioja winemakers, Jesús Martínez Bujanda of Conde de Valdemar, agrees. Martínez Bujanda, who has experimented extensively with Cabernet Sauvignon and made a one hundred percent Garnacha Reserva that is a knockout, said, 'My opinion is that Rioja should maintain its style with the Tempranillo variety dominant. It would be a pity if the growth of Cabernet Sauvignon in Rioja were massive and that the characteristics that make Rioja wines different were to disappear.'

Martínez Bujanda goes on. 'Tempranillo is the most important variety in Rioja. It is the essence of Rioja wine style and I think that it should continue to be. In my opinion, the most important change produced in Rioja in the last few years is not any experimentation with new varieties, but the revolution that has taken place in the way the wines are made.'

Twenty-five years ago most Rioja wines were uniform, with little difference from bodega to bodega. 'In a blind tasting, it was really difficult to distinguish one winery from another. In general, the wines were light, open in color and easy to drink. All that was the product of a short fermentation and very little maceration. Now we use longer maceration and shorter barrel aging to produce wines more full-bodied with a firmer structure. I think now it is much easier to identify wines from a particular winery, yet they are all Rioja wines.'

Martínez Bujanda added, 'I personally think that Rioja wines are much more interesting than they were years ago because there is a wider variety of styles. As for quality, they are much better.'

As frequent visitors to Rioja and longtime and appreciative drinkers of the wines, it does seem to us that at least some of the changes in how the wine is made have been for the better—and they have been changes within the framework of Rioja, not moves designed to chase the flavor of the month.

As an example, the new varietal Tempranillo wines from Berberana remain essentially Rioja and are recognizable as such, despite the fact that they are a single variety and were aged only six months in new American oak. The wine is very fruit-driven, yet very 'Rioja.' They have been quite successful with consumers as well and have won several awards, within Spain and internationally.

Even a traditional producer like Bodegas Montecillo has no problem using modern winemaking technology if it results in an improvement in the wines. María Martínez Sierra, the winemaker at Montecillo, said, 'Young Riojas have experienced a drastic improvement in quality thanks to an optimal control of fermentation, achieving much more aromatic wines. Aged wines are showing more body and deepness, due to longer maceration periods. Wines have also improved because of shorter oak aging periods and longer bottle aging.'

But on the issue of varieties, she isn't budging from the traditionalist position: 'I really believe that if Tempranillo is properly grown, it can be one of the best grapes possible. Handled right, it maintains good acidity and matures well. I think the Cabernet Sauvignon grown in Rioja has not produced any spectacular results to this point. People are beginning to realize that fine quality wine has nothing to do with being fashionable or trendy. The most important thing for a wine is to keep its own personality. Wine is a living thing.'

Guillermo de Aranzabal of La Rioja Alta puts a very practical spin on the question of Cabernet Sauvignon. 'As far as the future of Cabernet in Rioja is concerned, we think it is not going to be important, not only because it is in most cases illegal, but because the yield is lower than that of Tempranillo and it is more difficult to grow. Even if a winery were interested, growers are not,' he said.

However, La Rioja Alta does not simply follow tradition at any price. Last year they bought a small wine estate, Barón de Oña, a spectacular winery in the Rioja Alavesa. Unusual for Rioja, the wines are entirely estate-grown. The cuvée is traditional—about 90 percent Tempranillo with the rest Mazuelo—but the wines are fermented in temperature-controlled stainless steel tanks and aged for two years in small French oak barrels, used for one year at Château Margaux. They are held in bottle for several years before release.

Rodolfo Bastida, the assistant director of Bodegas Bretón has no problem with continued experiments with nontraditional varieties like Cabernet or Merlot. He warns, however, that growing conditions in Rioja are quite different than Bordeaux. He makes the interesting point that Tempranillo reflects the soil, the *terroir*, much better than Cabernet. 'It is such a delicate wine that you can see real difference from one field to the next, even if they are only a few meters apart,' he said.

However, like almost everyone we talked to in Rioja, Bastida has no problems using modern technology with the traditional grapes. 'This is the new Rioja, more fruit and less oak. Not too many people understand that yet in Spain,' he added.

Nor outside Spain, for that matter. The truth is that Rioja wines are much more complex, much richer and deeper wines than only a few years ago. That does not mean that there aren't a great many older Rioja wines that are really magnificent, but it does mean that in the future, the Riojas being made now should age even better with more individual style and character.

What Rioja has managed to do is change for the better while staying within the framework of Rioja. The better winemakers are pressing on with the business at hand, making the best possible wines reflecting the origin and potential of the grapes.

Some Rioja brands to look for include: Bodegas AGE, Bodegas Bilbainas, Bodegas Berberana, Bodegas Beronia, Conde de Valdemar from Bodegas Martínez Bujanda, Bodegas Bretón, Bodegas Marqués de Cáceres, Bodegas Campo Viejo, Compañía Vinícola del Norte de España (CVNE), Bodegas Marqués de Riscal, Bodegas Montecillo, Bodegas Marqués de Murrieta, Bodegas Muga, Federico Paternina, La Rioja Alta, Siglo, R. López de Heredia Viña Tondonia.

↜↝

The entire idea of 'making' a wine is most un-Spanish. In Spain, no one is called a winemaker, except by those wineries accustomed to dealing with Americans. In their place, you will find someone called a technical director or enologist. When the Spanish talk about winemaking, they use the verb *elaborar*, which means to elaborate or extend, not to create from primary material. This is not simply a matter of linguistics, but goes to the heart of the Spanish attitude toward wine. Wine is a natural, not a manufactured, product. It makes itself, and the enologist simply elaborates on something already in existence.

We once toured a large Spanish co-op with a group of American and British wine journalists. The enologist showing us about spoke adequate English, yet the group spent a great deal of time hung up over this point. One of the journalists was trying to determine when a certain step in winemaking procedure took place and the enologist was trying to tell him. But neither could follow the other's statements because of this distinction between making and elaborating. The Spaniard finally threw up his hands, cut short the tour and led us to the tasting room where we could talk about the wine in the glass, rather than how it got there.

One early winter's day, the process of 'elaborating' was about to begin at Bodegas Berberana in Rioja. We were to meet Angel Yecora, an enologist at Berberana, deep in the cellars of their very modern winery in the town of Cenicero. Yecora's mission was to lead us through the tanks of new wine and discuss how he would do the blending later on.

There are no formulas to follow, he said. 'The blending depends on the tasting, not on a recipe.' As in the development of sherry, the wine determines its own future. 'The time in barrel depends on the tasting, beginning now,' Yecora said. He was speaking of whether the wine would become a *crianza*, a young wine which would receive little aging, or a *Reserva*, or a *Gran Reserva*. 'It is all in the wine,' Yecora repeated, as we moved on.

Berberana had its beginnings in 1877 in the small village of Ollauri. In 1972, after decades of steady growth, they built a new winery at Cenicero with a total capacity of nearly six million gallons. It is one of the most modern wineries in Spain, with two huge underground storage areas containing twenty-five thousand oak barrels, an entire forest.

But Vecora had decided to make it easy for us by tasting only five wines, a Graciano, a red Garnacha, a Tempranillo, a Viura and a Mazuelo. We were focusing on the different grape varieties, without being concerned about different vineyards or growing areas. He thought this would be enough for us to handle.

It was pretty much a given that the Garnacha was destined to be a *rosado*, and already just a few months from the vine, that pleasant, rather acidic fruitiness that is the mark of a *rosado* was in evidence. The Viura was a high-acid white wine, rather simple, but intended only to add some acidic backbone to a final blend. The Tempranillo was very fruity and pleasantly round on the palate. The acidity seemed low on the finish, giving the wine a flabby feeling. But that's where the Viura would come in, and it wouldn't require much. The Garnacha, also fairly acidic, would help here, too. The Mazuelo sample was a deep, rich red, with an abundant tannic extract.

Vecora, like most other Rioja enologists, believes that with these five basic grapes, plus a little Malvasia and Garnacha Blanca, he can make about anything he wants in Rioja. He is very much against the idea of making a wine from a single grape varietal himself, feeling that it is in blending that Rioja really expresses itself.

After tasting samples of the five basic types, Vecora tapped a few more barrels, getting more and more excited about the prospects of the vintage. We were deep under the earth, going from barrel to barrel as Vecora demonstrated the difference between Tempranillo grown at low and high elevations (more acidic at the higher elevation) and speculated about how the wines would fit into future blends, or into the reserve program.

Many of the wines were surprisingly palatable despite being only a few months old. Because the Spanish are not infatuated with new oak barrels the way California winemakers are, young wine here doesn't have the bitter tannins that new oak imparts.

Bodegas Berberana is very much a working winery, not a museum. The floors are simple concrete, the lighting dim, to reduce energy consumption and keep things cool. The barrel storage area is designed for efficiency, including a central computer system for blending that looks like something out of Stars Wars. Yet there is something magical about tasting in any barrel room. It has to do with the smell of new wine, a cool earthiness that also comes from the casks and barrels that is very soothing, very satisfying.

It was past midnight when we left Mesón de la Merced, a rather posh restaurant about four blocks from the Plaza del Mercado in

Logroño. The dinner had been very good, but very reserved. We were there with a group of Americans, mostly there to taste the delights of Rioja, but perhaps a bit too self-conscious about those delights to enjoy them fully. Everyone was tired; it had been a long day, with another long day to follow.

Most had read what the guide books say about Logroño: 'Logroño lacks the charm that might be expected of the major wine-producing region of Spain.' Even worse in its way: 'Logroño remains a busy provincial capital. It is a manufacturing centre (textiles), and still produces its famous coffee caramels.' How damning is that faint praise! Would anyone want to linger in a city famous chiefly for coffee caramels?

But we moved from the restaurant out into an extravaganza, a burst of music and color. The very streets were being painted. Just past midnight, we had come upon the beginning of the eve of Corpus Christi. Starting at midnight, the Calle Mayor had been seized by painters with chalk. For blocks leading to the Catedral de Santa María de la Redonda, the narrow lane was divided into sections and had become a sketch board for fantastic scenes, more or less religious, relating to the theme of Corpus Christi. The sidewalks were crowded by onlookers, watching the work in progress. Apparently each shop took the section of street in front of its doors as a canvas.

There were bright angels with purple wings and violet halos gazing down upon green virgins, wearing glowing lavender shawls and clutching a golden Jesus to their breast. On the sidewalk, musicians played the guitar and shouted encouragement to the chalkers, who frequently interrupted their work for a glass of wine offered by friendly sidewalk critics.

I stood amazed. We had entered the Mesón de la Merced about 9:30 PM on a quiet evening in late May, eaten our way through a satisfying if rather boring meal, and emerged at 1 AM into a fairy kingdom. Fellini out of Disney. People in the bar next door spilled out onto the sidewalk to criticize, to comment, to offer drinks, to dart back inside for another quickly-emptied bottle.

My companions gazed bemused for a moment, then opted for the hotel, bed and sanity. I wandered like a lost child into the heart of the madness and never looked back. At 3 AM I was teaching hopscotch to a small tribe of Spanish children on the steps of the cathedral, sharing a bottle of rosado with a young couple who had come from Navarre for the Corpus Christi celebrations. They were farmers, their first child very visibly on the way. They wanted to know about California. Did we celebrate Corpus Christi in San Francisco? Was the wine as good? (Surely not, the young woman giggled.)

The children simply thought I was crazy, which was OK with them. They kept bringing us olives—one by one on toothpicks—from a nearby bar. In a few moments, the young couple from Navarre were joined by another couple who had made the trip with them. There was more wine and a roast chicken from somewhere. We made a picnic on the steps of the church while the children swarmed around us, shouting 'Hopscotch, hopscotch.' The chicken was delicious. It had been roasted with sprigs of rosemary and cloves of garlic stuffed in the cavity.

Near dawn, I was in the shower at our hotel. I was covered in chalk dust. I didn't want to wash it away.

❧

Bodegas Beronia is a Rioja winery with an unusual history. The name comes from the tribe of Berones, who gave the Romans a hard time in the third century BC. The winery was founded in 1970 by a Basque gastronomic society, whose members wanted to drink wine to match the food they ate. Unable to find acceptable wine at the price they wanted to pay, the society started their own winery near the town of Ollauri in Rioja Alta. It was so successful at making good wine that the shareholders decided they needed help. In 1982 they formed a partnership with González Byass of Jerez de la Frontera. The multinational sherry firm has taken over marketing and contributed some capital to modernize, but otherwise has left the winemaking alone. The results have been superb.

I arrived at Beronia the worse for wear. We had spent the previous evening in Logroño, with a long dinner as a kind of rehearsal for Twelfth Night celebrations, followed by a personal examination of a number of bars where one might find the best examples of that Rioja specialty, coffee caramels. At this point, it's unclear why we believed that the perfect coffee caramel would be found in a bar; or why, for that matter, Logroño was supposed to be known for such delights.

At any rate, my host at Beronia took one look at me at 10 the next morning and took me promptly to the dining room, calling for anise and coffee along the way. We sat down with a bottle of Chinchón and endless cups of espresso. Over the next two hours and a half bottle of Chinchón, I learned considerably more about Beronia, vineyards and winemaking in Rioja, than I would have while walking with a throbbing head through the cellars.

We talked about vineyards:

- The location of a vineyard is more important than what is planted in it.
- Most vineyard owners in Rioja have other crops planted and are not solely dependent on vines. Grapes are often not even the most important source of income.
- Only two vineyards in Rioja are larger than 250 acres.
- Because of rulings by the European Economic Community, no new plantings are now permitted in Rioja.
- An acre of land in Rioja costs about four million pesetas. In other areas of Spain, an acre of vines costs about one million. (At the time of the hangover symposium at Beronia, the peseta was about 125 to the dollar.)
- There is concern in Rioja about foreigners (French, mostly) buying up vineyards.

As we sipped our espresso and a third tiny glass of Chinchón, a man and woman began quietly setting a table across the room and an indoor grill was laid with vine cuttings. We were to be joined at lunch by a few people, at least one of whom, Ann, had been on the unlikely search for the perfect coffee caramel the night before. The sun was shining outside the wide windows, which overlooked a bucolic hillside setting of vines and sheep. All seemed well.

Chinchón, by the way, is one of Spain's two major brands of anise-flavored liqueur, the other being Anís de Mono, made in Badalona, just up the Costa Brava from Barcelona. Chinchón comes from the village of the same name about fifty kilometers from Madrid. Besides producing the life-restoring drink, Chinchón is a charming pueblo with a particularly pleasant Plaza Mayor, where bullfights have been held since the 1500s. There are few better places to sit in the sunshine, sipping liqueur at its source.

We were just beginning to feel guilty about neglecting the cellars when we smelled vine cuttings smoking on the grill and heard the cheerful sound of a bottle being uncorked. Good Lord! It was lunch time and I had actually made it through the morning without disgracing myself.

As you might expect, the kitchen at a winery owned by a Basque gastronomic society is capable of serving a better-than-average lunch. It was Rioja country food at its best. Every dish we had could be found elsewhere in Spain, yet each one had the Rioja signature. I was introduced to Pepe and María del Valle Pascual as they were laying *chorizo* and strips of red pepper on the grill. They had been at the winery for years, handling just about any sort of entertainment from a modern, but fairly straightforward, working cook's kitchen.

The pepper and *chorizo* were passed as a tapa before we sat down to lunch. Señor del Valle explained that the tiny, finger-sized *chorizo* was a specialty of Rioja, Navarre and the Basque country. They had less filler and more meat than *chorizo* from Extremadura or parts of southern Spain. They had also been well aged and were drier, but grilling brought out the flavor.

Señor del Valle was not so pleased with the peppers. They had come from Huelva in the extreme south, most likely grown under plastic. If we were to return in early summer, he could offer peppers from Rioja that would put these to shame. However, we found them delicious grilled and he agreed, adding that he would never serve them fresh.

We sat down to a serving platter of *menestra de verduras*, the basic vegetable stew of all Spain. It is served year-round, the ingredients varying with the season. Since it was midwinter, it was heavy on carrots, beans, potatoes, canned peas, ham, hard boiled eggs and plenty of garlic, of course. At other times of the year, it would include fresh peas, green beans, spinach, artichokes, other greens in season, perhaps beets or turnips.

There appeared a heaping platter of lamb ribs, served only with French fries. They had been grilled over vine cuttings to perfection, tender, juicy and loaded with flavors. These were, in fact, the lamb ribs that pilgrims have been traveling to Rioja to find for centuries. They were as miraculous as any saintly appearance. They were somewhat smaller than lamb ribs in the United States and somewhat fatter, but most of the fat was left behind in the coals, leaving only the deep flavor of the meat.

I asked Señor del Valle if the vines gave the cooked lamb its great flavor. He shook his head no. The flavor, he said, came from the lamb itself, which had been milk-fed, not just on one ewe, but two, a peculiarity of the north. He used vine cuttings because the heat could be quickly raised or lowered due to the fast-burning cuttings.

I would like to suggest that it is possible for American cooks to locate vine cuttings. Grapes are grown in most regions now, and for commercial winemaking in some forty-five states. In most places, after the vines are pruned, the cuttings are simply piled at the edge of the vineyard and burned. What a waste! A Sunday drive to the nearest vineyard anytime after mid-January will turn up enough cuttings to fill your trunk or station wagon in minutes.

Señor del Valle told us to forget about the knives and forks for the lamb ribs. We should eat them, he said, like we were playing the harmonica.

❧

In the cellars of La Rioja Alta Winery we were followed everywhere by a large white cat. Sometimes the cat would be peering at us between barrels, sometimes from atop a tall wooden upright. There were other cats in the winery, but only the one giant white cat followed visitors, it seems.

'The cats in the winery are completely wild and no one feeds them, or very little. Sometimes they might get some lunch scraps from cellar workers, but no more. They keep us clear of rats and mice and they don't drink any of the wine, so they are no problem.'

The young guide smiled. Gabriela Rezola had come in on her day off to show us the winery and whatever her expectations had been, was quite enjoying the unexpected opportunity to taste some of the older wines, as well as the new wine just put in barrels.

In early January, the entire town of Haro in Rioja smelled of newly-fermented wine, just as it did in the winery. It smelled much the same in cellars all over Spain, all over the world, no doubt, even those gleaming stainless steel pseudo-laboratories that try to give the impression all wine is made by machine, that pervasive smell of just-fermented wine will out.

It is the very stuff of life, as all wise cats know.

❧

We had followed the ripening vines through the heart of Spain, from Andalusia in the south, through La Mancha, ending finally in the lower reaches of the Pyrenees with the grape harvest finished except for a few scattered, mountain vineyards. After a weekend visit to friends in San Sebastián, we were on a weird mission, in search of the lost Basques of Bakersfield. We had read in a guide book that many Basques left Spain during the civil war and settled in Nevada and California. This we knew to be true. It was the next part that sent us on this odd quest, plunging down the steep mountain road from Roncesvalles toward the Spanish border town of Valcarlos.

The guide went on to say that many of these expatriate Basques had eventually retired to Bakersfield, California. When Franco died, they had left Bakersfield and returned to Spain, settling in and around Valcarlos. There, the guide book claimed, it would be easy enough to slip across the border into France should the political climate once more become uncomfortable. It all seemed unlikely somehow. Why would émigré Basques, accustomed to the mountains of Spain and California, inflict upon themselves the dry, dusty and polluted air of Bakersfield?

But before we could answer that question, there was Roncesvalles. It hangs hawklike at the head of the mountain pass that spills down into France, the route of Charlemagne's retreat, the route the pilgrims took centuries later on the way to Santiago de Compostela.

We had driven almost cross-country through the lower southern reaches of the Pyrenees for most of the day, having left San Sebastián on the Bay of Biscay early that morning. The main roads follow the mountain valleys south-south-east toward the fertile vineyards of Navarre and Rioja. In our small, rented Seat, 'the *Bota* Patrol,' we were cutting across those valleys, following breathtaking asphalt, gravel and dirt roads.

Once, a dirt road ended in the farmyard of a small whitewashed house, each window graced with a wooden window box full of blooming geraniums. Fruit trees were trained against a south wall, the fruit already picked, with only a few late leaves hanging on against the winter—bare, dark branches silhouetted against the white house. A few chickens pecked warily at the kitchen midden further down the hill. Beyond the farmyard, there seemed to be a faint trace of road sketched through a green cow-dotted pasture on a hillside, disappearing into a grove of trees higher up the mountain.

A man appeared around the corner of the house. He wore the typical Basque uniform—a baggy blue sweater over baggy colorless pants, topped off by a black beret. Was there an amused glint in his eye as he came upon the silly little red Seat sitting dispiritedly in the mud outside his door? Wordlessly, we offered him the *bota*. He accepted, and took a long deep squeeze of the wine that we had bought that morning in San Sebastián.

No, he told us, the road was impassable except for mules and horses. We showed him our detailed map of Navarre, which had the road continuing over the next pass until it reached C135, the main road to Roncesvalles. He shook his head. *'¡No pasar, no pasar!'* There had been a landslide a few years before and the road had not been repaired. We thanked him and started to get back in the car. 'Wait, wait,' he said.

He went into the house and returned with a pitcher of light red wine. He asked for our *bota*, which was nearly empty. He squeezed the last few drops out of it into his throat, then filled the *bota* with wine from the pitcher.

'It is better. It is from my nephew's vineyard near Pamplona. Try it now.'

I did, anxiously squeezing the *bota*, afraid I would spill a few drops onto my shirt and disgrace myself in the old farmer's eyes. Ann, too, squeezed out some wine in a clean, spinning spiral from bag to mouth. The sunlight glinted off the wine. There is a miniature painting in the wine museum at Vilafranca del Penedés in Catalonia showing a young peasant drinking from a *bota* with almost the same angle.

'It is better, much better,' I said. And it was. There are wonderful light red wines, sometimes called *rosado*, sometimes *clarete*, all through Navarre. A well-made wine from home can be better than a commercial version, since it retains its intense fruity flavor by being vinified in small batches, with no commercial shortcuts.

'Yes. Your bag is good but that wine was sour. '

He topped it off again and I turned toward the car, ready to retrace a few miles before we tried the next breakthrough toward Roncesvalles. I heard a harsh but feminine voice shout something in Basque and looked back. A small dark woman, like a frieze detail in a Scandinavian tapestry of life among the trolls, had appeared, taken Ann by the elbow and was leading her toward the house.

While they were gone, the farmer asked me to spread the map on the hood of the car. He stared at it in apparent astonishment. Finally, with a grimy finger he traced the route we should follow to Roncesvalles. Ann and the Basque troll woman reappeared momentarily with a quarter loaf of bread, some sheep cheese wrapped in a newspaper and a few parings of ham, cut from near the bone. We had one hit on the *bota* all around and were on our way.

But not for long. As soon as we were decently out of sight, we pulled to the shoulder of the road, found a dry spot in a pasture shared with dozens of suspicious sheep and picnicked. The cheese was the typical hard sheep cheese found all over Spain but brought to perfection in the Basque mountains. Its sharp, chewy acidity was a perfect counterpoint to the young, fruity, light red wine squeezed from the bota. Lovely. We watched the hawks scouring the meadows for rodents for a while, then got into the *Bota* Patrol to follow the route the old farmer had pointed out.

Within a few kilometers, we reached the gravel road which he had assured us would take us over the final ridge to C135. At the corner was a small country bar. It seemed a good idea to ask directions and perhaps replenish the *bota*. Several cars were parked outside, most with Pamplona license plates; it's a sign of good food when city dwellers drive out to the country to get it.

A blackboard was propped up behind the bar, with 'Hay caldo' scrawled on it. We had come to an excellent place to ask directions. *Caldo*, in Spain, can mean anything from a stock or broth, to a fairly substantial soup. It is based on anything from chicken to veal to fish, depending on where you are in Spain and what needs to be cleaned out of the kitchen.

'Hay Caldo' at that particular nameless country restaurant, turned out to be beef broth laced with pork ribs, white beans and potatoes, served in shallow white bowls. This version had flecks of fresh chard chopped into it, probably from plants growing in a pot on a south-facing window sill, since it was too late for garden greens. After a generous bowl of *caldo* and reassurances that the road was open, it was time to get serious about Roncesvalles and the Bakersfield Basques of Valcarlos.

✢✢✢

Roncesvalles is mostly an act of imagination—historical Roncesvalles, that is. The huddled monastery and attendant buildings draw their fame from the legendary battle celebrated in the French epic poem *The Song of Roland*. The story goes that in 778 the rear guard of Charlemagne's forces, led by the warrior Roland, were slaughtered at the pass of Roncesvalles after Roland blew his horn in desperation for help, which never arrived.

Eighth century reports were that Moors did the dirty work at the pass, but in fact it was the Basques, infuriated because Charlemagne had destroyed the walls and poisoned the wells at Pamplona when he withdrew. In any event, modern historians say that the battle might not have taken place at Roncesvalles at all, but in nearby Hecho.

In the twelfth century, when the pilgrimage route from France to Santiago de Compostela was established, it crossed the Pyrenees at Roncesvalles. Some guidebooks say that pilgrims to Santiago can still get a free bed at the monastery chapter house, but we wouldn't count on it. The ruins have been extensively rebuilt so that little actually remains of the original abbey or the *Colegio Real*, as the monastery's church was called. There is a museum, but it seems to be open at whim. A modern hostelry stands on the site of a medieval inn located within the original monastery walls.

Another Roncesvalles inn, Casa Sabina, sets a very pleasant regional table. The owner, Gabriel Guerrero, is a great booster of the wines of Navarre, and while his selection is not extensive, it is very good. He is also very proud of an elaborate *flan* dessert which, he claims, his wife prepares 'with her own hands and from her own recipe.' It may be that his wife makes it with her own hands, but I'll wager the recipe came from a food magazine, like *Comer y Beber*, or a London newspaper cooking column left behind by a modern pilgrim. The dish has a definite 'pud' feeling to it.

Whether his wife has anything to do with it or not, what appears on the table—apart from *flan*—is more than passable. We began with a simple *Trucha a la Navarra*, grilled trout wrapped in ham, the trout fresh from the nearby Irati River. Because the ham gave an added dimension to the dish, we opted for a delicious *rosado* from Bodegas de Sarria, as recommended by Señor Guerrero. The fruitiness of the wine matched well the sweetness of the ham and fish.

Between courses, Señor Guerrero insisted on bringing a platter of the famed *chorizo* from Pamplona, which deserves its reputation. Finally, there was *Cochifrito a la Navarra*, a basic lamb sauté which was masterfully done by the Casa Sabina kitchen. With the lamb we opted for a red wine from the Nuestra Señora del Romero co-op winery, made of a blend that includes a little Cabernet Sauvignon— a legal variety in Navarre. After Señora Guerrero's unusual pudding, we finished off with a glass of the house *pacharón*, wild fruit marinated in an aguardiente base.

Most of the standard guides detail the historic relics of Roncesvalles, but few make more than passing reference to the sheer beauty of the place. The exact site of the battlefield where Roland fell may be disputed by scholars, but no one can dispute the beauty of the breathtaking road that plunges from the pass just above the monastery toward Valcarlos and the French border. On the hillsides and steep ravines stand a few remnants of the great oak forests that once covered most of Europe. It's called the wood of Garralda, and it gives an idea of what northern Navarre and the whole range of the Spanish Pyrenees must have looked like in the days of Charlemagne.

Valcarlos seems mundane after the descent down valley through the trees. The village could be French, Swiss, even Austrian. Set in a narrow cut through the mountains, there seems little reason for its existence. Perhaps that is the very quality that attracted the Bakersfield Basques there—from one obscurity to the next.

We shot a game of pool in a small bar. A man there agreed that there were Basques in Valcarlos who had once lived in California. Both he and the bartender were indifferent to the point of rudeness. They had seen too many tourists asking the same questions. And there were too many mountains between Valcarlos and the Mediterranean, where people have time to answer questions. We finished our game of pool and our beers and left. In and out of Valcarlos in twenty minutes, back up over the pass, racing the twilight now in our *Bota* Patrol toward Jaca, the first capital of the kingdom of Aragon and one of the best meals we have ever had in Spain.

Aragon

Aragon terrain ranges from the near-wilderness region of Ordesa in the Pyrenees, one of the few places in Europe where there are still wolves and bears, to Zaragoza, only a few hours drive distant, which is one of Spain's most pleasant, most thoroughly civilized cities. The entire region is one of those unexpected pleasures that one often finds in Spain with little help from the standard tourist guides.

Except for Zaragoza, Aragon is a land of small towns, villages and rugged, often harsh countryside, reminiscent of the badlands of west Texas and northeast New Mexico. Aragon runs from the French border, south to the Sístema Ibérico mountains, which separate Aragon from Castile and Valencia. It borders La Rioja and Navarre on the west, Catalonia on the east. The Ebro river runs through the center of Aragon, winding pleasantly through Zaragoza to the Mediterranean. The river drains a large central valley, which is very fertile when properly irrigated. The climate ranges from desert heat in the south, to alpine in the north, with all shades and gradations in between.

In most guide books, Aragon is called the ancient kingdom. The reference is to a successful ninth-century revolt against the Moors led by a local baron in the Pyrenees foothills. A century later, Ramiro I enlarged his tiny Christian fiefdom into a kingdom, with its capital at Jaca in the north. In the early twelfth century, the Christians finally broke southward through the Moorish defenses and captured Zaragoza, which then became the capital of Aragon.

In 1154, a marriage allied Aragon with the Catalan counts of Barcelona and for the next two-hundred years, the combined states became a major power in the western Mediterranean, with its sovereignty extending from Valencia to Toulouse, and from Rioja to the Balearic Islands and Sicily. This was the height of Catalan power in the Mediterranean, with Catalan merchant princes playing a major role in the commerce of the entire region. (Although the Aragonese were not Catalan speakers, Catalan was their commercial language.)

Aragon's power went into decline after 1476 when Ferdinand II of Aragon married Isabella of Castile, uniting the two kingdoms to create the core of modern Spain. Isabella had no tolerance for Moors. She had them expelled from Aragon, and that peculiarly Spanish culture known as Mudéjar, collapsed. The *moriscos*, Moors who had converted to Christianity, made up almost twenty percent of Aragon's population, including much of the artisan class, and when they left the economy went into decline. The Moors had maintained a complex irrigation system around the Río Ebro in the great central valley of Aragon. That too fell into disrepair, and an arid semidesert replaced the rich agricultural fields of southern Aragon.

✦✦✦

Aragon shares some of its table with Catalonia, some with Navarre, some, even, with the French. The food has been described as simple, but that is a relative judgment. The ingredients are simple, yet they are combined in rich and complex ways. An example is *chilindrón*, probably the most famous dish of Aragon. *Chilindrón* is a lamb or chicken dish—lamb is preferred—braised with tomatoes and peppers and garnished with strips of sweet red pepper. Ingredients found in just about any Mediterranean kitchen, yet combined so as to create a marvelous dish.

Another treatment of lamb—*ternasco*—is indeed simple. It's baby lamb, usually cooked over a wood fire, with only salt, garlic and bacon fat for seasoning. In fact, the list of lamb dishes that figure prominently in Aragonese cooking is quite long, and includes lamb testicles, lamb head and lamb tails, which are called *espárragos montañeses*, mountain asparagus.

Aragon is well known for its charcuterie, especially *morcilla* or black pudding, which in Aragon is made with rice, cinnamon and pine or hazel nuts. The ham of Teruel is well known throughout Spain, and often featured in the tapas bars of Zaragoza.

Soups, especially winter soups, are excellent in Aragon. One of our favorites is a shepherd's soup with garlic, potatoes, bread and egg, as served at La Rinconada de Lorenzo in Zaragoza. *Presa de predicador* or preacher's game, is a wonderful soup made with beef, mutton, pork, chicken and sausages. There is still another delicious garlic soup in Aragon that is made with almonds and eggs, and there is also a kind of bread soup made very thick with tomato, pepper and *chorizo*. Other Aragonese winter fare includes various bean and sausage dishes that approach the consistency of a soup or stew.

✦✦✦

There are over eighty thousand acres of wine grapes planted in Aragon. A tour of its vineyards in the blazing heat of midsummer or the bitter cold of midwinter would lead one to believe that little could survive here, let alone a delicate grape. But wine grapes—and winemakers—turn out to be tougher than expected.

Aragon's best known wines are from the Cariñena denomination of origin (DO), which covers a large area, more than 50,000 acres, south of the city of Zaragoza. Until very recently the wines of Cariñena have been strong, dark and high in alcohol, made from the Garnacha grape. They often reached seventeen or eighteen percent alcohol and were much in demand for blending, especially in those regions of France not as blessed, if that is the word, with scorching summer heat. The trend in Cariñena in the past decade, however, has been toward making lighter wines by earlier harvest of the grapes and the installation of temperature-controlled fermentation equipment. By holding down the temperature of the fermenting must, it is possible to highlight fruity flavors and reduce the level of alcohol.

The biggest change taking place in Cariñena is the replacement of the traditional Garnacha with the Tempranillo grape from Rioja and the Macabeo grape from Catalonia. There is also more white wine being made than ever before, mostly from the Viura, another Rioja variety.

The DO of Campo de Borja, west of Cariñena, produces a short list of fruity reds and rosé wines. The tiny region of Somontano in the foothills of the Pyrenees is a small DO with only about 2,000 acres now planted. With its cool, foothill climate, it may have the potential to produce the best wine in Aragon. In fact it may already be doing just that.

✦✦✦

We had the good luck to arrive in Aragon in the early winter, driving from Navarre to Jaca; good luck, because Aragon, in our imagination, is winter country. Even the dusty plains south of Zaragoza put us in mind of winter. Perhaps it's the food, the rich stews and soups, the hearty meat dishes, the dozens of treatments of mutton and pig. Or perhaps it has to do with Aragon's fanciful place in the history of Europe. Aragon is medieval, remote, edged in ice and a bit austere. To us it's fantasy, and the landscape of fantasy is so often a winter journey.

Jaca fits that image well. Carved out of a hillside terrace above the Río Aragon, with mountains to the north and south, Jaca could be a sepia drawing of a chilly winterscape in a book of fairy tales. It was Aragon's first capital and the center of resistance to the Moors. It was also an alternate jumping off point for pilgrims in the Middle Ages bound for Santiago de Compostela. It is said that pilgrims going to and from Santiago filled the town, giving it an international flavor unusual for the time.

With a population of under 15,000, Jaca still has that feeling, although now the pilgrims are more likely to be en route to a ski trip in the Pyrenees, or to bird watch in Ordesa Park to the north. Or perhaps en route to the Hotel Conde Asnar, as we were that dark and bleak evening in early January. Or more precisely, the restaurant in the hotel, La Cocina Aragonesa. As the name suggests, it offers a typical Aragonese menu and has the reputation of doing it quite well.

We thought we had surely been led astray when we arrived. The Hotel Conde Asnar seemed a commonplace, rather modern establishment, with a loud television lounge opening just off the office entryway. But we had been driving for hours in a fine rain that threatened to turn to snow, packed into a tiny Seat—the notorious *Bota* Patrol—and it was Saturday night. There was no point in being picky. In fact, our room was comfortable, the water was hot, there was really no reason to complain. And within the hour, we discovered that the Aragonese table was a splendid place to be seated. It was a bit like I imagine a medieval feast would have been, without the cold drafts, the dogs and the fleas.

First the dining room. La Cocina Aragonesa was all dark wood, on two levels, divided by railings into several separate seating areas, with each area guarded by a ghostly knight in armor. There was a working fireplace and the light was dim, but it was still bright enough to see the plate—very important in unfamiliar restaurants.

There were no oppressive, hovering waiters, too often encountered in hotel restaurants in Spain. There was a comfortable, maternal-looking woman who knew the menu thoroughly and, even more surprising, knew the wine list too. And what a wine list! Not only the selection, but the pricing was so exceptional that we wanted to change all our travel plans and simply last out the month, drinking up all that lovely wine.

For openers there was a seventeen-year old Bodegas San Marcos Rosado from the wine town of Barbastro. Much too old to be drinkable, would be the common wisdom about a seventeen-year-old rosé and the common wisdom would be wrong again. Although the color was a bit faded and dull to the eye, the flavor was rich and nutty with chocolate tones on the finish. It was about ten dollars a bottle. We had it as an aperitif.

That was followed by a four-year old Señorío de Lazán Reserva Montesierra, a glorious red wine from the Cooperativa Somontano. The waitress suggested it since it had just been released and was not yet on the wine list. It was still young, but what deep, rich flavors! Mark it up at about five dollars a bottle.

We remained with it through the next few courses. First we had a *mousee de aiernos y cigales,* prawns layered with a green sauce and very delicately flavored, with just a touch of garlic. Then *hojaldre de puerros,* a thin-layer of house-made puff pastry baked in a ring mold, with a custard of leek, cheese and eggs. *Pan crujiente* followed, another pastry, filled with a *morisco* of crab, clams and prawns with a deep green asparagus sauce.

Another bottle of the *Reserva* accompanied a half-pheasant in a sweet Madeira sauce with puréed vegetables. We carried on with the *Reserva* right through a sea bass, roasted with sautéed garlic and served in a *caldo* with clams in the shell. The sauce had just a hint of vinegar, which gave it a piquant twist that balanced the sweetness of the fish and complemented the fruitiness and depth of the wine.

With the final dish, medallions of venison stewed with whole shallots in a rich brown sauce, we switched to a 1964 Campo Viejo from Rioja (younger versions are available in some US markets). It was a mark of the waitress' true appreciation of wine that when we asked what she thought was the best older wine on the list, she went outside Aragon for her choice. Yet she didn't go for the most expensive or the best known, for there were wines from Muga, La Rioja Alta and other, much better known Rioja bodegas on the list.

The Campo Viejo turned out to be a superior choice, especially with the venison. The wine had mellowed to a soft, velvety texture in the bottle that complemented the rich flavor of the venison. For a twenty-five-year-old wine of the quality of the Campo Viejo, I would have been prepared to pay well over one hundred dollars at almost any US restaurant—only, of course, it would not have been available. In Jaca, it was a bit under thirty dollars.

The dessert that night was the perfect finish: a fig mousse, prepared with dried figs, served with a hot custard sauce and covered by chopped walnuts. Our pleasure knew no limits. We finished off with a glass or so of the house aguardiente, flavored with plums. It left a warm, glowing, fairy-tale sensation in the mouth.

✦❀✦

An old black-shawled woman goes up and down the sidewalk of the shops of the Vía César Agusto in Zaragoza, with bent back and frayed straw broom, spending the gray morning sweeping away the dried mud and dust. The street is being torn up to build an underground parking garage, only a block from the mercado. By noon it starts to rain and there is nothing she can do against the tide of new mud slowly accumulating. She stands motionless in the doorway of the Hotel Marisol where, no matter how thoroughly guests try to clean their feet on the mat, they track mud up the carpeted stairs to the gleaming tile floors of their rooms.

Later that afternoon, the rain becomes a fine mist drifting down without any apparent promise of change from the monochrome sky. The old woman is gone from the doorway, but as we step out onto the sidewalk, we see her a few doors away in front of a small bar sweeping the fine, sandy wet mud steadily back toward the broken street.

✦❀✦

The history of the city of Zaragoza goes back to an Iberian river-crossing of uncertain age, called Salduba. From its position on the Río Ebro it was, and still is, a key to travel routes through northern and central Spain; from Tarragona and the Catalan coast to Rioja and the Basque country, and from France through the pass at Jaca to Madrid, Toledo and Cordoba in the south.

The Romans took Salduba in 25 BC and renamed it Caesaraugusta. Later, the Moors seized the city and altered the name to Sarakusta. After its recapture by the Christians, it became, as Saragosa, one of the most prosperous cities in Spain, an important commercial and cultural capital. The ruling body, the *fueros*, was for several centuries the most liberal in Spain. Zaragoza offered full protection to the Moors, so there are excellent examples of Mudéjar style in the churches and houses in the old town that escaped destruction by the French in the nineteenth century.

The city's commercial fortunes have been up and down over the centuries, but there has been one cultural constant: the fame of the Virgin of Pilar. The story goes that on the second day of January in AD 40, the Virgin Mary appeared here in a vision to St. James, who managed to get around a great deal. She left as proof a pillar. A basilica was later built around the pillar (the present church is the third on the site) and The Virgin of Pilar's fame spread throughout Spain. It is pretty much a toss-up whether more girls in Spain are named Montserrat, from the dark Virgin of Catalonia, or Pilar. I once met a woman in Barcelona named Pilar Montserrat. All bases covered.

October 12 is the Virgin of Pilar's festival day in Zaragoza, celebrated with fireworks, torch light parades, giant cardboard figures, and the usual madness that attends major fiestas in Spain. Or so I am told. I have never been lucky enough to be on hand for that particular party. But I have often created my own fiestas in Zaragoza, another wonderful Spanish city that somehow falls outside the normal tourist route.

Like Jaca, Zaragoza is a city of winter. It has always been raining in Zaragoza and it is always Christmas, or thereabouts. Lights gleam on brick and concrete, crowds of people jam the Corte Inglés, shopping on a scale that no American, however well-trained in the suburban malls, could claim to match.

Shopping, like most other things in Spain, is a family experience: Mom, Dad, the kids, Grandma and Grandpa, and probably a few cousins. And in Spain you don't go shopping in spandex workout clothes. In any of the big cities, shopping is a dress-up event, and the Spanish probably dress up better than anyone else in the world. It starts with the smallest children. Babes-in-arms wear outfits that must have set the family back a day's wages. There are high-fashion children's clothing stores on many shopping streets, and we're not talking about stacks of jeans and T-shirts. These are designer-label threads.

Most of Zaragoza was rebuilt following the Napoleonic wars in the early nineteenth century. It now has broad, graceful streets that invite leisurely strolls, leading the shopper on to the next window and then the next. After the shopping spree, a Zaragoza family can choose from some of the best tapas bars in Spain. There are several good areas for tapas.

Any of the streets leading away from the Plaza de Aragón toward the Puerta del Carmen or the Plaza San Sebastián are worth sampling. Closer to the river there are good tapas bars a few blocks from the cathedral, known as La Seo, and another cluster of good bars in the university section.

Two of my favorites near the Plaza de Aragón are San Siro on Calle de Costa and the Bar Cochera on Calle de Casa Jiménez. The specialty at the latter is the marvelous veal *pinchos*, a small skewer of lamb, goat, or beef sautéed with garlic and served on a piece of toasted bread, served with a glass of the full-bodied red wine from Cariñena. Just the fuel needed to launch you back into the shops.

There is an outstanding seafood tapas bar near La Seo called the Bar Casa Amachio on the Calle del Captún. It's a favorite hangout of Galicians, since most of the fish there comes from the Galician coast. There are lovely fresh oysters, clams, crab, all sorts of prawns and fresh fish. They are shipped by fast train or refrigerated trucks and have not been out of the Atlantic more than ten or fifteen hours by the time they are served. This is fairly typical actually. Even inland, much energy in Spain is devoted to seeing that fresh food is available in remote areas. It is ironic that other Europeans regard the Spanish as backward and inefficient. It is really a matter of priorities. When it comes to dealing with things they consider important, the Spanish can be as efficient as any northerner.

There are some very good restaurants around the wide, pleasant streets bordering the Plaza de Aragón. Others, such as the Mesón del Carmen, have achieved landmark status as typical Aragonese restaurants, while serving indifferent food. At one time Mesón del Carmen may have been worth a visit, but no more, at least not for dinner. There is a pleasant enough tapas bar there, with good *pinchos*, although it does try a bit too hard to look *típico*.

Visitors to Zaragoza, or to any other large Spanish city for that matter, should make the tourist office among their first stops. You don't lose any face by admitting that you are a tourist and you will come out way ahead. Too often gastronomic guide writers simply repeat with minor variations what has been printed in previous editions. But things change. Restaurants are sold to new owners, chefs come and go. Reviewing a restaurant isn't like reviewing a monument, after all. It requires some regular updating. And that's what tourist offices can do.

Just around the corner from Mesón del Carmen, is Rinconada de Lorenzo ('Larry on the corner', how could we resist?). This establishment offers outstanding Aragonese cuisine in a bistro-like setting with a friendly staff who know the food and wine and like to discuss it. They'll even attempt to do so in English. It's worth having a closer look at Lorenzo, if for no other reason than that it displays on one menu all the richness of Aragonese cuisine.

One triumph is the *migas*, a winter dish served throughout rural Spain, which usually consists of unmentionable animal parts preserved in pork fat, served with crumbled, stale bread. One must be trying real hard to be authentic, or have had a bit too much *vino tinto*, to tolerate more than a spoonful of this. But at Lorenzo it is served as a tapa; the unmentionables have been replaced with thin slices of excellent ham; the stale bread has been replaced with dry but still tasty bread crumbs; instead of pork fat, lamb kidney fat is used in the preparation; and fresh grapes are added at the last moment. The whole is served just slightly above room temperature and is delicious.

We were served an Aragon cava, a three-year-old Blanc de Blanc Brut Nature from Hinzón, absolutely dry, tasting faintly of apples and pears. If *cava* this good were put on the world export markets, there would be much higher appreciation of Spanish sparkling wine.

Another typical Aragonese dish was the soup at Lorenzo, a *sopa pastor*, or shepherd's soup, served in a *cazuela*, an earthenware casserole. It has a bit of everything—garlic, potatoes, bread, topped with an egg that has been fried in olive oil with slivers of garlic. This is a catch-all soup and only the cook's imagination or supplies at hand can limit the ingredients. Topping it off with a fried egg is an Aragonese trademark.

A specialty of the house is *morcilla*, blood pudding, made with rice, cinnamon and hazel nuts, one of the endless variations on *morcilla* to be found throughout Spain. Practically every area, almost every city, in fact, has a typical *morcilla*. In Asturias, for example, the traditional *morcilla* is made with bacon fat, onions, and pig and cow's blood. A version of *morcilla blanca* (white sausage) is the famed *butifarra* of Catalonia. In Jaén in Andalusia, *morcilla* is made with sherry, dried fruits and nuts. In several areas rice is used and sometimes sugar is added. In fact, almost anything in the way of fruit or cereal can be added to blood pudding. In

Galicia I have had *morcilla* with apples, in Extremadura with potatoes.

Blood sausages come out of the fall hog-butchering ritual, when blood is abundantly available in rural areas of Spain. In the United States it is next to impossible to find hog's blood at any time of year, but a good butcher may be able to procure cow's blood. It should not be frozen, as freezing will spoil the flavor. *Morcilla* does taste very good when properly made, although we have found the name 'blood sausage' repels some American cooks. Perhaps if you think of it by the French term, *boudin noir.*

✦◟◞✦

Driving east out of Zaragoza there is a promise of sunshine toward the Pyrenees after a night of gentle rains. Early traffic is light enough to permit us to stop the car for a few moments on the Puente de Santiago and look back down the Ebro toward La Seo, the cathedral, and Nuestra Señora del Pilar. A light mist rises from the water and a few birds, impossible to identify at this distance, work the rising currents of warm air for insects a few hundred yards downstream. There is light enough to reflect the tower of the cathedral in the water. Suddenly, a single narrow beam of sunshine like a heavenly spotlight hits the eighteenth century steeple, reflecting from the glass windows of the observation platform at the very top in a blaze of light.

Catalonia

Catalonia has enough geography to be a continent in itself. The terrain ranges from the spectacular Costa Brava on the Mediterranean in the east, very like the Big Sur coast in California, to the peaks of the Pyrenees in the north, to the flat plains of Aragon in the west, to the rugged back country of Tarragona in the south. From sea resorts to ski resorts, the land is remarkable for its beauty and diversity.

The coast is one of the most celebrated in the world. The Costa Brava between Barcelona and the French border is too crowded to contemplate in summer, stuffed to the surf line with Brits, Germans and Scandinavians, but in fall and winter its spectacular beauty can be better appreciated. There are good restaurants all along the coast and many places to rent sail boats, another way to escape the crowds. The coast south of Barcelona toward Tarragona and Valencia is a little less spectacular and less developed, but the coastal superhighway has opened it up to the most casual day-tripper.

Along the coast, the climate is Mediterranean and mild in winter; summers can be a bit muggy, especially in Barcelona which seems to have been built in a swamp. But the smaller coastal resort towns are quite pleasant, even in the peak of summer. Inland, the climate is more extreme, with snow at fairly low elevations in the winter and intense summer heat.

Catalans have always been the only real Europeans of Spain. You are in Spain, there is no doubt of that, but it is a far different Spain from Castile or the south. The centuries-old Catalan drive for separation from Madrid is not so much an attempt by the Catalans to wreck Spanish unity, which is a mythical concept in any event, but to assert the autonomy of the Catalan consciousness and reestablish Catalonia's independence.

Barcelona, the chief city of Catalonia, was the most powerful city in the Kingdom of Aragon while Madrid was still a muddy river crossing baking on the plains of La Mancha. For much of the thirteenth century, Catalan naval power was supreme in the Mediterranean, and Catalan princes ruled the Mediterranean coast from Valencia to Nice. The combined kingdom of Catalonia and Aragon, with Catalonia the dominant partner, held the island of Sicily and exercised tremendous influence in Athens and Northern Italy.

Through the centuries, the rivalry between Catalonia and Castile has been constant. Some of the bloodiest and most bitter battles of the Spanish Civil War were fought in Catalonia. Today, the competition is largely fought out in the commercial arena or on the soccer field, but it is still there.

Catalans are fiercely proud of their language, which on the printed page looks like a mélange of French and Castilian, but on the tongue has a harshness, like a French speaker using German. Catalan is spoken by about six and a half million people (more than Norwegian or Dutch, for example), and it is a major *faux pas* to refer to it as a 'dialect' of Spanish or Castilian. Besides Catalonia, it is spoken in about two-thirds of Valencia, a wide strip of western Aragon, the Balearic Islands, the Republic of Andorra, parts of the Italian island of Sardinia and the area of Roussillon in France.

Much more than language separates Catalonia from the rest of Spain. Historically, Catalonia was the most romanized of any area in Spain. There was minimal contact with the Moors, and it has always had closer contacts with the French and northern Europe than with the rest of Spain. In the nineteenth century, Castilians referred to Catalans as *Francos*. New ideas in art, literature, or social thought usually make their way into Spain through Barcelona. The social customs are also different. There are more self-service standup bars in Barcelona than elsewhere in Spain; more people look at watches, the trains run on time, and lunch and dinner proceed a bit faster.

Catalonia is Europe with a Spanish accent.

꘎

The cooking of Catalonia is rich and sophisticated, combining roots in the ancient Mediterranean tradition reaching back to Rome, with the influences of the Moors, the Orient and the New World. It is distinct from the rest of Spain, indeed from the rest of Europe, and is worth a great deal of attention.

For centuries, Catalan chefs have reached beyond the culinary borders of Catalonia, taking what they like and adapting it to the Catalan kitchen. During the twelfth to fourteenth centuries, Catalan seafarers brought back rice and other foods from the far east, introducing them to kitchens at home and throughout western Europe. One of Spain's first cookbooks, written in Catalan in 1477 by Ruperto de Nola, is entirely dedicated to Italian food. By the nineteenth century, Barcelona was well known for fine restaurants, many of which offered a French menu. And anyone who has ever tasted cannelloni from Barcelona will never again think of it as an exclusively Italian dish.

This turning outward to the sea and across Europe has expanded the Catalan table tremendously and made Catalan the dominant cuisine of Spain. Bear in mind that it should not be tied narrowly to Barcelona and its immediate area, but covers a wide area that extends across northeast Spain and into France as far as the city of Toulouse. Considered in this larger sense it is clearly a major European cuisine, combining the resources of the Mediterranean, the valleys of the Pyrenees, the pastures of Aragon, the rice fields of Valencia and the culinary heritage of Provence.

An additional culinary influence of the past twenty years has been the influx of workers from the farms of Andalusia, Murcia and Extremadura. Although chic Catalans would be reluctant to admit it, this migration has enriched the Catalan table with the vigorous peasant cuisines of those areas.

Out of this have emerged five Catalan kitchen 'basics':

- *Allioli*, a garlic and olive oil sauce served with grilled fish, lamb chops, snails, fowl, rabbit, prawns, bread, fingers, toes—in fact, just about anything. It is the most important Catalan sauce, found on almost every table. It is a mayonnaise-like blend of olive oil, pounded garlic and sometimes egg yolk, although purists reject the egg. The sauce is traditionally made in a mortar and pestle.

- *Picada*, a ground-up mixture of garlic, almonds or hazel nuts, sometimes bread, less often saffron.

- *Romesco*, the secret sauce of Catalonia. It probably originated in the ancient city of Tarragona as a humble fisherman's stew. Fishermen would make it while at sea, using the trash fish that they couldn't sell on land. Gradually, the sauce—almonds, red peppers, garlic, onions, tomatoes and olive oil—became more important than the fish, although in Catalonia it is still usually served with fish. Now every cook in Catalonia has his or her favorite recipe for *romesco* which they jealously guard.

- *Samfaina*, a blend of onions, tomatoes, peppers, eggplant and zucchini, sautéed in olive oil.
- *Sofrito*, onions and tomatoes sautéed in olive oil, occasionally with garlic or peppers. *Sofrito* is not exactly a sauce in itself, but is the base for other sauces.

+〜+

Since the opening of trade between Spain and the rest of the Mediterranean centuries before the birth of Christ, wine has been one of Catalonia's most important products. Phoenician and later Greek traders established outposts on the wild shores of the region from the eighth to the sixth centuries BC. Among their first civilizing tasks was the planting of vines, eastern Mediterranean varieties, and among their first items of trade was wine.

Catalan food, customs, even land laws have grown up around the vine. It grows at the very heart of Catalan culture. It is in Catalonia that the most thought and care is given to the matching of food and wine. This slightly self-conscious approach to the table and the wine barrel distinguishes Catalonia from the rest of Spain. Yet I must quickly add that it never reaches the point of unconscious parody that it sometimes does in the US.

Catalonia produces a greater range and variety of wine than any other region in Spain. There are red and white table wines, the sparkling wine called *cava*, dessert wines and brandies. At their best, the red wines of Rioja may be better than any single Catalan wine, but the overall quality of Catalan wines is higher than the wines of anywhere else in Spain.

There are six denominations of origin in Catalonia: Alella, Ampurdán-Costa Brava, the Penedés, the Priorato, Tarragona and Terra Alta. The wines of Alella were famous in Roman times and it is one of the oldest wine growing regions in Catalonia. The area of Alella is on the highly-developed coastal strip north of Barcelona. Like many wine producing regions in the world, it is struggling for survival against a rising tide of concrete. In 1967 when the coastal highway running from Barcelona to the French border was completed, the number of acres planted to vines was less than 3,500. Today only 1,000 acres are left and the pressure of development persists.

It is more profitable to build condos to sell or rent to the British, Germans and Swedes, than to maintain vineyards that have been in existence for over 2,000 years. But there have been some encouraging signs recently. Local councils have drastically reduced the number of building permits issued for sites on vineyard land. There has also been investment in the wineries, particularly in stainless steel fermentation equipment, which enables producers to follow the lead of Torres in the Penedés and produce lighter wines which tourists and, increasingly the Spanish, prefer. This is especially important for Alella, since most production there is in white wine, which benefits most from cool, controlled fermentation.

Grape varieties in Alella are the Garnacha Blanca, the Pansa Blanca and Pansa Rosada and Xarel-lo (char-el-o). There aren't too many red wines made here, but the Tempranillo, called Ull de Llebre in Catalonia, is widely planted. There is some *cava* made in Alella and also some very pleasant sweet dessert wine, which is made by adding sweet must to a dry white wine.

The district of Ampurdán-Costa Brava stretches from the French border high in the Pyrenees to the Costa Brava, with a total of nearly 15,000 acres of vines. The area is best known for its rosés, which account for over seventy percent of its production. They are made from the ever-present Garnacha and Cariñena. There are some white wines made from Xarel-lo and Macabeo.

The Penedés district, south and west of Barcelona, is one of the most important in Spain, not only for the ships filled with *cava* that go a long way toward balancing Spain's foreign trade, but also for a handful of excellent table wines that have established it as one of the world's finest wine-producing areas. There are some 110,000 acres of vines here. Table wine and brandy production are centered around the town of Vilafranca del Penedés with the *cava* capital a few kilometers away in San Sadurni de Noya.

Penedés is an old wine growing area. *Cava*, the Spanish sparkling wine, has had the greatest influence, accounting for the vast majority of the region's grape production. *Cava* is made from the white varietals Parellada, Xarel-lo and Macabeo. Traditional Penedés reds are made from the Ull de Llebre, Garnacha Tinta, Monastrell, Cariñena and a handful of other local varieties.

There is a very special dessert wine made in the Penedés region from a few vineyards near the beach resort of Sitges. The wine is made from the Malvasia grape, probably first planted on the coast by Greek traders in the seventh and eighth centuries BC. There is very little true Malvasia to be found. Some sweet wines on the market represent themselves as Malvasia but are, in fact, not made from Sitges grapes at all but from much cheaper and more abundant Moscatel grapes.

There is a good deal of experimentation going forward in the Penedés with plots of Cabernet Sauvignon, Chardonnay, Merlot, Riesling, Pinot Noir and Cabernet Franc planted by Jean Leon, Torres and a few other wineries. The innovations in the vineyard were preceded by changes in the winery that have had a profound effect on Spanish wine, both at home and in the export market.

The Torres' Viña Sol, when it was first introduced on the Spanish market in the 1970s, was a revolutionary wine. It confounded the view that Spaniards would only drink wood-aged, partially oxidized white wines. Using stainless steel cold fermentation, Torres kept the intense perfumed fruitiness of the Parellada grape, bottling it young with only a touch of oak. It was on the market less than a year after the harvest. Although critics declared that Viña Sol would never sell in Spain, it can now be found in almost every Spanish bar and is exported to dozens of countries.

Cabernet Sauvignon was first officially planted in the Penedés by Jean Leon in the early '60s. His hunch that the varietal would do well in the Mediterranean climate proved right. Leon's plantings were followed by plantings of Cabernet Sauvignon, Chardonnay, Merlot, Pinot Noir and even some Zinfandel, at various Catalan vineyards. It is this kind of research, backed by a willingness to experiment and go beyond traditional methods, that has brought the wines of Catalonia, and especially the Penedés, so far in so short a time.

The district of Priorato is quite distinctive. Much of its nearly 10,000 acres of vines are planted in a wild, scenic landscape of steep hills and valleys. Grapes are carried down the slopes in 100-pound bags and often taken to the winery in mule-drawn carts. Yield is low, even by Spanish standards, on the decomposed slate and volcanic soils of the region. Because of this small production and the ever-increasing costs of labor, many of Priorato's vineyards have been abandoned in the past ten years.

The red table wines of Priorato are well known in Spain for deep, rich colors and a great concentration of flavor. They respond well to barrel-aging, becoming richer and more intense with time. Because of their intense color and high alcohol content, Priorato wine is often sold to producers in the Penedés for blending. This is a pity. The producers could make a greater profit selling aged wine on the Spanish and international market, thus enabling them to keep the low-yielding, expensive vineyards planted.

Fortunately, a few Priorato firms have understood this and are making an effort to produce slightly lighter but still intense wines that are better suited to short-range consumption by a public that has grown increasingly less interested in aged wines. Some of these wines can be found in the restaurants of Tarragona and Barcelona.

Also, look for an unusual dessert wine from Catalonia called *rancio*. This is not a grape variety nor a wine growing district, but a style of wine made by an age-old method traditionally used in Catalan farm houses. A barrel of sweet, white wine called *la bota del raco*, the butt in the corner, is kept in the darkest corner of the cellar. The barrel is never completely filled, nor completely empty, and is renewed each year by the addition of young wine. Occasionally, the *bota del raco* is wheeled out into the open air and exposed to the sun for a time.

In some modern farm houses, the *rancio* is stored in glass or clay carboys called *bombonas* and spends most of its time on the roof or in the courtyard. Whatever the method of production, evaporation through exposure to air causes a concentration of alcohol and flavor that is remarkable. It is not uncommon to find such wines all over the Mediterranean but they are particularly good from the Priorato area, perhaps because they begin with a high alcohol content that tends to preserve flavor properties in the wine. Unlike those dessert wines of the world which have followed fashion and gone upscale, *rancio* is still an inexpensive way to finish a meal. In the area around Tarragona, they can often be found in local bars for as little as twenty to twenty-five cents a glass.

Rancio wines have been compared to Madeiras, dessert sherries, even the Banyul wines from the south of France, but they are much more intense and distinctive, so rich that even a very small glass can be satisfying. Because of the concentrated flavor, *rancios* often leave an impression of sweetness on the palate, but a true *rancio* is a dry wine. Sweet *rancios* are also available, made by the addition of a sweet must to a dry *rancio* which then undergoes additional aging. When *rancios* are bottled, they age very slowly and the rare bottle of aged *rancio* is a treasure.

Tarragona is the second largest wine growing district in Catalonia at about 60,000 acres. Like most of Catalonia, Tarragona's vintages were famous throughout the Roman empire. Now, much of Tarragona's table wine production could be characterized as elbow-benders, easy drinking wines of decent quality and low price.

Terra Alta is the southernmost district in Catalonia and the third largest, with about 40,000 acres of vines under cultivation. As far as quality wines go, Terra Alta is relatively unimportant, with most wines of fairly high alcohol content.

The Conca de Barbera, which has gained a provisional appellation status, is about midway between Barcelona and Lérida near the ancient town of Poblet in the province of Tarragona. Until very recently most of the wine made from the 23,000 acres of vineyards in the Conca have gone into bulk wine or to the *cava* houses of San Sandurni de Noya. Now there are plantings of Chardonnay, Cabernet Sauvignon and Pinot Noir, which grow well there. Local growers believe the area has a great future for those wines because of climatic conditions that encourage the growth of quality grapes.

⌇

Among the major food festivals in Catalonia each year are *La Calçotada*, held in early spring in the neighborhood of Valls, a few kilometers north of Tarragona, and the *Romescada* held at Cambrils, also near Tarragona, in April.

To understand *La Calçotada*, it is necessary to know how the *calçot* (cal-SOT), a Catalan variety of green onion, is grown. And that gives some insight into the Catalan attitude toward food. It all starts about eighteen months before the festival itself, in late September or early October, when onion seeds are planted at the waning of the moon. The seedlings are set out in January and grown until midsummer, when they are pulled from the ground and laid out to dry in bunches under the shade of a tree. In a few months the dried bunches begin to sprout again and they are then put out again in trenches and earthed up around the stalk, like Belgian endive. (This earthing-up actually gives *calçots* their name, which is derived from the verb *calcar*, 'to put on one's boots.' The young shoots are, as it were, wearing boots of soil.) By their second January the *calçots* are ready to eat.

The entire *calçot* season could be regarded as a long-running festival, since the original Valls celebration, which began on a small scale, has worked its way around to many of the neighboring towns. The actual harvesting season usually lasts into March or perhaps April. The *calçots* are grilled, ideally over a fire of vine cuttings. At the more upscale *calçot* feasts, they are served in curved tiles (like roof tiles) which look quite nice, but are a bit heavy and awkward as serving platters. More informally, they are served wrapped in newspapers.

However they are served, the important thing about *calçots* is that it is necessary to get very messy while eating them. Eating *calçots* is an acquired technique requiring years, perhaps decades, of practice. Colman Andrews in his book *Catalan Cuisine* describes it well:

'A *calçot* is grasped in the left hand by its blackened base and in the right hand by the inner green leaves at its top, then the black part is slipped off and discarded. The glistening white end of the *calçot* is next dipped into the . . . spicy nut sauce formerly called *salvitjada* and now known mostly just as *salsa per calçots*—then lowered into the mouth with one's head thrown back jauntily and bitten off about where the green part starts. As might be imagined, this is messy work and everyone wears bibs at a proper *Calçotada* and retires frequently to a nearby sink or pump to rinse off the soot.'

The *salsa per calçots* is a specialized version of *romesco*. Which leads to the next great Catalan food fiesta, the annual *Romescada* at Cambrils. The contest draws thousands of people, and many of the cooks are fishermen, since *romesco* began as a fisherman's sauce. There is much dispute about just when the *Romescada* began, but in its modern form it can only date from the discovery of America, since the capsicum pepper, from America, is one of *romesco's* major ingredients. Whatever its origin, the word *romesco* has three different usages in modern Catalan. First it is the pepper itself, sometimes called *nyora* in Catalan, *nora* in Castilian; it is also a sauce; and finally an elaborate seafood dish, in some respects the most interesting of all Catalan fish stews or soups.

❧

Cava, the Spanish sparkling wine, is not exclusively Catalan. Until the mid-1980s, any sparkling wine made anywhere in Spain that adhered to the French *methode champenoise* regulations was entitled to be called *cava*. Now *cava* can be made only in the Catalan provinces of Gerona, Barcelona, Tarragona and Lérida, or in Zaragoza, Navarre and a small area of Rioja. Nevertheless, over ninety-nine percent of all *cava* is made in Catalonia. *Cava* is made from the white varietals Parellada, Xarel-lo and Macabeo. Parellada adds crispness and ageability, the Xarel-lo adds body and color, and the Macabeo gives acidity to the finished *cava*.

Spain, like other countries that make sparkling wine, has adopted the regulations in force in Champagne regarding production. These regulations are collectively known as the *methode champenoise*. The key to *methode champenoise* is that the secondary fermentation takes place in the bottle, the same bottle you buy at the wine shop. There are a number of other technical rules of champagne production that need not concern us here.

The history of *cava* is curious. It is so dominant in Catalonia—between sixty and seventy percent of all the grapes grown there go into *cava*—that it seems part of the landscape. In fact, the first bottle of *cava* wasn't produced in Spain until 1872, and then in sincere imitation of champagne. It was made by José Raventós, the owner of the Codorníu winery, who traveled widely in France and was especially dazzled by the wine he found in Champagne. The old bubbly got to him in a big way. Back in Spain, he experimented with the techniques he had observed in France and produced his own sparkling wine.

The Raventós family had been in the wine business since 1669. Records show that in 1531, Jaime Codorníu bequeathed wine presses, barrels and vats to his heir. Two generations later, María Anna Codorníu married a Miguel Raventós. Codorníu is still completely owned by the Raventós family, making them one of the world's oldest wine dynasties.

There is great dispute over whether Codorníu is, as it claims, the world's largest producer of *methode champenoise* sparkling wine. Another giant Spanish *cava* house, Freixenet, which was founded in 1889 by the Ferrer family also claims to be the largest. I suppose the only way to know for sure would be to go around and count every bottle. It certainly doesn't make any difference in the bottle on the table tonight, so let's not worry about it.

What is astonishing is that despite the huge production, the quality level is high in both companies. Certainly, the inexpensive lines of Freixenet, Codorníu and other *cavas* are no match for most champagnes, but they aren't intended to be. Since the death of Franco explosive growth has taken place in *cava* exports. What the Catalans have managed to do with *cava* in twenty years is something the French were unable to do in centuries. They have brought sparkling wine within the reach of the everyday wine drinker. And remarkably, it is wine of fair quality too.

Companies such as Freixenet, through various promotional efforts and television ads, have positioned *cava* as a fun drink for anytime. One of the most successful promotions is Freixenet's creation of the 'little cellar boy.' A charming preteen lad is used in posters and commercials and featured in a children's book, explaining in color cartoons the history of *champagne*, how it is made and what a wonderful thing it is.

The use of a child in an advertising campaign to promote *cava* would create an uproar in the United States, where alcohol in any form is untouchable until the mystical age of twenty-one. But around the Mediterranean where the legal drinking age is when you are tall enough to get your nose over the top of the bar, there are fewer problem drinkers than in the US, Scandinavia, Russia and other countries where minors are forbidden alcohol. Children of the Mediterranean grow up with wine. It is as much a part of the meal as bread or olive oil.

The Spanish *cavas* have also created an entirely new taste range for sparkling wine. Although *cava* was more or less invented in Catalonia as a painstaking recreation of *champagne*, it has become an entirely different creature. Where champagne is austere and aloof, *cava* is friendly and embracing. *Champagne* demands attention, *cava* is willing to be taken for granted. In the mouth, *cava* has a distinct earthiness, combined with a forward, fruity freshness; the acid level is generally lower than *champagnes*, making it easier to drink.

Mind you, these are the less expensive *cavas*. At a higher level of more limited production, there are *cavas* such as Juve y Camps, Cavas Hill and Rovellats, as well as the top-of-the-line Freixenets and Codorníus, that will challenge any sparkling wine in the world. Yet even at the top, *cava* is a distinctive wine. It has more in common with California sparkling wine than with French. There is a fullness of flavor that is unmistakable. Part of this is simply that the grapes used in *cava* production are different from those in *champagne*, where Chardonnay, Pinot Meunier and Pinot Noir form the base *cuvées*. But it is also a question of climate. Like California, the grapes used for sparkling wine in Spain are riper than those in the colder climate of France. The riper grapes, of course, produce more fruit flavor.

The huge Spanish appetite for *cava* has led to a wonderful institution in Catalonia called the *xampanyería* or champagne bar. These are, in effect, tapas bars where the chief drink is *cava*. They often feature forty or fifty different *cavas*, most of them available by the glass. Some *xampanyerías* are upscale operations that could be in San Francisco, Paris or London. This is the usual approach in Barcelona, where there is likely to be British or American rock, or jazz, playing on tape.

The more traditional *xampanyería* often has a slightly raffish air that is characteristic of the best Spanish bars. There is that momentary hesitation at the door that most Americans feel when they see a floor filled with paper napkins, cigarette butts and other discarded debris. That is the usual way of disposing of trash when you have a drink and a bit of food at the bar—simply drop it by your feet. Someone will be along later to sweep it up.

✦~✦

A pleasant Sunday morning in May. In front of the cathedral in Barcelona, hundreds of people are moving gracefully through the intricate, balanced steps of the Sardana, that most Catalan of dances—controlled, precise, nothing left to chance or the aching strum of the guitar. The Sardana is one of the many ways Catalans proclaim 'No es Español,' to quote the common graffiti. Tourists from all over Europe crowd the edge of the dancers, spilling off the steps of the Cathedral, cameras at ready, wanting to understand.

Two Gypsy women, barefoot, wearing that constant, slightly aloof and arrogant Gypsy mien, watch the crowd watching the dancers. The older woman has a baby at her breast. Occasionally she turns to the tourists leaving the church, one hand clutching the baby, the other extended like a claw, mocking the universal gesture for alms.

From time to time, the younger woman, perhaps fourteen or fifteen, darts into the crowd. She stares her prey in the face, backing them against the wall of the church, or the unmoving curtain of tourists. There is danger in her face. Her eyes are old. She moves like a dancer, alert to the crowd before her, staring down her victims like the prima dancer of a flamenco troupe. She speaks rapidly, harshly, switching from Castilian to Catalan to

French to English to German, never bothering with Calais, her native tongue. She doesn't ask. She demands. The pockets of her dress are filled with silver.

◈

We once met a man who had supported himself for several years in Barcelona, teaching English to the whores in the Barrio Chino. As he describes it, he would stand at the mirror, writing English words in lipstick, while the women sat on the bed behind him, repeating the word or phrase. The Barrio Chino is a former working class district, near the foot of Barcelona's famed Ramblas. It is now given over to gaudy nightclubs, sex clubs and other places you don't want to take Aunt Sandy from Chicago.

But don't worry. There are plenty of places in Barcelona that you can take Aunt Sandy. Barcelona is a wonderful walking city, being mostly on the flat, and the chief walk, naturally, is down the Ramblas, that marvelous ongoing street fair that runs for about three or four kilometers from the Plaça de Catalunya down to the harbor. Many cities and towns in Spain have a Ramblas—the name is derived from a word meaning watercourse or stream— but none, anywhere, matches the Ramblas in Barcelona.

It ranges from the simply silly to the utterly bizarre, from whores of all sexes (the two major, plus several minor indeterminate), to religious fanatics who stand all day draped on imaginary crosses, arms extended, tears rolling down their cheeks. There are sidewalk painters, bird sellers, booksellers and sellers of items that even in liberal Barcelona could get you locked up. The rule seems to be, if you don't lean on people too heavily, the cops will let you play. That's on the Ramblas, mind you. Wander off into one of the areas close to the port, like the Barrio Chino or the Barrio Gótico, and the rules change, especially after dark. Take care. You are not likely to be physically assaulted, but you could be financially inconvenienced.

◈

I'm always a bit cynical about the tourist circuit stops, but I recall a late night visit to the Sagrada Familia in Barcelona, architect Antonio

Gaudí's unfinished testimonial to spiritual fantasy. It had been lightly raining, but about midnight the clouds were starting to break up as a cold north wind that felt like it came straight off the Pyrenees began to blow. Suddenly a full moon broke through and fell like a visible chorus of angels on the fantastic spires of the church.

I had gone earlier in the day for my first look at the Cathedral that anchors Barcelona in the Barrio Gótico. I remembered those gothic towers, thrusting toward God, the entire great church like a fortress, massive and magnificent, full of the importance of the men who designed and built it. Now in front of me by moonlight was Gaudí's incredible creation, hanging against the sky like a burst of obscure Catalan laughter from a dark room.

On another night of light rains, but with no moon, I discovered La Barcelona de Vin & Spirits, the gleaming, very modern *xampanyería* with wood walls lined with single malt scotches and over 200 different wines, including perhaps sixty *cavas*. I was trying to walk off a miserable San Francisco-New York-Madrid-Barcelona flight. I was alone, feeling sorry for myself and inclined to view life around me with misgivings.

Lunch had been at Los Caracoles, a well-known Barcelona tourist restaurant in the Barrio Gótico, where the food is usually quite good. My lunch companions had all seemed charming, witty, wise and well-dressed, whereas I felt unkempt, surly and difficult. On the way to lunch I had bought a rose from a Gypsy girl in the nearby Cathedral Close and, trying to strike a whimsical pose, had stuck it in my buttonhole. It had promptly wilted.

After lunch I went to one of the first bull fights of the season— almost like a spring training game. Predictably, it was terrible. Catalonia isn't really bull fight territory. Two of the bulls were actually sent back. My companion was a bullfighting aficionado going back to the days when bulls were still killed in southern France. She was thoroughly disgusted with the spectacle.

I was prepared for La Barcelona de Vin & Spirits to be a disaster, but instead it rescued my day. Beginning with the welcoming glass of Jaume Serra Brut Reserva and a plate of excellent *jamón serrano*, my spirits began to rise. I consulted with the barman about the prawns, which were small and taken from the Mediterranean. He assured me they were absolutely fresh and so tasty that he served them without sauce. He was right. They had been quickly boiled with the heads on, and the flavor was creamy and rich. They needed nothing but perhaps another glass of Jaume Serra.

Things were looking up.

The barman and I discussed the bullfight for a time. He had not been there, but his girlfriend had. She told him it had not been good. 'But,' he shrugged, 'it is only to be expected so early in the season.'

I agreed and ordered a plate of *caracoles del mar.* The barman recommended a glass of an unusual wine called Can Feixes, a Penedés blend of Parellada and Macabeo. It combined the qualities of those two grapes perfectly, the intense perfumy quality of the Parellada an ideal foil for the fresh acidity of the Macabeo. The sea snails were a little on the chewy side, but by that time balance and order had been restored in my soul. I was back in Barcelona, back in Spain.

❧

We were walking the vines in the mountain vineyard of Pontons about forty kilometers from Barcelona, deep in the heart of Catalonia's wine country. The low hills before us, worn and ancient outriders of the Pyrenees, bear a passing resemblance to the coastal ranges of California. There is the same extravagant rush of green in the spring, the same slow fade to brown in the fall.

Looking down from about eight hundred meters, the perspective becomes temporal as well as spatial. There is a scattering of small farm-steads; impossible, at a distance, to know whether they are still working farms or vacant husks emptied by Spain's rapid post-Franco urbaniza-tion. There are traces of old farm terraces, sight lines of abandoned roads intersecting still-used dirt tracks, all winding toward a paved road. The landscape has a used look to it, like an old shirt, worn and com-fortable with the years, thrown in the corner of the closet now but still there when you want it.

There is wildness in Spain. There are still wolves in Spain—in the mountains and in bad winters, in these lower valleys. Wolves are the last lonely symbols of a wilderness world far removed from vineyards, far from the smug hyperactivity of international food trends. Which is what makes Spain so unexpected. One can see in a field, perhaps first culti-vated by a Greek slave, the traces of the Neolithic in a footpath curving against the opposite hillside. Faint outlines break and cast new perspectives on the merely human landscape one sees in so much of Europe—and increasingly in the US as well.

But for Switzerland, we were in the highest vineyard in Europe. It is planted to white wine varieties, Parellada and Riesling. The man with me is Alberto Fornos who is the jack-of-all-trades for Bodegas Torres, the largest winery in the Penedés.

He is a dark, intense man, a native of Catalonia. He takes his work seriously, but also knows how to enjoy it. Since his English is perfect, one of the burdens of his job is to put up with visitors from England and the United States. He is also fluent in French and German. At the time, he was learning Russian. 'In case I should want to surrender,' he said.

We were doing a leisurely auto tour of his winery's holdings, from the home vineyards near Vilafranca del Penedés to these high mountain vines. There was a pale early February sun, which had just dipped below the row of pines at the southern edge of the vineyard. I was wearing a heavy sweater. As we walked along, Fornos kicked at the clods of dirt, occasionally reaching down to pick something up, then tossing it aside. We had known each other for some time, having met on previous trips to Spain. Fornos was relaxed. He had laid aside his 'public relations' persona.

We were enjoying a break from the car, taking the mountain air, appreciating the view down the valley with the small whitewashed stone house framed between pines at the foot of the vineyard. This was a new vineyard and the vines, which were trained to wires, had not yet been pruned. They were a bare, brown tangle; it was impossible to imagine where to start cutting to shape the season's growth. Fornos stared thoughtfully at what looked like a flat, oblong stone he had just picked up. He wet his finger and rubbed it.

'You remember me telling you that I worked for an American company for a few years, in communications.' He was vague, as he always was about this particular job.

'CIA, right?' I joked.

He smiled. It was an old game with us.

'Doesn't matter. I made a lot of money. But I had to quit.'

'Why?'

He shook his head, still rubbing what I thought was the stone in his hand.

'They wanted me to take forty-five minute lunch breaks. Be there at 8 AM, lunch at 12, back at 12:45, home at 5 PM. Couldn't do it. Now I work longer hours, but I have time to go home for lunch, a couple of hours. I take coffee, a glass of wine when I want. Have a talk with a friend,' he smiled across the vines at me. 'Now I get more work done in a day than I did with the American company and I have time to think about what I am doing. My daughter is fifteen. She comes home from school for lunch and I can eat with her. That's important.' He nodded. He had convinced himself long ago.

But his opinion is still debated in Spain, where many believe that they must act like Americans to become Europeans; become some sort of super-Europeans, in fact, to compensate for all those centuries when Spain turned its back on Europe. They feel they must give up those long, inviting lunches, the comfortable siestas occupied with sleep or some other refreshing activity, and bond themselves over to the heart-attack machines of modern business.

'Look,' he said, handing me the 'stone' over the row of vines. It was a rectangular shard of blue and white pottery, perhaps two inches wide by three inches long. 'My daughter has been taking a class in Catalan history. For her project she is collecting bits of pottery, so every time I go into the fields, I am on the lookout, you see. I've been helping her label things and I think this is fourteenth century. You can see a bit of the zigzag pattern that was typical then and the crinkled white finish is typical, too.'

'That will be a good find for her collection,' I said, handing it back.

Fornos shook his head. 'No, you keep it. She has plenty. They are common here, many much older than that. We Catalans have been here a long while.'

I still have that bit of pottery. I keep it on the mouse pad beside my computer where I can look at it, touch it, feel the ancient Mediterranean culture living thickly in the few ounces of dried clay and the flecks of paint.

I looked from the pottery toward the stone farmhouse.

Fornos, seeing my glance, nodded, 'Yes, it could have come from there. The house is at least that old. See, there are no wires leading to it.

No electricity yet.'

'Someone lives there?'

'A local man and his family. They work in the vineyards. That is their orchard, there beyond the pines. They keep a few sheep.'

As if on cue, a tall woman wearing a black shawl appeared around the corner of an outbuilding. A dozen or so sheep trotted along behind her. When she saw us, she stopped. Fornos waved, shouted something in Catalan. She shouted back, walked on through the garden, leading the sheep at a brisk pace.

As we drove back down the narrow road toward Vilafranca, Fornos was trying to explain the unique historical land holding system of Catalonia called *Rabassa Morta*, a system which developed as early as the ninth century. Whatever the reason for it, it worked for hundreds of years to put the small peasant farmer in virtual thrall to the vine, greatly influencing the cultural history of Catalonia.

Fornos explained it thus: the landed proprietor would lease land to a farmer but stipulate that it must be planted in vines. After the vines were established and producing, the owner would share the produce with the farmer, the percentage to be determined by the terms of the particular contract. The farmer could continue to operate the vineyard until the vines died, which could be more than a century.

This seemed to work fairly well, but the advent of a number of vine diseases, including phylloxera and black rot during the nineteenth century, forced growers to graft vines onto native American vine roots, which have a much shorter life span than vinifera, the traditional European wine grape. This led to all sorts of disputes and legal tangles, some of which are still being sorted out.

We had to slow down and creep along the edge of the road while a few dozen sheep occupied the middle. This time the sheep were in the lead, followed by a woman in a black shawl. She could have been the sister of the woman at the vineyard: the same angular, dark good looks, overlaid by a somewhat sullen expression. It was impossible to tell her age—somewhere between twenty-five and fifty. As we drew even, Fornos spoke to her in Catalan. She answered briefly and shook her head, frowning furiously.

Fornos chuckled. 'I asked her if they would like a ride. I don't think she has a sense of humor.' He drove thoughtfully for a few minutes.

'I really shouldn't have teased her,' he said. 'It is a very hard life out here in the country. And lonely, too. You know in the '50s and '60s, a lot of people left the country, went to live in Madrid and Barcelona. Until very recently, the big cities were ringed with shanty towns, little houses made of cardboard and castoff lumber. But the government started building houses and now most people have homes. But it left the country depopulated.'

He looked briefly in the rear view mirror, as if to be certain the sheep weren't catching up. 'At first, it was a disaster. The country people had no money, so they would rip out the appliances, the pipes, the sinks, to sell. But it got better when the government started schemes which allowed people to buy the apartments.'

We were only about sixty or seventy kilometers from Barcelona, a bustling, thoroughly modern city, yet it could have been the landscape of the Middle Ages: the black shawled shepherdess and her sheep, a straggle of vines below the road, brown upland pasture above. There were still signs of old terraces cut into the hillsides, but they were slowly eroding, receding into the brown undergrowth. It was odd hearing talk of housing projects in such a setting. I did not want to think about housing conditions in modern Spain, which seemed to differ little from housing conditions in modern St. Louis or San Francisco.

I asked Fornos about the terraces.

'God knows how old they are. Some may go back to the Romans. This was great wheat country then. But they are cut only wide enough for horses or oxen to work. Nobody farms the terraces any more.'

We stopped on a bare hillside where a rutted dirt road—little more than a path, really—led down into a thickly wooded canyon. Through the trees there were glimpses of a small, rapidly moving stream.

'If we had time, we could walk down there and I'd show you caves back up in the limestone cliffs on the other side of the river where people lived 50,000 years ago.'

We stood for a moment, listening to the wind in the trees, the sound of water drifting up from below. We walked a few yards down the dirt road. I looked hard into the canyon, waiting for a wolf to break through the underbrush, to disrupt the serenity. Back up on the road, the bleating sheep were drawing nearer.

'Look, we'd better go before she gets here,' Fornos said. She may have changed her mind and decided to accept a ride—sheep and all.'

✿

Some of the best sheer countryside in Spain can be found while wandering the back roads of the interior of Catalonia, perhaps taking a wayward route toward the great Monastery of Poblet, about fifty kilometers from Tarragona and over one hundred kilometers from Barcelona. The fortified Monastery of Poblet was founded in 1150 by Count Ramon Berenguer IV in thanksgiving for a victory over the Moors. It became an important symbol of Catalonia's power in the Middle Ages and was also the burial ground of a long line of the Counts of Catalonia.

The monastery was sacked and burned in 1835, during one of Spain's innumerable nineteenth-century civil wars. The greatest loss was the destruction of the 20,000-volume library, which contained books that were utterly irreplaceable. The monastery lands were sold off after that and restoration didn't begin until 1940. Even though little remains of the original building, it is still an impressive site, looming over the surrounding vineyards like a ponderous stone ship.

The Monastery at Poblet was of great importance to Spanish viticulture in the period of Catalan expansion in the twelfth and thirteenth centuries. New varieties of grapes from Italy, Sicily and the Middle East were planted there. The cellars at Poblet have been extensively restored and are a good guide to what winemaking in the Middle Ages was like.

The Monastery of Our Lady of Montserrat, about fifty kilometers from Barcelona, is set in a splendid site at about 1,000 meters elevation in the Sierra de Montserrat, looking out over the Penedés. It's a pity that it has been turned into another roadside attraction, with seemingly nonstop tour buses belching diesel fumes as they labor up the narrow, winding road to the monastery. There they join dozens of other buses, parked with engines running while tourists from all over Europe scramble for a quick look at *La Moreneta*, the Dusky One, the twelfth century wooden statue of a black virgin. Scholars, that is, say it's twelfth century. Any loyal Catalan will know the legend that it was first brought to Montserrat by St. Peter, later lost only to be rediscovered in the ninth century.

The legend of the Black Virgin, brooding for centuries atop the jagged, dramatic peaks of Montserrat permeates the Catalan consciousness. Meeting someone for an early morning coffee or blinking out into the sunshine after lunch, one looks toward the mountain and somehow, the day is better if those black peaks are in view. You know that Montserrat is watching over you.

ᐛᗢᐛ

If Montserrat is the spiritual face of Catalonia, Sitges represents whatever is the opposite of spiritual. Sitges is an improbable place, a beautiful, gently arcing, white sand beach backed by an amphitheater of wooded hills, with twisting, narrow streets fitting so snugly into the canyons and hillsides that they are almost impossible to spot from the very Victorian nineteenth century beach promenade. About forty kilometers from Barcelona and fifty from Tarragona, it's an ancient town, dominated by the Baroque church of San Bartolomé and Santa Tecia, which stands on a high rocky promontory thrusting out into the Mediterranean.

With its sheltered bay, it has been a haven for fisherman for thousands of years. These seagoing folk must have been surprised, perhaps even terrified, around the turn of the century when a Catalan cultural maven named Santiago Rusiñol formed a group of artists and literati who made Sitges their summer home. Rusiñol would probably have been surprised, in his turn, to find that modern-day Sitges is one of the capitals of the European homosexual community.

Sitges itself is, after all these centuries, still a wonderful place for a visit, from a few hours to several days. With a room rented in one of the pensiones in the old town, it is easy to fall into the rhythm of Spanish days. And there are miles of beaches, with the ones nearest the town center naturally being the most crowded. There are many nudist beaches in the area, as is usual on the Mediterranean coast of Spain.

The high point of the year in Sitges is *Carnaval*, just before Lent. We have never been in Sitges at *Carnaval*, but have it from a hard working spy that total madness reigns.

'It is very, very bizarre,' he wrote after the *Carnaval* of 1990. 'There is a quality to the celebrations that carries a certain edge of Spanish menace without actually being threatening. It actually adds to the pleasure, that hint of danger. It must be why people climb sheer rock cliffs without rope supports.'

'But you asked me about the food. I couldn't find anything special and I did look, since I was starving. I had hitched straight in from Valencia in the morning and got stuck for hours in L'Arboç. Do you know it? It's a small farming town about ten kilometers south of Vilafranca. Not a bad place to get stuck, but I shouldn't have been there anyway. I wasn't paying enough attention to where the driver was going.'

'Before retracing my steps to El Vendrell to get on the road to Sitges, I had a quick beer at a weird bar there called the Agricol. Why? I swear to God it was like being in bar in a college town in Iowa or Oklahoma (and I've been in both) which is pretending to be an English pub. There were dart games, a pool table and some English twit was playing acoustic guitar and singing Peter, Paul and Mary songs. Come on! But the owner was nice. When I told him I was hitching to Sitges for *Carnaval*, he bought me a beer on the house.'

'Anyway, I was hungry by the time I got to Sitges. I headed straight for the roast chicken booth, got a half and a bottle of cold beer and went to the beach. It was still daylight, but I could see things were weirding up pretty good.'

'As I chewed on my chicken bones, a whole troupe of lovely "ladies" passed dressed in stylish-looking sevillana dresses looking like they just stepped out of a travel film. Except these ladies had hairy legs. Or would have had if they hadn't shaved. But they sure looked pretty.'

'Back on the street, I found a bar, El Xatet, where the barman remembered me from the summer before and let me stash my backpack in the storeroom. Just to fortify myself for the night, I had a *ración* of *xato*, you know, that *romesco*-like salad with a glass (or was it three?) of *cava* and I was ready!'

'It was dark by this time and the streets were full of people. Sitges is the last major *Carnaval* in Catalonia before Lent, so there were people from everywhere more or less running around getting ripped out of their skulls, going off two-by-two down little alley ways, up to God knows what.'

'I bought a little black domino mask from a street vendor and slipped into one of the trendy bars on the Calle Dos de Mayo, what the locals call the Calle del Pecado or Sin Street. I spotted a girl from Barcelona who I knew slightly and attached myself to her group, all the better to get my drinks bought. There was about a dozen of them with Montse (of course her name was Montse) and they were all a few years younger than me. When they found that I was from California, was hitchhiking around Spain with nothing but a backpack and a happy smile, I became a kind of instant cultural hero.'

'It was one of those bars that I call early white concrete. All the rage, you may remember, in Catalonia. The seats were poured concrete benches against the walls, covered with pillows. There were low concrete tables before the benches and the walls were stressed concrete. Not that you could see much of anything that night. The place was totally jammed, shoulder to shoulder, thigh to thigh with people. There were hundreds of balloons bobbing around the walls and ceilings and occasionally one would pop and this would set the ladies to screeching.'

'Bottle after bottle of *cava* kept coming to our table and I was almost high on just sniffing the pot smoke in the bar. Anyway, I bailed out to the streets, where most everything was happening. Gays were dancing with gays, straights with straights, straights with gays, but mostly, you couldn't tell one from the other and mostly no one seemed to care. It was *Carnaval*.'

✦

Lérida (Lleida in Catalan) is one of Spain's lost cities. Our definition of a lost city is a place that the standard guidebooks overlook or vastly underrate. Spain is simply not as well known to travelers as France or Italy, so many places that are worth a visit are passed over with a sentence or two.

Lérida is only one of many Spanish towns that receive brief notice in the tourist guides but that repay a closer look. Not that the guide books get it completely wrong. Certainly cities like Córdoba or Cádiz or Seville have more to offer the visitor. Yet as the tourist pressure increases on the cities that are touted in every guide, the experience of visiting them becomes something less than a spontaneous response to the place; a certain element of self-consciousness comes into play. 'Here I am in Barcelona, looking at the Sagrada Familia. Isn't this grand?' The tourist becomes involved in looking at him- or herself looking at the sights.

Out in the smaller or more obscure towns, such as Lérida, Vilafranca del Penedés, Zaragoza, Logroño, the villages of Extremadura and Andalusia, the rainy byways of the Basque or Celtic north, the unexpected is found at every turn. One is once again able to simply live life as it comes.

The same applies perhaps in even stronger terms to food and wine. Anyone with an adequate supply of funds and the right guide books can go to the great restaurants, can seek out the great wines. And to some degree that's good because, naturally, great restaurants and wines receive a lot of attention. They are proclaimed far and wide, and often with good reason. But it is possible to worship too seriously at both the table and the wine barrel. There is also the added danger that as a restaurant such as Reno in Barcelona, or Zalacain in Madrid, takes on an international reputation, it subtly shapes itself to an international clientele, in the process losing the very thing that drew the international clientele in the first place.

✦✦✦

Lérida remains a lost city. The American Express Pocket Guide to Spain grudges it a mere two inches, remarking that there is 'little of ancient origin or artistic accomplishment to see.' Well, there are other motives to travel besides these.

Lérida is, in fact, a vibrant, welcoming city, the center of a rich agricultural zone that ships garden produce and fruit throughout Spain. The irrigation system, which to this day keeps the orchards and gardens so productive, was first put in place by the Moors, who held a hill top fort here from the eighth until the twelfth century. Even after the Moors were officially driven out, the *moriscos*, those Moors who converted to Christianity and remained, helped establish one of Spain's most prestigious universities here, which by the fourteenth century was known throughout Europe. But by the sixteenth century Lérida had begun to decline, at least in part because of Queen Isabella's expulsion of the *moriscos*. The French finally destroyed the Lérida citadel in the nineteenth century, and what the French left was finished off in the Spanish Civil War in 1936.

Lérida hosts a surprising number of good restaurants, including what we believe to be one of the best restaurants in Catalonia, Pati de Noguerola. Pati de Noguerola is first of all visually lovely. There are attractive dining rooms scattered throughout an old house, creating a feeling of dining in a private home. Each room contains only a few well-spaced tables, adding to the air of intimacy.

The food is an imaginative blend of Catalan country cooking and the latest trends from Barcelona, but there are no rough edges showing where the graft takes place. A thoughtful menu or recipe should be like a well-balanced wine; one should simply be aware of the pleasure of eating and drinking, not how its elements are put together. Pati de Noguerola serves one of the best *arroz negros* we have ever had. We always have it for openers, which is how the dish should be served. A specialty of the house is *col rellenado*, small cabbage rolls filled with pork, veal and egg, cooked in a casserole with vegetables.

An eggplant *flan* is an example of Pati's creative yet playful approach to food. The dish is more or less standard fare in Catalonia. It's made like a charlotte, with custard, often with bits of meat inside. At Pati there is no custard, and instead of meat the eggplant is filled with minced, sautéed mushrooms, then turned out of the mold and served on a base of tomato sauce.

Again, the treatment of partridge at Pati appears to be strictly traditional Catalan. Half a partridge is roasted, then dressed in a highly-reduced, dark brown sauce of red wine and stock. But at the finish, the sauce is flavored with black currants or whatever wild berries are in season. It surprises the palate with its piquant flavor.

Pati also does traditional Catalan preparations splendidly. Like the *lenquado con almendras*, a whole small sole, scaled and topped with toasted almond slices, or the *javali de cevet*, wild boar that has been marinated for two days in red wine, then roasted on a bed of vegetables and served in a brown sauce, thickened with puréed vegetables. *Bacalao Lérida* is, as you might guess from the name, a specialty of the region. It's chunks of salt cod in a *sofrito* sauce topped with diced apples, carrots and toasted pine nuts.

After a late lunch at Pati, we were not inclined to push on to the coast. Even though we had been to the restaurant on at least two other occasions, we had simply exited the freeway, driven straight to the restaurant, then back to the freeway. We had too slavishly followed the guide books and ignored the city. That particular day, we agreed that we had had enough of the road. We found a comfortable if unremarkable hotel just across from the river, near the old city, which sprawls up the hill toward the cathedral and the fortress site.

It worked out well. Lérida is a marvelous city for walking, and if there is nothing old to see, there is a very inviting pedestrian mall that rambles for several blocks behind the hotels and shops that line the river front. The mall opens up at the top into an attractive plaza where there is a tourist office. Just before that there is a cluster of small bakeries where delicious things can be found. One Lérida specialty is the light, fluffy anise-flavored roll called the *ensimada*, which is shaped like a snail and is undoubtedly connected with the great snail-eating feast held each year in early May, the *Aplec del Caragol*.

Snail lovers come from all over Spain for the event, which takes place along the banks of the River Segre. Snails are roasted in the thousands for this strange festival. There is speculation that it originated at some obscure point in history when Lérida was under siege and snails were the only thing to eat. Then again, the festival of snails could be related to the opening of the earth to new growth in spring, just as the snail becomes more active.

✛〜✛

He had been preparing himself for days, he told me years later over a glass of cava in a very upscale Madrid restaurant called Cabo Mayor.

'I was 10-years old, but nothing that I have ever done has been as exciting, as concentrated, if you now what I mean.'

He was now in his 40s, a very successful attorney, toying with the idea of running for national political office. His beautiful wife, a leading actress on Spanish television, smiled by his side, although what he had just said must have been painful for her, if she was even listening.

'I was told a few weeks ahead of time that I would be the top of the tower in the main plaza during Semana Santa in Vilafranca del Penedés. You know how they build those towers of men?'

I nodded. The castels were built in a rough square of four or eight men. The biggest, strongest men in the town formed the foundations, then the next row of slightly smaller men scrambled on their shoulders and so forth, up to a height of nine men, with the very top of the castle being a small boy. A small boy for two reasons. He was lighter, of course, so less a burden for those under him. Also, when he fell, he could be more easily caught.

'The biggest towers as you know are made during Semana Santa. All the eyes of the

the town would be on me. It was incredible. I have talked to bull fighters who say they feel that same concentration, that same sense of withdrawal from ordinary life that I felt for those few days. But, you see, I am not a good person to describe it or you. Because I was so inside myself that although I remember each second, climbing up the shoulders of the men, reaching the top and standing for a few glorious moments in the sun, looking face to face at my mother standing on the first floor balcony a few feet away, I cannot really say what happened that day. I could describe other fiestas, the crowds, the dancing, watching the tower grow like a living thing—as it is, I suppose—but not the one I was involved in.'

'Did you fall?'

'Never. Never. I stood for a few moments, then leaped into the arms of my older brothers standing below. Our tower came down perfectly, injuring no one.'

There was still intense pride in his voice as he looked back on his role in the building of a perfect castel.

No one really knows the origin of the living towers, which are built during fiestas throughout most of present and past Catalan territory. All sorts of ingenious theories have been advanced to explain them. Some believe the towers were invented as military lookout towers. That seems a little farfetched. Others have tried to relate the towers to relics of some religious ritual. None of the explanations I have heard seem to truly account for the sheer joyful madness, the incredible tension of the event.

As each step of the tower is completed, the tension grows, the swirling crowd clapping and shouting until near the finish, when the crowd becomes quieter, almost anxious, as the small boy climbs to the top, usually carrying a Catalan flag or something with the Catalan colors.

Some towers are carefully planned, with each person's role as a building block known in advance. These are for the major festivals. But tower building can also be spontaneous. One never knows when it will happen or exactly why.

I was sitting quietly once in the Ramblas at Vilafranca del Penedés, having a single espresso, writing postcards, the complete tourist, in fact, when a group of young men ranging perhaps from early- to mid-teens came running into the Ramblas at the upper end, from the old part of town. It was late afternoon of a perfectly ordinary day in early spring. There was no official fiesta going on or contemplated that I was aware of, but these young men had obviously been holding their own fiesta, no doubt with good cause.

When they reached the center of the Ramblas (it is only about two blocks long) jackets and shoes were discarded amid much laughter and shouting. They were beginning to draw a crowd already—housewives shopping for dinner, men from nearby bars, coming out, drinks in hand to see what all the shouting was about.

Four of the largest teens linked arms, forming a small hollow square. Quickly, three more levels formed, but the impromptu tower was already leaning worse than Pisa. As the next 'level' started up the tower, the whole rickety structure suddenly began to stagger sideways, almost doing a circle dance as the foundation struggled to maintain balance and keep the whole thing upright. It was hopeless. In a few seconds, the tower crashed into a leafless plane tree at the edge of the Ramblas and the structure collapsed, with some of the upper floors caught in the branches of the tree.

Even before I was sure no one was hurt, I was helpless with laughter, as were the other watchers. The whole episode had taken about three minutes, start to finish, and now the broken bits of the tower lay about on the concrete, giggling and gasping.

A barman came rushing out with a tray of glasses and several bottles of cava that one of the onlookers had ordered. It was then I learned the true origin of tower building. Never one to pass up a glass of cava, I joined the small group, joking and laughing with the teenage boys.

'Why did you do it?' I asked one of them.

He looked at me as if I were crazy. How could I not know?

'Because it was fun.'

⌒⌣⌒

Vilafranca del Penedés is the Napa of Catalonia, one of the most important wine cities in Spain, yet it is completely overlooked by some guide books. And we can't really find fault with editors for ignoring this commercial but superficially rather charmless city. There are some very good restaurants in Vilafranca del Penedés, as there should be in a major wine producing center, but the veteran tourist of California's wine country will look in vain for the expense-account restaurants, the countrified shopping malls crowded with antique shops and T-shirt emporia. There are no cute little bed-and-breakfast places, so filled with antiques that you are afraid to move. In fact, there may not even be a room to rent.

This is also true of other major wine areas like Logroño and Haro in the Rioja. Even Jerez de la Frontera, where the British taught the Spanish to capitalize on sherry as an incentive for tourism, has a severe shortage of hotel rooms during the *Feria*, the international horse show in May, and the harvest festival in September.

You may end up staying in a bare bones truck stop motel, but you will eat well, as we did one cold January night at the Celler del Penedés just outside Vilafranca. There had been a light dusting of snow on the vineyards that afternoon, which had chased the pruners out of the fields.

Dinner was long and extraordinary, opening with *escudella d'anec,* a winter soup with duck, potatoes, garbanzos, leeks and sausage. It was warm and inviting and would certainly have been enough by itself. But we didn't stop there. The season was right, so we followed with *rovellons,* a kind of wild mushroom, grilled in olive oil and sprinkled with olive oil, garlic and parsley. *Rovellons* are extraordinary. The mushroom has a red/orange cast and grows in the foothills in scrubby underbrush. It is the object of many freezing tramps into the hills in late autumn and early winter. The best of these autumn treasures appear after the first rains during the time of *scirocco,* the drying winds from North Africa.

The next course was a *cazuela de conejo con caracoles,* a wonderful casserole dish of rabbit and snails based on a *picada* of almonds, garlic and chilies. The almonds give it away as an old dish, as does the combination of snails and rabbit. Finally, there was *perdiz dessosada en col,* which was presented in the *cazuela*—boned partridge with shredded cabbage stuffed into a huge softball-sized cabbage leaf. Contentment was spreading fast. We considered a fast drive over to Sitges for a walk on the beach and perhaps a coffee and brandy to end the evening

But we were reluctant to leave the restaurant. It's a huge rambling building, divided into a number of cozy rooms, each containing a half-dozen tables, probably seating about two hundred people overall. It looks like a potential tourist trap but is quite the opposite, being a favorite of the locals. And from the first night we were taken there, it has been one of our favorite Spanish restaurants. The ceilings in the bar are thick with dozens of hams from all regions of Spain; there are old farm and vineyard tools hanging on the walls, along with painted tiles, old plates and enough Catalan memorabilia to send an antique dealer scurrying for his checkbook. A couple of the rooms have fireplaces, but all have the feeling of being candle-lit and warmed by an open hearth.

At any rate, there we sat, contemplating a turn of virtue by skipping dessert, when the waiter appeared with a fresh ice bucket and a half bottle of Cavas Hill Rosado. (We had opened with a half bottle of Cavas Hill Brut de Brut, a magnificent Penedés sparkling wine).

'It is from the two gentleman across the room,' he said, indicating two men at a corner table, who gave every impression of being well fed and contented, puffing on cigars with coffee and brandy before them. It wasn't too clear why we were being treated, but I told the waiter we would be delighted if the gentlemen would come over and have a glass of *cava* with us. They came to our table and explained that they were surprised at how well we had ordered. We were obviously foreigners, so how did we know Catalan food?

After introductions all around we learned that they were dealers in mushrooms and truffles, specializing in the giant *rovellons* and the rare Catalan black truffles, the *tofona negra*, which the French and Italians will cheerfully tell you doesn't exist in Spain. At any rate, the glass of *cava* led to another bottle, and that led to a simple dish of *mel i mato*, a dish of honey and soft white cheese, probably one of the oldest desserts in the world, and one of the most satisfying.

It was served with a glass of *rancio* from the small village of L'Arboc, only a few kilometers away. We mentioned that we believed the wine to be quite good, and one of the men nodded. 'Yes, to be sure. But have you tasted the other *rancios* in the cellar here?'

We admitted that we had not, and the waiter sent for Señor Clave, the owner of Celler del Penedés, who appeared from somewhere in the depths of the kitchen, looking a bit shop worn, like a working cook is apt to look after a twelve-hour shift. It was now about 2 AM, only a few tables were left and he could safely step out of the kitchen.

This of course demanded another bottle of *cava* and an extensive exchange of compliments regarding the restaurant, the quality of the *rovellons*, and what splendid Americans we were. In time, we got around to the cellar and the tastings of *rancios*. The wines were superb. And the only place they can be tasted is at the Celler del Penedés in Catalonia.

It was past 3 AM when the last barrel had been sampled. It was suggested that we should top off with a brandy, but we had to plead an early appointment the next day and parted, but only after Señor Clave had pressed into our not unwilling hands a small jar of black truffles packed in brandy and a huge bag of *rovellons*, still smelling of the earth.

We slept well.

✦

Down a dirt road outside Vilafranca del Penedés to the tiny village of La Bleyda and a rambling indoor-outdoor sort of place, called El Merendero.

The root *merienda* goes back to the Latin *merum*, which means pure.

In fact, the modern Italian word *mero* means unadulterated wine. But in Spain, wine is rarely drunk by itself. There is usually a bit of food at hand, perhaps only bread and olives, but something. So in Spain, *merienda* has come to have the meaning of a snack, or a meal of simple foods. Not snack in the American sense. To Americans, 'snack' means food taken on the run, but in Spain, *merienda* involves food shared with friends.

And there were plenty of friends that night. There were, in fact, two cars of us; yet that isn't as many as it sounds, since we were traveling in Seats, the Spanish Fiat. Friends of friends kept showing up and joining our table; others hopped away to nearby tables. Conversation was an arcane mix of English, Castilian and Catalan, with a smattering of French now and then as the *lingua franca*.

Even during the Franco years, the Catalans hung onto their language, although Franco tried to establish Castilian as the language of Spain. Today, there are at least two daily newspapers published in Catalan and one of the major Spanish television networks broadcasts in Catalan. Catalan is the language of the vineyards in Catalonia.

It is an indication of the fierce regional pride of the Spanish that the repressed languages sprang up in full bloom as soon as Franco's linguistic rules were relaxed. They had all been spoken at home, right through the Franco years, when those guilty of speaking Catalan, Basque, or Galician in public could end up in jail.

While waiting in the small bar of the restaurant for a large table to clear, we were crowded into a corner near the open brick oven, which was built into the wall. Everything El Merendero served came out of that oven, grilled over or roasted in the embers of vine clippings.

Cooks knelt on the floor in front of the oven moving food in and out. The heat was intense, which is probably why we kept ordering a delicious chilled white wine, made a few kilometers down the coast at Tarragona. If we had asked for the vintage date, we probably would have been shown the door. It was a simple *vino blanco*, with no pretensions at all but a charming willingness to please.

The air was filled with smoke from the oven and, of course, from cigarettes. If you are not prepared to put up with a little tobacco smoke from time to time, best to steer clear of Spain—or most of the Mediterranean region, for that matter. The idea of a nonsmoking section in a Spanish restaurant is laughable.

Across the room, a swarm of small children clustered around two ancient pinball machines. Above the clang of the machines, a television set was blaring but no one seemed to be watching. Beyond pinball machines and television sets the common noise was the human voice, raised loudly and constantly in argument.

The talk turned, as it often still does in Spain, to the Civil War of the 1930s. My Catalan friends were poking perhaps not such gentle fun at us for spending part of the afternoon riding around in a Jaguar with a winery executive from San Sadurni de Noya, the *cava* center. We told them his sad story. The family, like many wealthy Catalans, had been pro-Franco. When the general finally died, they had been so terrified that they fled to Portugal into the welcoming arms of the dictator Salazar and had only returned to Catalonia when Salazar was overthrown

Now they were back in Spain, getting even wealthier under a centrist Socialist regime, but still not feeling quite comfortable with it all. After all, hadn't the name of the Avenue Franco in Barcelona just been changed to El Diagonale? What kind of name was that for a street?

This got one of the more radical members of the party, a young woman just out of school, started on a list of problems the workers of Catalonia still faced. Oddly enough, two of the more urgent were the US military bases in Spain and the Spanish presence in NATO.

But never mind. In the nick of time we were called to table. After demanding more wine, switching now to red, plus plenty of bread, *allioli* and *romesco*, we began the feast.

At El Merendero the *romesco* was made to order, as was the pungent *allioli*. We opened with *calçots*, followed by a salad of *bacalao*, the dried salted cod fish, ubiquitous in the Iberian peninsula. Salt cod is a northern dish and was probably first brought to Spain by the Basques, who ranged clear across the Atlantic and were fishing off Newfoundland centuries before Columbus was born.

The meal went on, of course, as Spanish meals have a way of doing. But by midnight we were done with the main dishes, which were simply grilled but absolutely delicious pork and rabbit. The meat had not been much meddled with: drizzled with olive oil, a handful of herbs thrown on it as it grilled, a bit of salt and pepper. The rabbit was served either halved—split from nose to tail, with head left on—or whole, on a trencher of bread.

After lively discussion, our party left. One car of celebrants left for the nearby resort of Sitges to paddle in the Mediterranean—one of the first beach parties of the Spring—and to drink brandy. The rest of us stayed behind for a few *porrones* of Malvasia and *postre de músico.*

Postre de músico is a simple dessert made of dried fruit and nuts. It is said that the dish goes back to the Middle Ages, when musicians wandered the countryside, singing for food and maybe a bed. The Spanish hold music in such reverence that even the poorest household would try to give something to the players, if only a handful of nuts and dried fruit.

We love drinking from the *porrón.* It is a bit tricky, but once you get the hang of it, it's quite fun. It is almost impossible to describe. It's a glass vessel with a long, tapering drinking spout and a large straight neck that you pour the wine into and use as a hand grip. The *porrón* is raised above the head and held a few inches from the mouth. The mouth must never actually touch the *porrón.* Very bad form, that. A thin stream of wine is released when the *porrón* is tilted—about the diameter of a pencil lead. As the drinker becomes more confident, the *porrón* is extended to full arm's length so that a stream of wine perhaps twenty to twenty-five inches long is pouring into the mouth. You can drink an amazing amount of wine that way as well as run up some staggering laundry bills.

Malvasia is a local dessert wine, made from the grape of the same name, probably first brought to Spain by the Greeks or the Phoenicians. In Catalonia a very sweet dessert wine is made from the grape, with the principal vineyards only a few kilometers from our table. It has a ripe, golden color. In fact, one of the brands imported into the US is called Malvasia de Oro.

It was well past 2 AM by the time the last *porrón* was empty, the last plate taken away. We were not the last to leave however; several tables of locals were still there, drinking coffee and brandy and talking quietly. The Spanish are nocturnal creatures.

But the oven had been banked and closed and a young boy was mopping the bar area. We took our last coffees outside and sat at a table under the deep black sky. There was a full moon, but no artificial light to be seen. A small hill blocked the few lights of Vilafranca. It could have been a thousand years ago. And surely there were wolves in the next ravine, sniffing the rabbit-thick air of the Catalan night.

✛⌒✛

As much as we admire the wines made from French varietals in the vineyards of Catalonia, we have a great deal of misgiving about the decision to plant them there. As we have already argued, there is enough Chardonnay and Cabernet Sauvignon in the world. The strength of the wines of Catalonia comes from its indigenous grape varieties. Great Cabernet Sauvignon has been and will be made in Catalonia. But haven't we lost something by this internationalization of the wines?

In reply to this kind of criticism, winemaker and author Miguel Torres writes in his book, *The Distinctive Wines of Catalonia*:

'Certain French experts have commented that our viticultural policy could mean the loss of identity of our traditional wines. They argue that the important thing is to keep the character of the wines that were made here one or two hundred years ago...

'That point of view can be very respectable, although naturally we do not agree with it. In the first place, it could be said that this consideration should be extended to areas like California, Chile, South Africa, etc., which have also introduced lately high quality European vines with great success!

'On the other hand, Cabernet Sauvignon wines, for instance, made in Bordeaux, in California, or in Catalonia, will always be easily identified due to the differences of soil, climate and, also, as a consequence of the criteria followed in each country, as regards vine cultivation as well as vinification and aging of the wines.

'Possibly, that new Catalan viticulture should be classified, despite so many years of history, with the relatively new wine countries: here, we have had to start from scratch . . .'

There is much truth, certainly, in what Torres writes, but it is important for Catalan wines to maintain their identity. By planting the same grapes used in France, there is a natural tendency to accept the French standards as to what is and is not a good wine produced from those varietals. As close observers of California winemaking, we know that for many years California struggled to find its own identity, always comparing what was made in California with what was made in France and striving to achieve a 'French' quality, thereby blurring even the geographical distinctions that Torres cites.

Clearly, the decision to plant the classic French varietals has as much to do with marketing as with wine quality. For example, in 1982, at a famous wine judging in France, the Torres Gran Coronas Black Label was awarded top prize over a number of first growth French Bordeaux red wines. This was the event that pushed Torres into the international spotlight. That wine contained no Cabernet Sauvignon. It was made of Garnacha, Ull de Llebre and Cariñena. Today, the Torres Gran Coronas is 100 percent Cabernet Sauvignon and is a completely different wine.

On the other hand, Catalans have always been innovators and experimenters, in food and wine as in other areas. Certainly much of the excitement surrounding the new Catalan kitchen can be credited to this bold approach.

✛∿✛

The Picasso Museum in Barcelona. Near the old cathedral. Go when it's raining and look out the windows onto pots of geraniums on the balconies of nearby apartments. Imagine yourself in a movie about Picasso. Two young boys in blue pants are sitting on a bench in the Blue Room. They are very still, looking at the pictures; they become the pictures. On another bench an old woman knits lace, watching the blue boys on the bench watch the pictures.

The Mercado San José in Barcelona. There is a light late-morning rain. A crew of street workers have built a fire from wood scraps in a barrel. They are grilling their lunch: fish from the mercado.

Olives. There were 22 different kinds of olives for sale in the mercado at Vilanova.

Cats. One lazy afternoon we counted 29 cats from the back balcony of our son's apartment in Vilafranca. It was the day the hot water failed and we showered cold. The corner of the bed was propped up with a volume of Lord of the Rings.

Gaudí. An astounding architect. Roots in the Gothic and science fiction. Look for Gaudí's buildings along the Ramblas in Barcelona before you see the Sagrada Familia.

George Orwell. Keep Homage to Catalonia on your bedside table or in your knapsack. Don't read it. Jot down the telephone numbers of strangers you meet in bars on the inside front cover. Lose it at the airport.

Valencia

Of the three chief cities of Spain, Valencia has more in common with Barcelona than with Madrid, yet there is a strong rivalry between the two Mediterranean ports. If you gain the confidence of a *valenciano*, he or she will almost certainly let you know that Valencia is far superior to Barcelona. They will bristle if you suggest that the local language is a subset of Catalan as spoken in Barcelona, and will insist instead that it is a separate, though related, language.

The strong regional ill will between the two cities seems to go deeper than the usual Spanish regionalism. *Valencianos* feel that Barcelona has unfairly gained a certain historical stature by its resistance to Franco's forces in the civil war. Few outsiders realize that Valencia was the last major city to fall to Franco.

There is a bustle to Valencia that must come naturally. It has been a major trading port since before Roman times, shipping wine and food throughout the Mediterranean. The modern Valencian port of Grao is the highest volume port in Spain. Valencia is also an auto manufacturing center, and makes and exports goods such as jeans, shoes, carpets, textiles and computers. But none of these industrial exports are as important as food and wine.

Valencia lends its name to a long strip of the Mediterranean coast, as well as an inland area ascending into the mountains where it meets New Castile and La Mancha. The entire district, south along the coast through the province of Murcia, is known as 'the garden of Spain.' A seemingly endless supply of rice, fresh vegetables and citrus fruits is shipped from here, with the famed Valencia oranges only the tip of the market basket. The coastal zone is also called the Levante, an ancient name for the area that, politically, includes the provinces of Castellón, Valencia and Alicante, as well as the northern parts of the province of Murcia.

Valencia is an ancient city. The Phoenicians and Greeks traded and planted grapes all along the Levante, but it was the Romans who established Valencia as an urban center in the second century BC after driving out the Carthaginians. The Moors, who arrived early in the eighth century, loved the Valencian coast with its seemingly endless spring, its lakes and its streams flowing down from the mountains in the rainy season. They lost it briefly to the legendary hero El Cid in 1094, but won it back only six years later and held it late, resisting the Christian Reconquest until 1238 when the Aragon-Catalan expansionist tide rolled over them.

Valencia's rich history of craftsmanship in metal work and ceramics owes a great deal to Moorish craftsmen, who remained in the city after the Christian Reconquest. They were finally expelled in 1609 by Philip III, and Valencia suffered a commercial decline that lasted several centuries—perhaps until the popularization of *paella*, which to the casual observer is easily Valencia's major industry.

Moorish Valencia was part of the enlightened Al-Andaluz caliphate, governed from Seville, and great advances were made in agriculture under Arab rule. The Moors, taking an irrigation system that had been created by the Romans, expanded and perfected it into a water delivery network that is still in use today. Water use is so important that the Arabs established a special court to settle disputes concerning water. That court, now called the Tribunal de Las Aguas, still meets every Thursday at noon on the steps of the cathedral. It has the final word on all water rights relating to the Valencian irrigation system.

The thirteenth-century conquest by Aragonese-Catalan forces left *valencianos* speaking the Catalan language and with some of the bustling work ethic of the Catalans, nicely tempered, however, by more southern attitudes.

As elsewhere in Spain, you are never far from mountains. Occasionally, they break through the coastal plain, forming high cliffs above the Mediterranean, but mostly they parallel the coast. Inland, summers are relatively cool in the hills away from the humid coastal plain. It is becoming fashionable in both Madrid and Valencia to spend a few weeks in this area to escape the heat of the city. Most of the wine grapes grow in the mountains. They like the same kind of weather that people like, so the cooler summers are good for them, too.

One of the region's most prominent geographic features is Lake Albufera, which skirts the shores of the Mediterranean just outside the city of Valencia. Albufera is a large freshwater lake, steadily nibbled away by rice paddies and other less scenic developments. When the rice fields were established by the Arabs in the eighth century, the lake was twice as large as it is now, a wilderness of fish and birds. Today, the rice paddies share the marshy lake shore with automobile plants and housing developments. Albufera itself remains surprisingly unpolluted. There are a number of good restaurants around the lake, which specialize in fresh water shellfish, eels and snails.

On a sunny day, it is a pleasant enough outing from the city—only a ten or twenty minute drive. In bad weather it takes on a gloomier appearance, with the kind of flat, pearly light associated with the low countries or northern France. One can brood over a glass of wine and imagine century after century of men, Romans and Arabs with their attendant slaves, draining, dredging and diking the vast marshy lake to put food on their tables. Cooks of the world would argue that it was a good thing; but probably not the sandpiper, busy on a mud flat just outside the restaurant window.

The sandpiper and his kin have seen the marshy shoreline and the incredible rocky coast of Valencia disappear at an ever increasing rate. The drainage projects of the Romans, begun almost 2,000 years ago, are being completed by faceless international businessmen planting only resorts. Perhaps it would be more bearable—for the traveler if not the sandpiper—if the resorts were not so boringly like one another.

The hydrology of Lake Albufera is complex and dates back to Arab times. The name itself is Arabic, meaning small sea. It is divided from the Mediterranean by a narrow sandbar called the Dehesa, which is cut by three drainage channels, two natural, one man-made. The drainage channels can be opened or closed to allow water to flow into the Mediterranean. Although Albufera is the largest fresh water lake in Spain (about 7,000 acres) it is very shallow, ranging from three to eight feet in depth.

The rice paddies, one of the factors threatening the existence of Albufera, also attract enormous numbers of birds and bird watchers to the lake. About 250 species of bird, including ninety regular breeders in the area, have been recorded here.

A far greater threat than rice paddies is the growing contamination of the lake by industrial poisons and domestic and agricultural sewage. Albufera has long been a battleground, with conservation groups and duck hunters usually ranged against local authorities, who too often risk the threat of long-term disaster in exchange for the quick peseta. In the early 1980s, Albufera became a natural park, with very stringent protective measures imposed by the government of Valencia. At the moment, conservationists classify it as an area 'in stress.'

But like the sandpiper, one must eventually eat, putting one's global conscience aside. It's a good idea to follow the sandpiper's lead and go for the local cuisine. Probably the most famous Albufera dish is *all i pebre*, which is eels, fried in garlic and pepper sauce. The sandpiper has to settle for the eels solo.

✛✛✛

Most people think of Valencia in terms of oranges. If they are a bit more sophisticated about Spanish food, they will know that *paella* is a Valencian dish. But if they stop there, they will have missed the richness and abundance of Valencian cuisine, from the mountains to the sea.

Paella—the basic ingredients are rice, saffron and olive oil—has certainly come a long way from its peasant origins. Invented perhaps over a shepherd's campfire in the mountains behind Valencia, it has become an international icon for Spain much as pizza is for Italy. The name comes from the *paellera*, the pan it is cooked in. A *paellera* is round, shallow and flat-bottomed, about two inches deep. *Paella* is only one of many dishes prepared in a *paellera*. The dishes are commonly those in which a liquid stock is all absorbed by rice.

Much of Valencia's rice cookery developed during times when Lent was strictly observed. *Paella* no doubt owes something to older Lenten dishes of dried cod and rice. But as the dish became popular it took on a livelier aspect. Americans are most familiar with the seafood *paellas*, loaded with fish, shrimp, even lobster. In Valencia, one is more likely to meet with a country *paella* of chicken or rabbit, garden vegetables, snails perhaps, fresh rosemary and white beans.

In Valencia, preparing and cooking a *paella* has become 'man's work,' much like the weekend stint at the barbecue in many American families. In the same way, there is infinite secret lore concerning the best way to go about cooking a *paella*. Great numbers of tireless angels dance on infinite pin points over whether the *paella* should be finished in the oven or brought to completion on top of the stove, or over an outdoor fire. And if an outdoor fire is used, should it consist of vine prunings or orange wood? There are great debates over the precise ratio of water to rice, when to add the water, and even how to add it.

Beyond *paella*, there is a galaxy of other rice dishes on the Valencian coast, we have had to stop counting them somewhere around 200.

+‿+

But don't forget the orchards. Begin with the oranges, which, depending on variety, are harvested nine months a year. There are very few Valencia oranges grown in Valencia, by the way. The actual Valencia orange makes up only about two per cent of the crop. There are any number of different varieties grown, with one kind or another ripening during nine months of the year, beginning with the Clementina in September.

What most people mean when they talk or write of the Valencia orange is the sweet orange, which is a mutant of the bitter orange, and was introduced into the west by Portugal in the fifteenth century. In fact, Elizabethan England called the sweet orange the *portyngale*. The navel orange is a further mutant of the sweet orange, as is the mandarin and the tangerine.

The orange, which looms so large in the image of Valencia, is a native of south China. By the first century AD it was in India and from there spread via Arab sea trade routes to North Africa and to Rome.

There may have been oranges is Spain during Roman times, but the first certain records date to the ninth century when the Moors began planting huge groves of bitter oranges between Seville and Granada. The bitter orange was originally grown for ornamental and aromatic uses, but the juice was also used as seasoning in several meat and fish dishes, including the famous *pato sevillana*, or duck Seville, which is by all odds the origin of the French dish, *duck a l'orange*. This bitter orange is also the orange used in orange marmalade.

One of the first records of orange exports from Spain is a shipment to the port of Southampton for Eleanor of Castile in 1290, who must have been yearning for a taste of the sunny south in the bitter fogs of London. The most famous orange merchant in England was, of course, Nell Gwynn, Charles II's very well-known 'Protestant whore.' Her oranges were of the sweet variety. Gwynn and the other 'orange girls' were notorious in the theater district. Louise de Kéroualle, the Duchess of Portsmouth, who shared the king's bed with Nell, said of her, 'Anybody may know she has been an orange wench by her swearing.' One assumes that the duchess was not implying that oranges had anything to do with Nell's use of language.

The orange reached the New World quite early. Columbus, on his second voyage in 1493, planted them on the island of Hispaniola. They were first planted in Florida in 1539 by Hernando de Soto. According to Waverly Root, the Seminole Indians took to the fruit and served red snapper steamed with fresh oranges to the naturalist William Bartram when he visited the Florida tribe in 1791. There is a Spanish dish much like this.

However, oranges are just the beginning of the Valencian orchard and garden. There are apricots, apples, asparagus, anise, peaches, melons, grapes, grapefruit, plums, pears, cherries, olives, garlic, capers, saffron, onions, mushrooms, peas, broad beans, green beans, tomatoes, lettuce, cucumber and on through an entire shopping cart of vegetables and fruits.

❀

Whatever the dining occasion, rice remains at the heart of Valencian cuisine. Valencian cooks are so famed for their rice dishes, that in recent years Japanese chefs have apprenticed in Valencian restaurants in order to learn the techniques of proper short-grained rice cookery.

The Moors first planted rice in Andalusia in the eighth century, then in Valencia a short time later. From Valencia, rice culture spread to Italy and by the fourteenth century, rice was extensively cultivated in the Po river valley. There are at least a couple of reasons for the spread of rice cultivation from the Mediterranean coast of Spain to northern Italy. Spain had long been active, militarily and politically, in much of Italy, beginning with the conquest of Sicily in 1282 by Peter III of Aragon. And at various times over the next few centuries, Sicily and the Kingdom of Naples were under Spanish control.

It is possible to detect a Spanish influence on certain dishes normally thought of as Italian. For example, Elizabeth David, in *Italian Food*, states that compared with other rice dishes, Italian *risotto* is 'of a totally different nature and unique.'

Anytime one sees the word 'unique' it is a good idea to get suspicious. Precious few things in the world are truly unique. The techniques for preparing a basic *risotto* and the Valencian dish, *arroz abanda,* are almost identical. But there is an even more direct link between Spanish rice cuisine and the famed *risotto* of Italy, and that is *risotto alla Milanese. Risotto alla Milanese* is one of the rare uses of saffron in Italy and in some forms can look very much like a *paella.* Especially with the addition of, as David suggests, 'chickens, duck, game, lobster, mussels, oysters, prawns, mushrooms, truffles, goose or chicken livers, artichoke hearts, peas, aubergines, almost anything you like.'

There is a story concerning the invention of *risotto alla Milanese,* which is repeated in Anna del Conti's book *Gastronomy of Italy.* 'In 1574, the daughter of the craftsman in charge of making stained glass for the windows of the Duomo was getting married. One of the apprentices, who had a passion for adding saffron to the molten glass, hit on the idea of making the plain *risotto* for the wedding dinner turn gold like his windows. He gave some saffron to the host of the inn where the dinner was to take place and asked him to mix it into the *risotto.* The result was a most beautiful golden *risotto.*'

Although del Conti calls this a pretty legend, she suggests that the true origins of the dish 'lie in the east and it reached Italy via Sicily.' It seems quite possible that it did, indeed, reach Italy by way of Sicily. But it reached Sicily from Valencia, where the technique of slowly adding liquid to rice probably originated, as well as the addition of saffron.

✚〰✚

Today, Valencia's orange trade is much larger—about twenty times larger—than its wine business. But Valencia and other ports of the Levante have been shipping large quantities of wine since the sixth century BC, long before anyone around the Mediterranean had ever seen an orange. Today, roughly half of all Spanish wine exports are from Valencia, which even most Spanish are astonished to learn.

In a national survey taken in 1985, only 2.4 percent of Spanish wine drinkers knew anything of Valencian wines. The ever-upbeat *valencianos* take this as a good sign. At least, they note with an optimistic smile, the wines don't have a bad image in Spain—simply no image at all. Even in Valencia itself the wines are often neglected, with ninety percent of the total Valencian production going to the export market. One is more likely to find the wines of Rioja or La Mancha or the

Penedés on local restaurant wine lists than Valencian wines. This has
held down the price of Valencian wines. Quite good wines can be pur-
chased in bottle for under two hundred pesetas, or less than two dollars,
in the local markets and shops.

Perhaps part of the reason for the invisible image of Valencian wines
is that the vineyards are hidden away, with the only farm icons in sight
being orange groves and rice fields. Oranges do not grow above the four
hundred meter level and that's where the vineyards begin. And since
tourists to Valencia rarely get above sea level, they rarely see its vineyards.

It must be frustrating to Valencian winemakers, who have made
tremendous gains in the past decade. Probably no area of Spain, except
possibly the Penedés, has more modern winemaking technology than
Valencia. And it shows. The wines are fresh, fruity and delightful, perfect tablemates with the garden and seashore freshness of Valencian cuisine.

There are five denominations of origin in the Levante: Alicante,
Jumilla, Utiel-Requena, Valencia and Yecla. Together they produce more
wine than any other region of Spain except La Mancha.

The region of Alicante, closer to Murcia than to the city of Valencia,
is best known for a wine which rarely stands alone. The *vino de doble pasta*
is not a wine to order with a double serving of spaghetti, but a deeply-
colored blending wine, shipped in concentrated form all over the world
to beef up local vintages. It needn't concern us much unless we happen
to be in Norway and wonder where the red wine on the table came
from.

The Valencian wine most likely to be found in the United States is
from Jumilla, a mountainous inland region in the northern part of the
province of Murcia. In the past, big, high-alcohol red wines from Jumilla
(made mostly from the Monastrell grape) were popular in Spain, especially in the south. In the last few decades, Jumilla winemakers have
begun producing wines of higher acid that are fresher and not as alcoholic and heavy on the palate.

Yecla is the smallest denomination in the Levante, lying inland from
the city of Alicante. It produces wines quite similar to Jumilla.

At the moment, the region with the potential for the best quality
wines is Utiel-Requena, in the mountains at the extreme western edge

of the province of Valencia. In fact, the area has more in common with New Castile and La Mancha than the coastal province, and there is a strong political movement to split away from Valencia and join the province of New Castile.

The wines that come from Valencia DO are quite drinkable in an honest, anonymous kind of way. They make their way all over the world, from Africa to Scandinavia to the Far East and Eastern Europe. Over ninety per cent of the wines shipped from the Valencia DO are sold in bulk—that is, sent to another nation and bottled there, often without any Spanish identity at all.

In a technical sense, they are well made, very easy to drink; what you might call friendly wines. An English writer called them 'working man's wines,' and that seems fair enough; seems, in fact, to fit well with the rough but friendly and bustling egalitarianism of Valencia.

✦✦✦

There is a certain attractive seediness about the city of Valencia. It seems, on first impression, to have more in common with a Mediterranean port city in France or perhaps North Africa, than in Spain. There is a tropical core to Valencia, in mood if not always in climate, utterly lacking in Barcelona, or even Madrid, despite the extreme summer temperatures in the Spanish capital. Perhaps it is that Valencia is a bit theatrical; even the modern buildings look as if they were designed more as backdrops to some human drama than as department stores, banks, or other places of business. One expects to see Peter Lorre, brooding over a glass of wine at a sidewalk café, mysterious men in trench coats appearing briefly behind you on the sidewalk only to disappear down a narrow alley when you look back.

We were once slightly lost in the older part of Valencia near the *mercado*. We knew, in a general sense, where we were and where we were going, but in the tangle of narrow streets, it is easy to become confused. It was just dusk, on the first day of the *Fallas*, the week-long carnival held every year in Valencia in mid-March. This celebration dates back to the Middle Ages when Valencia was a city of craftsmen. It springs from a custom of the carpenter's brotherhood: gathering to burn accumulated wood shavings on the Day of St. Joseph, the saint of carpenters. The term *fallas* comes from the Latin *facula*, or torch.

Over the centuries, craftsmen began making objects just to burn. Often images of unpopular political figures were created, only to go up in flames. Finally, the wooden images were replaced by pasteboard or plaster floats made by artisans or merchants from different sections of the town. Over time the floats have became more and more elaborate, even bizarre, and the entire thing has taken on an air of fantasy. The streets are filled with gigantic grotesque figures, wandering to and fro. There is a fine madness in the air, punctuated by the sights and sounds of fireworks, all building toward the fiery climax of the evening of March nineteenth, when the floats and figures go up in flame.

During the week of *Fallas* the heart of Valencia becomes evident—it is a Spanish city through and through. No one approaches fun with more seriousness yet with a greater sense of style than the Spaniard.

But that night, whatever street we turned into seemed to lead to an even narrower one. Rationally, we knew the people around us were perfectly friendly, yet shadowy figures in doorways took on an unexpectedly threatening air. A trio of whores standing outside a bar drinking beer and laughing were suddenly laughing at us.

It was all nonsense, of course. In a few minutes, we had come out into the Plaza de Zaragoza and the sinister looking man who had been following us turned out to be an Englishman, a fellow guest in the hotel, trying to catch up with us to ask directions. But the feeling persists that in Valencia, anything is possible. And good heavens, it is Peter Lorre. And he is getting up, smiling that delightful elfin smile, to meet you. But no, sorry. It isn't Peter Lorre after all. It is only a local Rodríguez rising to meet another Rodríguez.

Rodríguez is the name *valencianos* give to the slightly bewildered middle-class, middle-aged men, on their own for the week or weekend while wives and children escape the heat up in the mountains or at a beach cottage. As one Rodríguez described it, the tradition consists of groups of men meeting to drink wine or coffee, have dinner, share a good gossip and home to bed early, because while the family plays at the beach or in the mountains, the wandering Rodríguez must be back at the office the next day. Perhaps the custom is left over from Arab days, when the males gathered in the streets to talk, while the women stayed safe behind the walls of the houses. If it is, it should be added to the long list of customs that Valencia owes to the Moors.

✦

Valencianos, in general, love cooking over a fire pit and eating out-doors. The local version of the chamber of commerce reports that there are 320 days of sunshine a year in the area—many of those days quite warm—so weekends and holidays become occasions for great bursts of outdoor celebration. This may last until dawn in the warm summer months, with all hands snatching a few hours sleep before the next day's *al fresco* lunch, perhaps at a fashionable cottage at Lake Albufera.

The whole area around the lake, on the higher ground above the rice paddies, was once market gardens, or *huertas,* as gardens are called in Valencia. As the gardens were slowly lost to urban expansion, the grow-ing Valencian middle-class bought the old garden cottages, called *barracas,* and remodeled them to make weekend or year-round homes. The cot-tages are simple A-frame structures, with whitewashed walls and thatched roofs of marsh rushes, or rice straw.

The rich, sandy soil around the lake yields two vegetable crops a year in the mild Valencian climate. Only a few decades ago, the residents of the cottages supplied vegetables for the tables of Valencia. They would set out long before dawn in horse or donkey-drawn carts for the *mercado central* in the city.

The Valencia market is one of those marvelous iron and glass build-ings that looks as if it might have been designed as a railway station somewhere in southern Germany or northern England around the turn of the century. Its vastness—almost 10,000 square yards—is filled with such splendid goodies, especially in the spring, that it's worth getting out of bed before dawn to catch it at its peak.

Entire aisles are devoted to hams and sausages, including *morcilla,* the famous blood sausages, sometimes stuffed with onions and pine nuts. There are huge *alonganiva de Aragón,* a sausage made in a U-shaped loop; and *choricitos,* little round sausages in a long loop, tied off every two inches. At the next aisle, you can find whole oceans, beaches, bays and estuaries of shellfish, including tiny blood-red shrimp called *quisquilla,* gathered from the city's beaches and served in tapas bars, traditionally with a glass of cold beer.

Various sorts of marine snails are on hand, also *langostino* and *cigala,* which looks like a seagoing crayfish. Endless fish, large, small and of virtually every fish shape and color; fish that are untranslatable but supremely edible. There are a half-dozen different kinds of salted or smoked tuna, each tasting a bit different because of a different smoking technique. Here you find the delicious *mojama*, a dried tuna ham which is a favorite tapa in Valencia served with the steely local rosé or *fino.*

There are cheeses from the mountains made of sheep and goat milk, booths filled with garlic crowded next to peppers, potatoes, every kind of green and leaf imaginable. In the spring, you can buy crisp, pencil-thin asparagus, which the Spanish call *espárago trigo*, wheat asparagus, because it often grows on the margins of wheat fields. The peppers can be especially dangerous. A pepper called the *padrón* is often grilled and served as a tapa. The particular mystery of this pepper is that it is impossible to tell from the shape, color, or size whether it will be sweet or hot.

Booth after booth is filled with tomatoes that actually taste like tomatoes, an agreeable sensation one frequently meets with in Spain. However, there are dangerous signs. Spanish farmers have learned that northern Europeans will pay the same price for green tomatoes as for ripe red ones. Green tomatoes are easier to pack, ship better, and, of course, can be grown faster. But for the Valencia market, at least, tomatoes continue to be picked ripe.

If it is early in the day, one can easily get stuck in the market's pastry section. Valencian pastry chefs and bakers are famous for delights such as *tarta cristina* or *pan quemada.* Once past the sweet delights, you come upon an amazing selection of *empanadas* of all sizes and stuffings. One particular standout is a stewed artichoke *empanada* made with a whole wheat crust. Another yummy is a red pepper and *bacalao empanada* wrapped in something like a thin pie crust.

Once, in a mid-morning fit of hunger after several hours' wandering through the market, we loaded a bag with pastries and *empanadas* to take back to the hotel. We should have been satisfied with the free samples the ladies of the pastry booths kept pressing on us, but greed won out and the bag was filled. Wisely, we also got a bottle of a local Valencian sparkling wine, slightly sweet, yet not so sweet as to compete with the pastries, but blending perfectly with them. We sat in the middle of the slightly oversized single bed the Spanish call a 'matrimonial,' ate pastries and *empanadas* and drank bubbly.

✦

Pedro de Arechavaleta de Peña is very much a modern Valencian businessman. He has been involved in global sales of everything from irrigation equipment to wine. Yet Pedro, one of the people who first introduced us to the wonders of Valencia, thinks nothing of whisking sixty or eighty kilometers down the *autopista* for a lunch that might last three hours.

One brilliant summer day, we drove south from Albufera where the coast arcs out toward Denia and Cabo de la Nao in a lovely sweep of sand, rocks and palm trees, with groves of oranges clinging to steeply terraced hillsides. Pedro noted that it is a good thing oranges make such a fine cash crop, otherwise the hillsides would most likely be growing cookie-cutter retirement villas for northern Europeans. One silver lining of the tourist presence is that this particular stretch of coastline has more good seafood restaurants per kilometer than any place on earth. The variety on offer is amazing, as is the quality almost everywhere. But Pedro was heading for a particular restaurant in Denia called La Pegola.

'It is very hard to get a table,' he explained, 'and they were not answering the telephone this morning, so I couldn't try for reservations.'

As we moved a steady 160 kilometers an hour down the *autopista*, Pedro discussed how the Spanish do business.

'Car telephones will not happen here. Why should I want to talk business when I am out of the office? Going to lunch is to get away from business—yes, even if it is a business lunch. Perhaps some business gets done, but it isn't why we get together.'

When we reached La Pegola, Pedro directed us to wait in the car. He would have lost face if seen in the company of *dos Americanos*. He disappeared inside the restaurant for about five minutes. This was around 12:30 in the afternoon. No one, of course, would dream of arriving for lunch before 1:00 or 1:30. Pedro was not trying to get us in on the spot, but to make reservations for later in the afternoon. Finally he emerged, beaming.

'I did it. He pretended he didn't remember me even though I was here only two weeks ago and bought him a cognac after lunch. But when I mentioned my wife's family, he said we could come at 2:00.'

It had made his day. He had been a victor in a peculiarly Spanish hustle. Pedro is not *valenciano*, but Basque, so he begins any sensitive local negotiation with one strike against him. His wife, however, comes from generations of *valencianos*, going back, perhaps, to El Cid himself. Her family name is like a talisman, finding tables in restaurants where there are no tables.

And, it was worth it. La Pegola is right on the Mediterranean, with a sweeping view toward Ibiza; but the food is so good little thought was given to the view. There is no menu. The waiter simply begins to bring food. First, there is a salad with lettuce, tomatoes, peppers, pickled fish, radishes and grated carrots. On the day we were first there, it was followed by *gambas*, served Spanish-style with heads on. After eating the body of the shrimp, we picked up the head and sucked out the nutty-tasting substance inside.

Then came the *arroz abanda*, which La Pegola is famous for. The name *arroz abanda* means simply 'rice on the side.' Fish stock replaces water in cooking the rice, and originally this stock-cooked rice, with saffron added, was served to the side of the same fish that went into the stock. Now if there is fish served, it is usually freshly grilled.

La Pegola's *arroz abanda* was beyond wonderful. It was rich and crunchy, outrageously good. The crunch came from the *quemada*, the slightly burned rice at the bottom of the pan, which is scraped loose and mixed with the rest of the rice. The rice was the Valencian short-grained variety, the only kind that should be used in *arroz abanda* or *paella*.

The chef had not spared the olive oil in his *sofrito*, and *calamares* and *merzola* (a local Mediterranean fish) were sparsely mixed into it. Wonderful! And with a little planning, most anyone can get a table at La Pegola without knowing Pedro's in-laws.

❦

Late spring and we were high in mountain vineyards about one hundred kilometers west of Valencia near the small town of La Portera, about ten kilometers off the main highway between Valencia and Madrid. The map reads local road number 330, which leaves the main highway at Requena. Lunch that particular windy day of high blue skies was lamb chops and local sausages, grilled over an open fire with only sprigs of fresh rosemary as garnish. The rosemary had been gathered by the four-year-old son of the jefe, the vineyard manager, and was thrown over the white coals of the vine cuttings just before the chops were removed from the grill.

There was a huge platter of chops and sausages for four of us, and a huge bowl of salad, fresh from the garden, enough salad to satisfy even Americans, who are often heard complaining that they simply can't get a fresh green salad in Europe. And bread. That was all.

The salad consisted of several kinds of garden greens and a few freshly gathered wild greens which the jefe's wife—who looked like she had just stepped out of a painting by Goya—could find no Castilian words for. Her husband was a small, spare man who talked about his latest experiments in the vineyard as if we were at a seminar at the viticultural school of the University of California at Davis.

'And how do you think Chardonnay will do at this altitude?' he asked. 'I believe it could have a good future here. The microclimate is right for it, according to some reports I've seen. I've planted a few rows. I'm going to put it on a high wire and open up the center, pull the leaves, to let plenty of air circulate, because sometimes we get rain near the harvest and the Chardonnay is very thin-skinned. It rots easily. It should do well on the English market too, a Valencian Chardonnay, don't you agree?'

And there, just there, we were at the heart of modern Spain. A man who moments before had been grilling freshly-butchered lamb chops very much as they had been grilled in these mountains for thousands of years, was easily up-to-date on his viticulture and wine marketing.

We were so deep in the country that in the conversational silences you could hear the thin, high scream of a hawk, hundreds of yards away. The jefe's little boy sat on his lap and gnawed at a lamb chop bone, while his wife poured fresh glasses of a fruity, slightly chilled red wine that danced a delicious duet with the lamb across the palate.

The boy slid off his father's lap and dashed out the door, waving his arms furiously at a half-dozen magpies who had gathered around the remains of the open fire, picking at the scraps of lamb. He threw his lamb bone at the birds and watched in amazement as one of them seized it and flew away. He ran crying to his mother, who laughed and gave him a crust of bread, dipped in red wine.

Basque Country

The Basque country as a state of mind is larger than the political entity. Politically, the three Basque provinces are Guipúzkoa, Vizkaya and Alava, but the Basque cultural influence extends south, well into Navarre and Rioja. The Basque culinary influence reaches around the world.

Language is the first item that separates Basque country from the rest of Spain. The other languages of Spain—Castilian, Catalan, Galician, Andaluz—are all linked through the common mother language of Latin. Basque is altogether different and is not related to any other European language, or even to Indo-European. It has vocabulary in common with Berber languages of North Africa and languages still spoken in the Caucasus. Most fascinating is the research, based on blood types and skull shapes, that suggests that the Basques may, in fact, be descendants of Cro-Magnon man, the original European.

The Basques were already isolated in the steep valleys and mountains of the Pyrenees when the Romans arrived. Although nominally under Roman rule, they were pretty much in a constant state of rebellion. They have continued to resist any government imposed from outside their mountain territory.

The land itself is beautiful. The Basque country, along with the rest of the northwest, gets plentiful rain off the Atlantic. The brown, bare hillsides of the rest of Spain are replaced by a landscape as green as Wales or Ireland. At lower altitudes, the winters are mild, the summers balmy.

In the summer, the coastal cities and towns are shoulder to thigh with northern folk from all directions who come to bake winter from their pale bodies and sweat the ice from their souls. Avoid them. There is no point in going there for the beaches. There are better beaches in other parts of Spain. Go to the Basque coast in the late spring when the vines and other plants are in flower, take an umbrella and wander the old section of San Sebastián, sniffing carefully at the door of each bar. Find one that smells good, order a *tapa caliente*, a glass of *txakoli* and watch the rain fall. It's good for the vines and keeps the northerners away.

✦

Basque cooking is really two separate cuisines, one of the mountains and the other of the sea. Many Americans are probably most familiar with the Basque restaurants of the American west, where Basque immigrants went in the late nineteenth and early twentieth century to work on sheep ranches. This hybrid Basque-American cuisine is remotely related to the simple mountain fare of the homeland, which is quite similar to that of Rioja, Navarre and Aragon.

This upland fare is quite different from the coastal table, which has developed into one of the world's great cuisines by emphasizing the region's tremendous selection of seafood and fresh produce. This style has recently been called *Nueva Cocina Vasca,* or Basque nouvelle cuisine, which is guilt by association as far as we're concerned. Perhaps the influence of Paul Bocuse, among others, has helped Basque chefs to break away from old-style dishes. But the basis of the mislabeled 'new' Basque cuisine has always been present in the flavors and native foods of the region. If it is a new cuisine, it is one that respects the older traditions and builds on them—a story we have read all over Spain.

The Basque country offers an extraordinary wealth of raw materials for the kitchen. From the sea: crab, hake, shellfish of all sorts, baby eels, tuna, *bacalao,* squid, bream, clams, mussels, oysters, lobsters and edible sea barnacles. From the land: beef, lamb, goat and pork. Game of all sorts, but especially quail, rabbit and venison. Because of the relatively mild maritime winters, fresh local produce is available most of the year.

In the past, corn flour or corn meal was an important item in the Basque diet, though its use has faded except in the countryside. For reasons that are not quite clear, the Basques took to corn quite early compared with other Europeans, who thought of it as pig food. Corn grows well in the Basque country's mild coastal valleys, and is not so subject to rot from damp weather as is wheat. A kind of corn mush or porridge called *morokil* is still served to Basque children. In the deep countryside, a corn bread called *talo* is also made. *Talo* is exactly like the Mexican *tortilla,* prepared and used in the same way, even crumbled into milk as a kind of instant soup as is done in the parts of Mexico.

Basque bakers are proud of the local wheat flours, especially that from the Bardenas Reales region of Navarre. It is in great demand by pastry bakers all over Spain. But they also import the hard durum wheat from Canada, especially to use in breads.

The eggs are quite good, perhaps because egg production has not yet reached the factory stage achieved in the United States. Most chickens are still fed on corn, which produces tastier eggs with a bright yellow yolk. There are also outstanding local hard and semi-soft cheeses, most made from ewe's milk.

One of the surprises of the Basque kitchen is mayonnaise, which the Basques have transformed from its humble role in home kitchens to a marvelous restaurant sauce. Mayonnaise is so basic to the Spanish kitchen that, in other regions of Spain, it is usually considered beneath the notice of restaurant chefs. (A fate it shares with chicken dishes. Hardly anyone in Spain would think of ordering chicken, a staple of the Spanish home diet, in a restaurant.) But in the restaurants of San Sebastián and elsewhere in Basque country, mayonnaise is suddenly met with on all sides. There is no ready explanation for this. Perhaps it's the weather. In most of Spain, it is too warm to risk using it in settings where it might not be consumed for several hours. Or perhaps it's simply that the Basques produce a lot of eggs and mayonnaise is a delicious way to use them.

Mayonnaise is, in any case, so common in Spain that the Spanish claim to have invented the sauce doesn't seem entirely out of the question. Some say that mayonnaise was taken to France by the Duke of Richelieu, who was the leader of the French invasion force that seized the port of Mahón on the Spanish island of Menorca in 1756. As the Spanish tell the tale, the Duke was very taken by a certain Menorca lady, who tempted the Duke with a special sauce, as well as certain nonculinary devices. The Duke, so the story goes, later popularized the lady's sauce in Paris, calling it sauce *mahonnaise*.

One of the most famous of Basque dishes is *elvers*, or young eel, called *al pil-pil*. Frankly, we can't stomach it, even though there are few foods or dishes we have ever turned away from. These young European eels are spawned in the Sargasso Sea and almost immediately start back across the Atlantic to their home river, where mom and dad eel originated. (True aficionados claim to be able to tell in what river the young eels were caught.) It takes three years for the journey. They enter the rivers of Basque country in the fall and are netted and trapped in great numbers. After very laborious preparation they are converted into a dish that looks a great deal like a bunch of earthworms and tastes like rubber bands. The great virtue of the *al pil-pil* recipe is that its flavor, or rather lack of flavor, is enhanced by garlic, oil and hot red pepper.

✦✧✦

Most of the wines drunk at the Basque table—at least on the coast— are white wines from the province of Alava, which pokes down into Rioja. They are fairly simple, straightforward wines that go well with seafood. In the mountains, the hearty red wines of Navarre are likely to be the drink of choice. There is one wine that is truly typical Basque and that is *chacolí*, in Castilian, or *txakoli*, in Basque. It's a highly acidic wine, very like the Portuguese *vinho verde*. It shows at its best in the many tapas bars of San Sebastián. Like *vinho verde*, it is low in alcohol, eight or nine percent, so a lot of it can be consumed with little effect. The taste is a bit odd. Someone described it as tasting like flat beer. That isn't far off, although with food it tastes better than one would expect.

In Basque country, the vineyards are a sea of mud in the spring. During a normal winter, the vines stand with their feet in water for weeks at a time. This does them no harm and in fact does one very good thing. The constant wetness disrupts the breeding cycle of the phylloxera root louse, so it has never established itself in the Basque country's wet, mountainous vineyards. Consequently vines here can be grown on their native roots.

Rain squalls sweep into the Pyrenees all through the summer, but rarely break over the high peaks into the more famous vineyards of Rioja and Navarre. Vines there are often stressed by drought by the end of summer. There is seldom such stress on Basque vines.

Txakoli is made from the Ondarrubi zuria, or Ondarrubi beltza, white and red versions of the same grape. *Txakoli* is usually made as a rosé, a blend of the red and white. Perhaps the real 'wine' of the Basque country is fermented apple cider, delicious with many of the local cheese and egg dishes.

✦✧✦

Seville is regarded as the tapas capital of Spain and its reputation is deserved. But if the tapas lover has an overwhelming urge for a nibble while in Basque country, there is plenty to satisfy. There are, in fact, a few surprises in store. The first, as noted above, is mayonnaise, a food rarely seen around a tapas bar anywhere else in Spain. On the Basque coast, from San Sebastián to Bilbao, there is a liberal lathering of mayonnaise—shrimp with mayonnaise, tuna with mayonnaise, vegetables with mayonnaise, vegetable paté, fish paté, many different egg dishes—all with mayonnaise. Mind you, the Basque version of mayonnaise is a far cry from the jello-like substance available in a supermarket jar.

We sat once in the Bar Asador Gambara in the old section of San Sebastián watching the mayonnaise maker make gallons of the stuff. The Asador Gambara is one of the best tapas bars we've ever been in. It has a restaurant which we have intended to try every visit to San Sebastián, but somehow we can't get past the bar.

It's an attractive space, with an almost American look of light wood and tiles. At certain hours of the day it fairly hums, moving toward critical customer mass, with people lined up two to three deep at the tiny bar and spilling out into San Jerónimo street. The bar itself is staffed by three to four very fast-moving young men, including the man on the mayonnaise machine, and the kitchen is filled with women who all look like fashion models.

As is common everywhere in Spain, cold tapas are displayed on top of the bar, where you can help yourself if you wish. Don't be afraid to grab whatever looks good, especially if the barman in your section is busy. Just try to keep track of what you have so you can settle your score in an honest fashion. Hot tapas come from the kitchen.

A specialty in San Sebastián is a tiny croissant, about the size of a baby's hand, with a piece of ham or cheese or a small sausage wedged inside. They are finger food and a delicious two bites, max. At the Bar Asador Gambara—and everywhere else in town—they claim to have baked the croissant on premise. That's doubtful. They are most likely from one of the excellent bakeries in San Sebastián, perhaps the Bollería Reciente on the Calle Mayor, just around the corner. This looks like a simple storefront bread and cake shop, but below there is a huge basement, filled with baking ovens that go twenty-four hours a day. The Bollería Reciente turns out a marvelous *turrón* called *vasco pasas*, Basque *turrón*, with raisins and a thin sugar glaze on top. They also do various whole-grain and health breads, which are gaining some popularity in

Spain, especially in areas where northern Europeans travel.

The 'homemade' bread at the Bar Asador Gambara probably comes from Bollería Reciente as well. But they do marvelous things with it, offering a range of *bocas*, finger sandwiches, with ham, cheese and green or red peppers, served with a teaspoon of mayonnaise on top. Or something with eggs. The Basque are mad about eggs and serve them with just about everything imaginable—shrimp, sausage and, of course, mayonnaise.

Encouraged by the fare at Asador Gambara, we abandoned plans for dinner and set out on a tapas crawl. Our base was the Pensión Amaiur, next to the Church of Santa María, just off the Plaza de la Trinidad. The steps of the church of Santa María make a good home base for a walk around the old quarter. All through the late afternoon and far into the evening, people come together here to meet friends, to make plans, to set out for the night.

About 8 PM, we zigzagged around a corner to the Zirika at 46 Fermín. We picked the tapas bar by the number of people inside. If we had trouble getting up to the bar to order, it seemed like a good place to be. The bar at the Zirika was so filled with tapas plates that there was hardly room to sit a glass of wine down. We began with a puff pastry tartlet about the size of a silver dollar, stuffed with finely chopped *bacalao*, red pepper and garlic. It's called *bacalao al ajo arriero*, or salt cod mule driver's style. It takes its name from the days when mule drivers carried fresh seafood over the mountains from the coast. Like today's truckers on the interstate highways, they insisted on eating well and simply, and this is one of the dishes from that era.

We could easily have spent the evening at Zirika, but that would be in violation of basic tapa rules, which insist that you must move on. Before doing that, we sampled a few other tapas, notably a *mejillones rellenos*, a stuffed mussel dish common on the Basque coast.

Next stop was the Bar Eibartarra at 24 Fermín, where we sampled a thin potato *tortilla*, served on a slice of bread with strips of red pepper across the top. This style of tapa is called a *montadito*, which means literally 'to mount.' The Eibartarra also served a superior *txakoli*, which had been made just for them.

The specialty at the Bar Txiki at 9 Calle de Lorenzo is *bocas*, lots and lots of little sandwiches, including one that is shaped like a swan. Very campy, but fun to eat and good. It consists of a small piece of bread, covered with a slice of hard-boiled egg, then mayonnaise, and finally the shrimp vertically-mounted on the mayonnaise in the shape off a swan. Very nice *rosado* at Bar Txiki, from Navarre.

There are several tapas bars on the Plaza Constitución, a block away from Calle de Lorenzo, and standard guides will tell you it's the best place for tapas in San Sebastián. It's not really, although it is the most expensive. There is one excellent bar here called Tamboril, which is a kind of Basque drum. They serve an especially wonderful tapa, a finger-sized pickle, stuffed with fresh tuna and topped with an anchovy held in place with a toothpick. Yummy and bizarre. Tamboril also has some excellent puff pastry, little tartlet shells stuffed with various bites and a fine hot tapa of whole tiny mushrooms on bread.

We finished at the Casa Igara, a most old-fashioned bar that looks out on the steps of Santa María. The people here were older, not so stylish-looking. The language of the bar was Basque rather than Castilian. The tapas were plain, unassuming, more like something from a country bar in Extremadura or Andalusia. There were hams hanging from the ceiling, jars of olives and pickles sitting on the bar. Not a drop of mayonnaise was in sight. Coming straight from the glitter of the trendier bars, it seemed dull and uninteresting. We ordered a plate of ham and olives, a glass of *txakoli*, and settled ourselves. Outside, we could look straight across at a shop called 'Trips' which looked very California—full of rather pricey things that no one could really need made by people who didn't care. It was profoundly depressing. Sitting in old Spain looking out the window at the new Europe.

We turned back to the bar and discovered it was literally a kind of museum. A small back room had a few tables; perhaps they served lunch there. The room was lined with shelves and cabinets displaying everything from religious relics to old winemaking equipment and odds and ends from ancient Basque kitchens. True, it was a small space, perhaps twenty by thirty feet, but well worth a look. And it is rare that one has a chance to tour a museum with a glass of wine in hand.

There was a kitchen, closed for the night, at the back of the museum and a group of women sitting around a table. Bread, ham, cheese and wine. One of the women was nursing a baby, a bright-eyed black-haired girl. When she has her own baby will the Casa Igara be a souvenir headquarters for the trend-conscious of the next century?

Just to shake the gloom, we decided on one last glass of wine and then an early evening. We settled on a small bar in the Plaza Trinidad, next door to our pensión, and had a small glass of *rosado* which went down well for only forty pesetas, about twenty-five cents. Having started about 8 PM, we finished off at about 11, having visited ten different tapas bars and having at least one tapa and one glass of wine each—small glasses—in every bar. Total cost for the evening, just under $30.

There is a delightful Baroque whimsy to be seen in some of the decorative effects of the tapas in San Sebastián. A prawn posing as a swan, gliding in a mayonnaise lake. We are one step removed from food as mere nourishment here, balanced on the edge of a culinary fantasy that bears, after all, a very Spanish accent.

A long taxi ride from the old quarter of San Sebastián is the ancient fishing port of Pasajes de San Juan. One despairs of ever reaching it. There are interminable miles, or so it seems, of decayed factories. There is a gray dreariness of row houses (some mad scheme of Franco's ministers, no doubt intended to appease the sometimes surly Basques), which gives way to shipyards that seem somewhat cheery—there is at least some activity to be seen. At last, the taxi pokes its way cautiously onto a narrow, twisting street off the main road, leaving behind the signs with arrows pointing toward 'Francia.'

It had been a dry winter. Now there was an early spring rain falling, which made the narrow street we turned into seem almost like a car wash rain tunnel. The width of the taxi barely cleared the buildings on either side. There was a long stoplight. We waited while a few cars and Vespas emerged from a street even more dark and narrow. Finally, the light changed and we edged into the dark opening. We began to have doubts about the Restaurant Txulotxo, which, we had been assured by a taxi driver the evening before, has the best and the most typical Basque food in the entire San Sebastián area.

This wasn't just any taxi driver. He belonged to a *cofradía* or dining society. The *cofradía* are usually open only to men, although recently a few have agreed to admit women. The societies started in the nineteenth century and have their own kitchen and dining room. Members are called *tripasais*, which means someone who looks after his belly. We were the driver's last fare the previous day and he was anxious to get to his club, where a special feast was on for that night.

'Ah, but it will not compare with the feast we held on King's Night this year,' he said. 'That night, the wine flowed so freely that we had to wear rubber boots to keep our feet dry.'

Suddenly the taxi burst into the light. It was fairy rain, a fine light rain falling through bright rays of sunshine. Before us lay a narrow finger of bay, the passage of St. John, perhaps one hundred yards wide, with a few streets of stone cottages wandering up the hill on either side of the water. Sunlight broke through the rain, and the factories, shipyards and dull row houses were out of sight, behind a wooded ridge and centuries away. But for our taxi and a few other cars, we could be deep in the past. Basque fisherman sailed from the Pasajes de San Juan to fish for cod off the Banks of Labrador in the thirteenth and fourteenth century, hundreds of years before the wily Columbus sold Isabella his passage to India get-rich-quick scheme. These fishermen probably introduced salt cod into Europe.

We were early for lunch—just past one—so were able to get a table by the window at Txulotxo, overlooking the bay. There are only a dozen or so tables in the restaurant, which is operated by a Basque family with the help of a Portuguese daughter-in-law who is an expert on witches. We learned this at the end of the lunch—a meal which goes by the impossible name of *apalaurreaudiak* in Basque—when she told how the Portuguese witches of her home town had once put a curse on her husband's shirts during a visit. When her husband opened his suitcase, he discovered that all of his shirts were filled with holes.

The lunch, as served by our student of witches, was incredible. From the elegant *txangurro*, crab steamed in a yummy sauce, then put back in its shell, to *cigalas*, a type of crawfish taken directly from the bay outside the window, the flavors were superb.

There was a delicious *sopa de pescado*, which was an entirely different kettle of fish than the Mediterranean version, being almost a fish stew rather that the lighter *sopa de pescado* one finds in Catalonia or Valencia. This dish could be prepared anywhere with access to fresh or frozen fish and clams or mussels. It is a rich, thick soup with strong-flavored fish to match the abundant onions and garlic. A fisherman's stew, it should be hearty and filling, the kind of fish dish that you can eat with a light red wine.

There isn't much you can do about getting the next two dishes on your home table. But if you find yourself hungry on the Basque coast, two dishes which you must try are *chipirones en su tinta* and *cigalas*. The first is squid cooked in its own ink. At the Restaurant Txulotxo they serve a whole squid, about the size of a baseball, just taken from the bay. Squid, done properly, has an almost sweet feeling on the palate, simply bursting with flavor. It is possible to get squid and squid ink in other parts of the world, but rarely such a large one and rarely so fresh.

Cigalas, I'm afraid, are impossible to duplicate outside the Iberian peninsula. They are like a sea-going crawfish, only a bit bigger. They are found on both the Atlantic and Mediterranean coasts of Spain and are absolutely delicious. Bite into one and you can taste the sea itself.

Our main dish was *merluza a la vasca* or hake, Basque-style. *Merluza* is found all over Spain. In fact, it is quite likely Spain's favorite fish and can be done in a number of ways, even as simply as a Spanish version of fish and chips. The Basques prepare it exceptionally well. Any good Basque cook can come up with a half-dozen recipes for *merluza* without a second's hesitation. It's a white, firm-fleshed fish. One can substitute cod, haddock or whiting for *merluza* in most recipes.

The Englishman Jan Read, the dean of Spanish wine writers, has turned up a nice story concerning *merluza a la vasca* in *The Wine and Food of Spain*. Read cites a letter written in 1723 by Doña Plácida de Larrea of Bilbao to a friend living in Navarre. 'Doña Plácida specifies that the fish must be caught from a small boat by hook and line, and describes how she stewed it in an earthware *cazuela* and served it with cockles and crabs in a green sauce made from parsley, and with a garnish of asparagus, a present from friends in Tudela.'

Read gives this as evidence of the 'origin and date' of the dish, but we suspect its origin reaches much farther back than the eighteenth century. The green parsley sauce also identifies it with a dish called *kokotxas en salsa verde*, which is a specialty of San Sebastián. The *kokotxas* is the tiny bit of delicate, very perishable *merluza* flesh taken from the fish's throat. These uses of a green sauce with *merluza* are found nowhere else in Spain.

After a lunch lasting more than three hours, our apprentice witch of a waitress realized that she was dealing with serious eaters. We had watched the sun move across the bay and had finally even changed tables in order to get the last few rays of light as the early spring sun ducked low above the ridge toward San Sebastián.

We were ready to pass on dessert, having gone through several bottles of an excellent Rosado Viña Ecoyen from Señorio de Sarria in Navarre. It seemed more like siesta time than sweets time. But we were wrong. We were presented with a menu of desserts and a bottle of *aguardiente* from Galicia, which is used in the famous Galician witches' brew called *quemada*. Although *quemada* is said to have originated in Galicia, it is found all over northern Spain and down into Murcia. At its simplest, *aguardiente* is poured into white china wine bowls and a match is put to it to burn off some of the alcohol. Oddly enough, when the flame dies out, the *aguardiente* is still cold.

We have had more elaborate versions in Catalonia where a bottle or so of *aguardiente* is poured into a large cazuela with sliced lemon, roasted coffee beans, and perhaps other fruit as well, then a match is put to the whole thing. It looks quite spectacular and warming on a cold day, and doesn't actually do any damage to the spirit under the flames.

It was past five and the Pasajes de San Juan was in shade by the time we finished. Four hours at table, each better than the last. Especially since we learned that we didn't have to take that long dreary taxi ride back to the old section of San Sebastián. There was a water taxi just below the restaurant that cut the journey back in half in a five-minute run across the bay, where a taxi was waiting.

And so to siesta.

***

It was a small café in the very industrial outskirts of San Sebastián, catering to taxi drivers, truck drivers, local day laborers. We had stopped to ask directions, and once there, decided on a cup of espresso and a small brandy. The waitress was flirting with one of the two drivers at the next table. When he left to go to the toilet, she grabbed his jacket and took it behind the bar.

'Tell him the witches took it,' the young girl giggled to his mate.

The man frowned. Suddenly the fun was gone.

'Don't joke about witches. You young girls know nothing about witches.' He looked around the Formica and stainless steel café as if an old hag on a broomstick might pop out

from behind a curtain.

Ann, sensing a story and recognizing his accent as Galician, said she had heard there were many witches in his homeland, but surely there were no witches in a big city like San Sebastián?

He looked glumly at her.

'You are American?' he finally asked.

'Californian,' Ann corrected, being stubbornly provincial.

'You don't have witches in California?'

'Well, I'm not sure,' she answered. 'At least, I don't know of any.'

He nodded. 'Yes, one does not know of witches until you met them.'

He leaned forward and nodded his head briskly, as if he had just made up his mind,.

'I could tell you about witches—or at least one witch, right here in this city.'

'We would like to know,' Ann said. 'Please tell us.' She ordered another brandy all around, as the other driver had just returned. The girl meekly handed over his jacket without a fuss.

'It was when I first left Galicia for San Sebastián, almost fifteen years ago. I was looking for a job then and took a room in a boarding house. There was a young woman there, a cousin of the manager, I believe, who kept flirting with me, but I had no money and no time then for women. Besides, I had a girlfriend back home. And on top of that, she was ugly as the devil, with a big wart on the end of her nose. Can you imagine?'

He took a sip of bandy, as if to ward off her ugliness.

'Anyway, I must have made her angry. One morning at breakfast I noticed that she was gone. When I asked, the manager said she had gone back to her home in the mountains. When I went upstairs to dress for a job interview, I went to the closet for a freshly ironed shirt. Now you will never believe what I found.'

Again, he looked over his shoulder and all around the café. The young waitress had given up any pretense of waiting on other customers and was standing wide-eyed beside the table, listening.

'I had four shirts hanging in the closet, all just laundered, you understand. The buttons had been cut from all of them. Neatly cut as if by a small knife. I saw at once it was witches' work and called the manager. He knew what I was thinking because without even being asked, he said his young cousin had left at noon. My shirts had not been returned to me until about six o'clock, several hours after the girl had left.'

He paused, as if his point were proven.

His mate nodded. 'Yes,' he said. 'That was the work of a witch for sure. They can do things like that at a distance. You are lucky she didn't do worse.'

The man nodded. 'I think so. Later, I found the buttons in an ashtray in the hallway.'

The manager had them sewn back on at his expense. He knew it was his cousin. I tell you, I got out of there in a hurry, the next day. I didn't want her thinking of more mischief. '

The two truckers finished their brandy and left. Ann asked the waitress if she believed the story.

'But it must be true,' she said. 'Only a witch could have done that.'

Celtic Spain

The three regions of the Celtic north are Cantabria, Asturias and Galicia. They stretch west from Basque Country along the Atlantic. Galicia is the largest of the three, with a long coastline running south to Portugal. Driving west from San Sebastián, through Santander and on toward Oviedo, one plunges into fairyland—Celtic territory. A landscape of intense green hills and craggy mountains and tiny hamlets tucked up under the shadow of rocky cliffs. Spain, at least the Spain of Hollywood films and travel posters, is left behind.

The Cordillera Cantábrica, a jumbled mountain range that stretches from the Pyrenees to Portugal, forms the southern border of Asturias and Cantabria. The range, one of the largest wild areas in Europe, runs more or less parallel to the Costa Verde and on south to the edge of the Meseta, the high upland plateau that dominates central Spain. There are wave after wave of hills covering over eight million acres. There are bears and wolves here, one of the few places in Europe where both these creatures are still found in the wild.

For centuries the Cordillera has formed a barrier, a natural frontier that has not only made it difficult for governments in Madrid to extend control over this wild, Celtic northwest, but also stopped the Moors as well. A small Moorish force did make one brief excursion into the mountains and was defeated at Covadonga in 722 by Pelayo, a chieftain who later became the first king of Asturias. After that defeat—which is recalled in local history as a major battle but was most likely a skirmish between an advance guard of Moorish cavalry and back country folk—the Moors retreated south of the mountains. This gave Christian forces the opportunity to regroup and begin the centuries long war of Reconquest.

In modern times, the region has not prospered. Galicia is the second poorest area in Spain, next to Extremadura.

✦❧✦

The Spanish Celtic kitchen benefits from a wide range of local produce rarely met with on the table in other parts of Spain. There are cool season vegetables such as turnips, carrots and cabbages, and a number of different beans and lentils. The wheat, rye and oats grown here are used in delicious traditional breads. And over 250 varieties of apple come from Galicia alone.

Like their Basque neighbors, the Spanish Celts have a rich selection of seafood, including hake, tuna, salmon, squid, sardines, scallops, oysters, clams, and shellfish of all kinds. There is also good freshwater fish, mainly trout. The pig is the most popular domestic food animal, with many tasty variations played on the themes of bacon, sausage, ham and salt pork.

There's plenty of game in the northwest, with long stretches of forest and mountains harboring partridge, pheasant, duck, quail, rabbit, deer and boar. We've left the olive far to the south and are well into butter country here. There are also a number of excellent local cheeses, most memorably a superb blue cheese called *pasiego* from the valley of Pas in Cantabria, which can be found in shops all over Spain.

The absence of Arab influence is evident in Spanish Celtic cooking. It is, in some respects a rich cuisine, closely related to peasant-country fare north of the Pyrenees. There is no winter growing season here, except perhaps for a few greens. The food is hearty, not very subtle, but very satisfying. It keeps away the winter cold.

There are wonderful fish stews, and an unusual turnip stew from Asturias called *estofado de buey,* which includes calf's feet in the list of ingredients. One of the area's most famous dishes is *fabada,* a ham and bean dish, which is also made in Galicia with beef. Many typical Spanish Celtic dishes feature local ciders, such as *lubina a la Asturiana,* a dish of fish, clams and cider. The region's wonderful blue cheese is used in a sauce called *salsa de cabrales,* which serves equally well as a dip for vegetables, a salad dressing, a steak sauce, or all by itself as a dessert course. Surely one of the most versatile sauces in the world.

They eat a lot of mussels in the coastal areas of Celtic Spain. Mussels fresh from the sea are a sentimental favorite of ours, since we practically lived on a version of *mejillones a la mariner* during the mid-1960s in Monterey, California. There are few things in life, maybe two or three, more wonderful than a mussel just minutes out of the water.

Wonderful dishes are made from the pig, including *empanada de lomo a la gallega,* the famous Galician pork pie, delicious served hot or cold. The Galicians were great travelers in the nineteenth century. Galicia was a poor area, and Galicians often left for Latin America, where in some areas the word for an immigrant from Spain is still *gallego*, regardless of what part of Spain the new arrival is from. The *empanada de lomo* was a lasting Galician import to Latin America, where most countries have some version of it.

✢

Galicia is the only area in the Celtic north to make wine in any appreciable quantity. Some of this wine is good, very good, in fact, though little of it makes its way outside the area. There are two geographical denominations of origin, the Riberio and the Valdeorras. There is also a separate denomination for wines made from the Albariño grape, wherever it is grown. The Albariño is the same grape as the Alvarinho of Portugal, from which the delicious, low-alcohol, slightly petillant *vinho verde* of that country is made.

The red wines are usually light and fruity, low in alcohol, high in acid. The best white wines have been compared to the wines of Alsace and of Muscadet. They have a similarity to Riesling, which may be more than a coincidence. There are dozens of grape varieties, most seldom seen elsewhere. Often, local wines are produced from tiny plots by farmers without the capital to invest in modern equipment. These wines can be quite good on occasion, but typically the reverse is true. Most of this wine is sold in unlabeled bottles in local markets or bars, and the first sip is often a real adventure.

But the real 'wine of the country' throughout these Celtic regions is fermented apple cider. The *sidra* of Galicia and Asturias is much appreciated throughout Spain, and is especially popular in the bars of Madrid. These dry ciders actually make a delicious pairing with grilled fish and shell fish.

✢

The road had seemed fine for the first few kilometers. A narrow blacktop ribbon, twisting and snaking its way through a green, heavily wooded landscape. Although it had rained all night, the rain had slowed to a few scattered showers by dawn when we left Orense in a rented car. I was later happy that we had spent extra car-rental money on a front-wheel drive Peugeot.

At the time, the sun was beginning to break briefly through the cloud cover. We were predicting picnic weather by noon. Not only was sunshine in view, but there was a good prospect of supplementing our basket of bread, cheese, sausage and bottled wine, with what we had been told was the best Albariño wine in Galicia. We were on a peculiarly Galician search for wine straight from the barrel. Not that there isn't plenty of bottled wine in Galicia. It is simply that Galicians consider it inferior and adulterated.

'What they put in the bottles!' The barman made a grimace and pretended to spit on the floor. 'It is the dregs, what they sell in bottles. For the real, the true Albariño, you must go to where it is made.' He was the owner of a small bar in Orense where we had stopped the day before for our late afternoon *merienda*—a light snack and a glass of wine. We noticed that he took the wine, the classic Galician Albariño, straight from the barrel. We complimented him on his wine, which was delicious, one of the best Albariños we had tasted. The flavor was fresh and appealing, a bit like a French Muscadet with a dash of very good Riesling.

Many Galicians believe that the grape was originally brought to the area by pilgrims to Santiago de Compostela in the early Middle Ages— perhaps the eleventh or twelfth century—and that it is actually a true Riesling. There is no California wine quite like it. It is low-alcohol, so I ordered another glass all 'round.

The barman nodded his approval of our drinking habits and I told him of our search for the real Albariño; that I had been informed all over Galicia that to get the best wine, it is necessary to go to the winemaker. At which he launched into his condemnation of any wine in bottles, 'You don't know what they might put in it,' and praised his producer.

But he would not tell us who that was. He simply smiled slyly and said, 'He lives so deep in the country, you could never find him. And now,' he waved at the rain falling steadily outside the open door, 'perhaps the road is closed.' We couldn't get the information from him, try as we might. Even another round of wine didn't loosen his tongue.

Gallegos are like that. And it is a quite un-Spanish trait. In most of Spain, a bar owner would have at once produced the winemaker's name, address and telephone number, along with directions to his house. The usual Spaniard is so convinced of the absolute superiority of his baker, his tailor, or his wine supplier, that he wants to share it with the world. But that's Mediterranean Spain. Moving into the Basque-Celtic northwest, that openness falls away. One enters the geography and the mind set of northern Europe. Clearly, two passing tourists were no threat to the bar owner's supply of wine. Yet the habit of secrecy was so deeply ingrained that he couldn't break it.

We stayed the night in Orense at the Padre Erjioo on the Plaza Eugenio Montes. Nothing special. A typically nondescript, fairly modern and overpriced hotel. But since we were only staying the night and it was raining, we didn't want to look for a pensión in the attractive old quarter. We fell into conversation with a young man at the hotel bar. He was from Burgos in Rioja but had married a Galician, and they had lived now for several years in Orense, where he was an attorney.

'That barman is my brother-in-law,' he said, laughing. 'He is amazing, and you have him pegged just right—a typical Galician. I would never dare say this to my wife, but her family is so secretive they hate to tell you the time of day.' He believed it had to do with the widespread Galician belief in witches. Every Galician knows, it seems, that the more a witch knows about you the more damage he or she can do. Therefore, tell nothing.

'My wife has cousins out in the country who burn hair and nail clippings so the witches won't find them and have power over them. And, you see, the winemaker who supplies my brother-in-law is married to a witch, or so they say. So, of course, my brother-in-law must be especially careful.'

He took out a note pad and quickly drew a map showing where the winemaker lived and told us his name. In true Galician fashion (even though he was only adopted Galician), he made us promise not to put the name in writing. He knew we were journalists but had apparently never read Joan Didion's maxim: 'Never trust a writer.'

At any rate, we left shortly after dawn, driving northeast on the C-546 toward the small town of Monforte de Lemos. Lemos is a lovely town. There is a tenth century monastery there, and some bits and pieces of a castle that once housed the Counts of Lemos. We stopped for a time and I thought how pleasant it would be to live in Monforte de Lemos, where history seems to have simply stopped some time ago.

But we were in search of the perfect Albariño, so we pushed on. We took the narrow paved road toward the village of Sober, an unlikely name for a town noted for its wine and vineyards. Our destination was in the hills above Sober where lived, we were told, the winemaker and his wife, the witch.

About that time, just past mid-morning, the sun disappeared for the day and the rain returned in earnest. We had also reached that point on the young attorney's hand-drawn map where we were to turn onto a dirt road that led up into the hills. There was to be a farmhouse where local cheese and wine were sold. But that was not the wine we wanted, he said. We should stop there, buy some of the local blue sheep cheese and ask if the rest of the dirt road was open.

A tiny old man in a shapeless gray sweater met us at the farmhouse door and led us down a long hallway into a kind of lean-to at the side of the main house. There were no windows in the shed, but he switched on a bare overhead light bulb. Cheeses were everywhere, hanging from the ceiling and stacked on shelves, cheeses of all shapes and sizes. Most were blue sheep cheeses, but there was also goat and cow cheese. In the dark, almost airless room, it was like being in a cave of cheese.

The smell of the cheese mingled with the sharp, almost acidic smell of wine. Wine barrels lined three walls of the room, raised slightly from the floor on a slab of concrete with a tiled drain running in front of the row of barrels. The drain ran through a screened hole in the wall into a pig pen outside. The room was perhaps twenty by twenty-five feet. An ancient dark table ran down the center. A cutting block and knives sat on the table, equally dark and stained with generations of cheese.

Yes, we were told, the road was open. But it led nowhere that anyone would want to go. Also, if it continued to rain, high water could close it at any moment. Besides, it was dangerous country. '*Muy peligroso.*'

'Why dangerous?'

The old man who was wrapping the cheese shook his head and just repeated that it was dangerous country, rain or no rain.

We took a chance. 'Witches?'

He looked up at me sharply and tightened his lips, finished wrapping the cheese and placed it on the table.

'Could we taste some of his wine?'

'Of course.'

There were several varieties, and as we tasted and talked about the wine, we gradually gained his confidence. I made a face at one of the wines, a Garnacha I thought. 'Sour, too thin,' I said.

He nodded. 'Yes. I told the fellow I didn't want his wine. But his wife makes good cheese and if I want the cheese, I have to take the wine as well.'

'It is Garnacha?' I asked.

'Yes. It doesn't grow well here at all. It needs sunshine and we don't have much of that.' He waved toward the rain.

'Do you have any Albariño wine?' I asked.

His eyes lit up. 'Yes, it is my own. But I keep it in the back. It isn't for everyone. Come.' He waved Ann and me around the table, through a door at the rear of the room, down a rain-spattered gravel path beside the pig pen (which was a model of cleanliness, by the way) and into a small barn behind the house. There was no electricity. He left the door open to let in light and also lit several candles which stood on a table.

'Here is my wine,' he said. There were a half-dozen barrels stacked in a pyramid against the rear wall, behind a table that looked like a duplicate of the table in the cheese room. Either of them would probably fetch a year's income for the old farmer in one of the trendy antique shops of London or San Francisco.

He opened the spigot of one of the barrels and poured out three half-glasses of the wine. It was stunning. Even better than the wine in the bar the day before.

'This is the best Albariño I have ever tasted,' I said. I was surprised, but then I had never expected the search for the perfect Albariño to lead me so far inland. It is commonly believed that the best Albariño is grown near Pontevedra in the Val de Salnes, only a few kilometers from the Atlantic. In fact, there is a yearly festival held the first Sunday in August honoring the grape in the seaside village of Cambados.

He thanked me, but not profusely. He knew the wine was good and was clearly very proud of his tiny cellar. 'I have been making wine for over fifty years, but last year was my last vintage,' he said. He explained that his wife had died the year before and there was simply 'no more joy' in his home. He was selling it all and moving to an apartment in Pontevedra to be near the sea.

'I was born there and I want to die there. I brought the cuttings of the Albariño with me when I moved here fifty-five years ago. They originally came with my grandfather from Portugal. I will sit and watch the sea all day and wait to die,' he said matter-of-factly. He could have been talking about the weather. There was no self-pity in his voice, nor any of that self-conscious cynicism found more and more in people of retirement age in northern Europe or America. Simply an acceptance of the end. His life had finished its circle.

He explained that his nephew was buying the property from him and would sell the grapes to the local co-op. 'It is a pity to lose such fine wine in the co-op blend,' I said.

'It is true,' he replied, 'but my nephew is a doctor. He has no time to make the wine. At least, my vines will continue to live.'

He poured another round. The flowery perfume of the wine was so intense, I could smell it from eight feet away. 'If you like my wines, perhaps you could take them to your country and sell them. You could send me a little of the money? They are the last wines of Marcelino Juan Castroviejo, for that is my name.'

I explained to Señor Castroviejo that although I was proud to taste his wines—and that they were, indeed, wonderful—I was not a wine importer and was a very poor businessman. I told him I would speak to friends in the wine trade. 'But the wines of Galicia are not well known in America,' I told him.

He nodded, sipped at his glass and smiled slightly. 'At least, my last vintage is a good one.' His mood brightened. 'Let me show you the vineyards,' he said and motioned us into the rain.

I have rarely been wetter. Ann thoughtfully said that she would stay behind and finish her wine, as it was far too good to abandon. I would probably have simply drowned but for the fact that his vineyards were rather small. I had started the day wearing hiking boots, so my feet managed to stay dry as we slopped down the rows of vines. Señor Castroviejo wore the knee-high rubber boots commonly seen in the often wet Galician countryside.

'Look.' He seized the end of a vine and pulled it down to face level. 'Look, it has begun. And I will not be here to see the finish.' It was a tiny speck of green beginning to form near the end of what appeared to be a dead brown branch. Señor Castroviejo let it go and the bursting green tip swung back up toward the wire, turned toward where the sun would be if it weren't for the steadily falling rain.

Not surprisingly, none of the importers I contacted in London or the United States were interested in six barrels of Albariño wine from Galicia. I exchanged a few postcards with Señor Castroviejo, but I learned that he died only six months after our visit. It would have been about the time of the harvest in Galicia. I know nothing of the circumstances of his death. I like to think that he was sitting on a terrace above the sea, watching the endless Atlantic roll onto the coast of Spain, with a glass of his excellent Albariño at hand.

We never made the trip up the dirt road that day. Señor Castroviejo's wine was so good that a further search would have been a waste and an insult. The grail is where you find it.

Extremadura

Extremadura is a harshly scenic land of mountains and high valleys lying between La Mancha and the Portuguese border. To the south is Andalusia, to the north Castile. It is a very poor region today, although centuries ago untold wealth in the form of conquistador gold flowed into Extremadura from the Americas. It was a battleground for centuries between the Christians, advancing from Castile, and the Moors, falling back to Andalusia.

In the nineteenth century, the entire region was so underpopulated that the government in Madrid encouraged mass immigration from Galicia in an attempt to resettle entire villages which had been abandoned. But even the Galicians, accustomed it would seem, to the most grinding poverty, couldn't deal with the harshness of Extremadura. Summer heat may climb over one hundred degrees daily. In winter, frigid winds howl through the mountain passes.

Spring—late March or early April to the end of May—is the best time to visit Extremadura. The weather is ideal, with high blue skies and intense green fields crowded with wildflowers, including brilliant displays of a red poppy that seems to grow everywhere in Spanish roadside ditches, kitchen gardens, and in the tracks of wandering shepherds. The hedgerows and trees are thick with birds, and the stately stork may be seen adding a stick or two to its towering nest.

The name Extremadura means 'beyond the River Duero,' and it was the frontier for several centuries in the wars against the Moors. As the Moors withdrew to the south, new towns were settled, old towns reclaimed.

During a lull in the years of battle, about 1300, a shepherd near the mountain town of Guadalupe stubbed his toe, so it is said, on a piece of wood sticking out of the ground. He took a closer look, got his shovel and dug up a small statue, perhaps half life size, of a black virgin who became known as the Virgin of Guadalupe. Her discovery was hailed as a miracle. Doubtless the carved image had been buried at some point to save it from destruction by the Moors.

A few years later, in 1340, King Alfonso XI invoked the Virgin of Guadalupe before a key battle against the Moors at Salado. Alfonso was triumphant; he dealt the Moors a defeat from which they never recovered. He ordered a monastery and church built at Guadalupe, near the field where the statute was found. Today, there is a hostel at the site, the Hospedería del Real Monasterio, and in the monastery, which was restored by the Franciscan order in 1908 and is very much an active institution, a very good restaurant for local specialties.

The Black Virgin of Guadalupe's usefulness didn't end with the defeat of the Moors. She came to represent the mystic concept of the *Hispanidad*, the community of language and culture linking Spain with the New World. Papers were signed in Guadalupe authorizing Columbus' first voyage to the New World, and the first American Indians to be converted to Christianity were brought to the Guadalupe monastery for baptism.

A few hundred yards from the monastery's church is a modern mural painted on the side of a wall, showing the baptism of the Indians, who look very saintly and noble. The mural is not very well painted. The style is naive, simplistic, almost cartoon-like. Yet there is a strength in the simple painting that represents very accurately the spirit of Extremadura.

Inside the church, the Black Virgin herself has a faintly tacky appearance, like an oversized and overdressed doll, looking down over the church from her modern enamel work throne within the small room known as the *camarín*, high above the altar. The throne turns about, like a tabletop lazy-Susan, so that the Virgin can be shown to tourists who have paid their one hundred pesetas and climbed the narrow stairs behind the altar for a closer look.

Despite all these tourist trappings, there is, even to a nonbeliever, an air of mystery here and a feeling that somehow one is close to the center of the Spanish soul. It has to do with an oddly-combined fanaticism and fatalism, probably more evident in the Middle Ages, but still to be found in the modern Spaniard. Extremadura seems to lend that spirit to its people with a brooding almost cinematic intensity. In spirit, and very much in appearance, it is akin to the high plateau regions of northern Mexico, the American southwest, and that vast heartland of the American west that runs right up to northern Canada.

In many parts of Spain, one can see a geography that the early Spanish explorers and exploiters must have recognized in the Americas. In

Extremadura, especially in the Trujillo-Guadalupe area, it seems almost possible to recognize a philosophic kinship as well. There is an underlying hardness, a rocky reality wrapped around a deep spiritual core that has as much to do with the interaction of the people with the land as with the land alone or the people alone.

Extremadura is the poorest area of Spain. In the past, the sons and daughters of its farmers left for Madrid or Seville as soon as they could break away. This was also true in the sixteenth century, when Extremadura was the homeland of the conquistadors. Cortez, Pizarro, Balboa, de Soto and the lesser-known of their ilk were all born in Extremadura. Perhaps economics sent them off to the New World, but Extremadura has a long military tradition, bloodily based in the battles against the Moors.

This tradition of warfare and the search for instant wealth in the form of gold and silver had another effect, common throughout Spain but especially evident in Extremadura: the development of a warrior class that disdained commerce, farming, or any ordinary labor. This attitude, remarkably similar to that of the warrior caste in High Plains Indian culture (did the Cheyenne and Commanche learn more than how to sit on a horse from the Spanish?) contributed to an already impoverished economy. Huge estates produced nothing but a few hundred sheep or pigs a year, while the owners searched for gold in the New World, or fought the Pope's wars in Sicily, Italy, or the Low Countries.

Sometimes, these often illiterate warriors struck it rich. The city of Trujillo, which is called 'the nursery of the conquistadors,' is filled with the mansions of those who made their fortune as conquerors and colonizers—the most famous being Francisco Pizarro, the conqueror of Peru. Pizarro was the son of a swineherd and butcher who married an Inca princess, only to be murdered a few years later in his palace in Trujillo, the victim of political intrigue within his own command. The conquistadors are still heroes, still remarkable legends to most people in Extremadura. There is little questioning of what they did, or the effect on the Indians of the Americas.

If there is anything critical in the local attitude, it is a faint suspicion. Where did all that gold go, after all? All that Inca silver? There is the nagging feeling that somehow they have been cheated of a legacy.

⌥

One can sit in the Plaza Mayor in Trujillo, surrounded by the mansions of men who made their fortune by murder and worse in the New World, gazing at those ponderous, absurd storks nesting in church towers, and calmly contemplate the incredible folly of mankind. But after a bit, it's time for lunch and a glass or two of wine.

⌥

There is a schizophrenic aspect to the food of Extremadura. Most is fairly simple—country dishes very close to their peasant roots. But there is, surprisingly, a centuries-old tradition of *haute cuisine* in this ancient territory, a medieval tradition developed in the monasteries of Extremadura and still found at its best in its monasteries and *paradores*. It is more, however, than just a curious relic, because it is now cross-breeding, as it were, with local country fare to form the beginnings of an Extremadura cuisine.

Some of this monastic fare has, in fact, made its way into French cookbooks through the works of Auguste Escoffier. It seems that during Napoleon's Spanish war, a Benedictine monastery at Alcantara was sacked by French troops marching toward Portugal. A French officer salvaged from the flames a cookbook manuscript, which he sent to his wife, who passed it along to Escoffier. It contained such unusual recipes as pheasant and partridge stuffed with duck liver pâté and truffles. The truffles, a specialty of Extremadura called *criadillas de tierra*, or balls of earth, were marinated for days in port. The legend goes that Escoffier declared this recipe alone worth Napoleon's entire disastrous peninsula campaign.

To be honest, Extremadura's wine and food are not yet world class, but they are in that exciting stage of early self-awareness that leads to unexpected and delicious results. It's a situation found in many parts of rural Spain. A culinary exploration of Extremadura is for the adventurer, for someone who can travel without the usual gourmet guides and enological maps, for someone willing to risk palate and stomach on dishes and wines that haven't received the slick magazine seal of approval.

There is an abundance of raw materials for the kitchen. In late spring, garden produce begins to fill the market stalls of the towns.

There are heaps of tomatoes, peppers, potatoes and baskets filled with herbs—rosemary, thyme and marjoram. There are freshwater fish, mainly trout, and famous local hams. Extremadura is the homeland for *cerdo ibérico*, a delicious ham from the black Iberian pig. According to locals, the special flavor of the *cerdo ibérico* comes from the wild acorns and herbs the pigs feed on in the rough, hilly terrain.

This rich and varied local cornucopia is the instant attraction of the *extremeño* table. One can sample it best, perhaps, at the regional market in Mérida, just a few blocks from the *parador*. But almost any nameless corner café or bar—what the Italians would call a *trattoria*, the Spanish, a *restaurante casero*—can be counted on for tasty, honest *extremeño* fare.

✦~✦

Wines have been made in Extremadura for at least 2,000 years, or since the Romans arrived. Until recently, the wine attracted very little attention outside the area.

One of the most common wines in Extremadura—as elsewhere in Spain—is *clarete*. Grapes used in this rosé-style wine vary from region to region, but in Extremadura it is made mostly from white wine grapes, including Palomino, the principle grape of Jerez, and Morisco, a common red grape throughout central and southern Spain and Portugal. Other winemakers might add Garnacha, Palomino negro or Tinto fino to boost the color of the *clarete*. In short, they use what is available and are more concerned with where the grapes grow than their names. There are some outstanding white wines, made from Palomino, Pedro Ximénez, Alarija, Bomita, Airén and Marfil.

Typically, the small wineries of Extremadura ferment the wines in open cement vats, sometimes sunk into the floor of the winery. Following fermentation, the wines are drained off into 500 liter oak casks—usually American oak—where they age for eighteen to twenty-four months.

Both the white and red wines develop a *flor* somewhat similar to the *flor* that blooms on the wines of Jerez. The *flor* is visible on the surface of fermenting wine in the vats, and has a browner appearance than the white *flor* of Jerez. Oddly enough, the fermented wine, which is clear for the first twelve to fifteen months of its life, suddenly becomes clouded and muddy looking in the casks, then clears in three or four months, when it is bottled. No one can explain this, but odds are the wine is undergoing some sort of delayed fermentation, either alcoholic or malolactic, perhaps having to do with a peculiar life cycle of the local wild yeasts. The wine has a fairly high alcohol content of thirteen to fifteen percent, and a definite sherry-like appearance and flavor, yet with a most un-sherry like fruitiness.

The best red wines of Extremadura by far come from the wine growing area of Badajoz, a few kilometers from Portugal. Near the town of Almendralejo is Extremadura's only classified wine growing district, the Tierra de los Barros. As the name implies, the soil here is a heavy clay that retains water well. A good thing, because the rainfall is very low, easily meeting Los Angeles standards in that department. Clays from this remote area are shipped all over Spain for potters.

Most of the wine production is from a white varietal locally called Cayetana blanca, a very high-yielding grape, from which a low acid but high alcohol wine is made. Most is sold in bulk for blending or for brandy distillation, and if this were the only wine in Tierra de los Barros, the area wouldn't be worth a second glance.

However, there is a wine made from Spain's workhorse red wine grape, the Garnacha. Around the town of Salvatierra de los Barros, in the south of the district, a small quantity of a very flowery, intense red wine with deep rich colors is produced. Over the past decade it has gained a loyal following in Spain and a tiny amount is being imported into the US under the Lar de Barros label.

There was a flurry of modern interest in wine growing possibilities around Cañamero in the 1920s, when many small wineries were opened and new vineyards planted. But the wine of Cañamero, in common with most of Extremadura, remains virtually unknown outside the immediate area and a few knowledgeable buyers in Madrid, where the white wines have become somewhat fashionable.

Locally, it can be found in the Parador Nacional Zurbarán and the Hospedería del Real Monasterio in Guadalupe. The *parador* in Mérida has a better kitchen than the one in Guadalupe, but a much less adventuresome wine list, with heavy homage paid to Rioja at the expense of local wines.

The more trendy *madrileños* have also discovered wines from the remote mountain village of Montánchez, north of Mérida. The town is famous for its hams, but there is a red wine here that also grows a *flor*, like a sherry. Most of it is still made in the huge clay *tinajas* or *conos*. It has a very sherry-like character, which is startling to the palate. The eyes see red; the taste buds say, no way, this is sherry.

✦

It's an unsettling experience to top a small rise in the road deep in the springtime green countryside of Extremadura and have to brake for a formation of storks, those birds from the mists of childhood marching across the road in the here and now. They stand between three and four feet tall and are quite formidable looking. One feels happy to be inside a car, not face to face in a bog, their preferred habitat.

The storks nest in the bell towers and on the roofs of houses and hotels in towns and villages all through Extremadura. It is possible to watch a male and female white stork go calmly about the business of feeding nestlings within a few feet of a huge iron bell clanging away in a church tower.

But there are birds everywhere in Extremadura. Even on a casual driveby through the open countryside, half a dozen birds can be added to a lifelist. The Spanish no longer net small birds, as is common in Italy and parts of France. It is illegal everywhere now in the European Economic Community, but in some areas the practice is still followed. In Spain, King Juan Carlos is an ardent conservationist, which may have some effect on the practice. Once, a small bird, roasted whole, was a common tapa.

We were on our way to lunch at a restaurant in Trujillo called La Troyla. We had driven from Seville to Guadalupe the day before, following National Route 630 over an easy pass through the Sierra Morena and down into Extremadura and another Spain. Extremadura seems remote and mysterious, a bit unexpected after the Arab fantasies of the postcard south.

Driving up from Andalusia may not be the most scenic way to approach this lonely, sometimes stunningly lovely countryside. The scenic route would be through the high mountain passes traveling west out of Toledo, on the route of the ancient Roman road to Lisbon. From Seville, it's a long flat drive, through towns that could be in Kansas or Nebraska, through streets filled with Spanish cowboys driving pickup trucks missing only the gun racks. The distance, which looks easy enough on the map, begins to stretch out. The highway is two-laned, jammed with trucks carrying the gardens of Andalusia north to France and Germany.

But we had arrived in amazingly good order in Guadalupe, in time for a wonderful dinner in the Hospedería del Real Monasterio, where we were staying. The friar there, who is also the chef, is a fund of knowledge about the local foods, intent on preserving the traditional monastery cuisine of centuries past. When he stopped at our table for a glass of wine after dinner and learned of our interest in the local foods, he recommended La Troyla.

La Troyla is family-style Spanish dining. There is no menu, although the waiter will offer a choice of entrées if asked. A bottle of *gaseosa*, a kind of Spanish 7-Up, was immediately plonked on the table along with a bottle of a local red wine called Viña Zanjo—a do it yourself wine cooler. It is possible to get other wines once the waiter understands that there is an interest. In fact, by the end of the meal, he is likely to bring a bottle of wine that his uncle or brother made. If that passes muster, there will probably be another bottle that he himself made. These are simple wines, to be sure, and one can taste the grape in them; at the risk of sounding trite, it is honest wine, and goes remarkably well with the food. Here, as in much of the countryside of Spain at the simpler restaurants, these wines are never bottled but are taken directly from barrel or carboy.

In some mysterious way, Extremadura's local winemakers are able to achieve an astounding feat: working in a hot climate, with overripe grapes, they make a wine that is high in acid (as a rough rule, the hotter the climate, the riper the grape, the lower the acidity of a wine). Perhaps this acidity is the result of the young wine's exposure to air while fermenting or perhaps it is simply built into the local, obscure grape varietals.

With the wine came a simple salad and a *tortilla de patata*, a Spanish potato omelet. Those first two dishes are standard. After they are finished, there is some variation. On this occasion, the waiter brought delicious tuna *empanadas* with very thin wrapping skins, almost like wonton skins. Loaves of bread were set at the table and quickly renewed as needed. The bread of Extremadura is a little gummy because of the quality of the local wheat, but very tasty with a smooth, velvety crust. Each local baker marks the bread in a different way, like a trademark.

The tuna *empanadas* were followed by white beans with *chorizo* and *morcilla*, and the next course, a local version of *gazpacho*, was served in huge bowls in the center of the table from which you could take all you wanted. But don't take too much! We are just beginning.

Next came *caldereta de cordero*, a plain lamb stew very typical of the region, with potatoes and red peppers. The stew alone was worth the visit.

As a kind of palate-cleansing sorbet, there followed *migas* with *chorizo.* This is one of the most basic peasant dishes of Spain and is found everywhere, with local variations. In Extremadura it is a bit more refined than elsewhere. At La Troyla, it is a dish of bread crumbs, chopped red peppers, either sweet or piquant, and *chorizo*, fried with garlic in olive oil, sometimes lard. It tastes better than it sounds. It was our second dish of *migas* for the day. We had ordered *migas* for breakfast that morning at the monastery and had been served a very traditional dish, heavy with pork fat.

There followed *cabrito frito*, a simple dish of fried kid served with a green tomato salsa. *Cabrito frito* is a traditional market dish in Spain, served at the end of the day after the market is closed. A group of farmers at the market will go together early in the morning to buy a goat, which is then butchered and cooked for a joint feast when the work is finished.

Finally, a simple dish of *prueba de cerdo* or 'pig test meat' was served. These thin slices of pork are traditionally cut from a freshly butchered pig to test the quality of the meat—should it be cured or cooked fresh?

For dessert, there was *flan* served with a sauce made from a local liqueur called Bellota y Arellanos, which is made from acorns. A glass of the liqueur was served with the *flan.*

The food at the *comida casera* in Trujillo was simple gustatory pleasure on an almost unconscious level. Regular patrons would know what to expect and would certainly want no changes. The quality of the raw materials was superb. The meat, the vegetables, were of very high quality. When we mentioned this to the waiter he seemed surprised that anyone would notice. That kind of quality is taken for granted in most of Spain. Anything less would be remarkable.

The following night, we had dinner at the Restaurant Nicolás in Mérida, where they serve a version of *caldereta de cordero* that has left the countryside and come into the city. It is more refined than the version at La Troyla, the flavors are more focused and intense. It is a dish that is beginning to be aware of itself. The wines at Restaurant Nicolás, just down the street and around the corner from the Parador Nacional, come in corked bottles and the waiters can discuss vintages and styles. They do not bring out their own homemade wine at the end of the meal. For sure, something has been gained. But something is also lost.

✦

We stopped one afternoon in the small town of Cañamero, about halfway between Trujillo and Guadalupe, on a pleasant winding country road which will appear on a detailed map of Spain as C401. The road twists up, into, and over the Sierra de Guadalupe, looping back to the main Madrid-Lisbon road.

It was late afternoon, the heat of the day was broken, and it was time for a plate of olives and a glass of wine. We fell into small talk with a man perhaps in his seventies, sitting at one of the little round café tables that crowded the sidewalk. He was a coin collector and we traded him a few American coins, dredged from the bottom of purses and knapsacks, for a glass of the local wine.

Somehow the conversation got onto the civil war. He said he had fought with Franco. 'Because they were the first to get me. If I hadn't gone with Franco, his soldiers would have killed me.' He had been through the whole war, including the horrific siege of Madrid and the street to street, house to house fighting there.

'I killed many people,' he said, shrugging and rolling the wine in his glass, 'but I never got accustomed to it.'

'Do you think it has made any difference, the civil war? Does it matter now?'

He thought for a bit and looked carefully around him, 'Then, I thought it mattered. I thought it was necessary. But now, I don't know. I don't think it mattered after all. We would still have been doing this,' He waved a hand vaguely at the buildings around, the street, the televised soccer game in the dark bar behind him. But he had clearly grown a bit uncomfortable with the subject.

'Do you like our wine?' he asked.

'Very much. It is made nearby?'

He laughed. 'It is made right across the street by the man who owns the bar. Come on, I'll introduce you.'

The owner was a gentleman named Miguel Valle Gómez and we fell at once into deep discussion of his vineyard and winery, which was also his home. It was, indeed, just across the street. His wines were quite good, particularly his whites, which were clean with a good acid balance.

We invited the civil war veteran to join us for a glass with Señor Valle. We toasted King Juan Carlos. We could see, through the open door of the bar, the man's vineyards across the street and a corner of his house where the wine we were drinking had been made in the basement two years before.

'To the vine.' We raised our glasses.

Wandering down a twisting narrow street in Guadalupe, just at dusk. Past houses with signs announcing honey and wine for sale. Old women dressed in black (where are the young women?) sitting stiff-backed, knitting lace on narrow front porches.

At the bottom of the hill, an old man sitting very still doing nothing. Thinking we were lost, he explained carefully in slow Spanish how to get back to the main plaza. We thanked him, followed his directions, and found ourselves with a different view of the mural showing the baptism of the Indians. In the half light of dusk, approaching it from below, it took on an heroic, other-worldly look.

In a bar across the street from the monastery, the young crowd was drinking beer and listening to American rock music. They were waiting for the disco to open. Guadalupe has a population of under 3,000. There are three discos. The young women dance to rock and roll while their mothers and grandmothers knit lace to sell to the tourists or to give to the Black Virgin.

Later that night we could hear the goats crying in the hills all around Guadalupe. That day, many of the kids had been taken to market. The goats cried until dawn.

Madrid

In Spain, all the old roads give the distance to Madrid and all roads lead to and from Madrid. It is not an ancient capital. It is young as a major city. It isn't as glamorous as Barcelona, as fabled as Seville, yet there is a gritty honesty to Madrid that can't be denied. Although its faults become very obvious to anyone who spends even a few hours there, Madrid has a rough magic. It easily ranks with the world's most exciting cities—Rome, London, Paris, San Francisco, New York, you fill in the blank. Whatever your favorite city, you'll find Madrid the equal. It isn't simply the laundry list of great museums, great restaurants, great opera and theater. Like all great cities, it is greater than the sum of its parts.

Madrid was established as the permanent capital of Spain in 1561 by Philip II. Before that, the capital of Spain (if one can speak of Spain as a unity then, or even now for that matter) was wherever the court happened to be. Toledo and Valladolid were favorite royal roosting places.

It isn't clear why Philip chose Madrid. It is, more or less, the geographical center of the country, so it may have been an effort to promote a feeling of unity. He also enjoyed hunting in the area. Whatever his reasons, critics ever since have enjoyed pointing out that it was a sorry choice. Madrid has been described as an obscure village with no history or importance. I suspect that these critics have simply spent too many hot summers in Madrid, because its history goes back to settlements of prehistoric people along the Manzanares river.

The Moors built a fortress there and called it Majerit. It was captured in 1083 by the Castilian king, Alfonso VI, who promptly discovered a statue of the Virgin just outside a granary, or *almudín*. He converted the local mosque into a church and dedicated it to the Virgin of Almudena, who has been the patroness of Madrid ever since. That's a pretty good start for the city's table.

All that history is very well, but a great many people simply cannot take Madrid at any price. They complain of the heat in summer, the cold in winter. They complain of the traffic, which is near gridlock for twelve to fourteen hours a day in the center of the city. They complain of the expensive (compared to the rest of Spain) restaurants and hotels.

And this is all true. What you rarely hear anyone complain of is the people, the *madrileños*. One would have to be a prime grouch indeed to find a grouch in Madrid.

And for all its size, for all the appearance of modern urban life, the pace in Madrid is reasonable. There is time to stop and look around. There is eye contact between strangers on the broad sidewalks. If anyone in Madrid is in a hurry, they are probably from New York or Barcelona.

***

Whatever the season, if you don't eat well in Madrid, you simply didn't try. So much of the harvest of Spain finds its way to Madrid, like a delicious national smorgasbord, that it would be a pity for us to ignore the Spanish capital, simply because there are no vines growing in the Prado.

And there are restaurants there that know exactly what to do with all the harvest bounty. They range from grimy tapas bars around the Plaza Major, to trendy upscale hangouts on the grand avenues, to the unlikely mall-like setting for one of the best restaurants in Europe, Cabo Mayor.

Like most national capitals, the nation's regional dishes can be found in Madrid. There are restaurants that specialize in all the regional cuisines of Spain, and other restaurants, a few, that try to bring them together. There is even a tapas bar that calls itself The Museum of Ham.

The best raw kitchen materials in Spain—from the coast, from the garden, from the farms—are sent to Madrid. Whatever the season, the best will be in the Spanish capital.

***

Wine lists in Madrid's white tablecloth restaurants will lean heavily on Rioja with a scattering of Catalan wine from the Penedés. Maybe a few bottles from France, overpriced of course, and the waiter will probably tell you that they are not available anyway. In the mid-class restaurants and the tapas bars, there will be the honest wines of La Mancha. These are often sold straight out of barrel, usually are non-vintage, and are quite drinkable. And very, very cheap. A generous glass, three to four ounces, will run thirty to fifty pesetas in a tapas bar. A good quaff, as the Brits say. There will also be plenty of sherry on hand.

Much of the red wine in the small bars and cafés of Madrid is made nearby in Mentrida, the most northern of the wine denominations of La Mancha. The demarcated vineyards lie at the feet of the Sierra de Gredos, in the provinces of Toledo and Madrid. The chief grape—almost the only grape—is the Garnacha, which covers over ninety per cent of the vineyard area. The wines are usually drunk while still very young with only about one-third sold in bottle, the rest in bulk.

If you have ordered white wine, it is still almost local—seventy-five to one hundred kilometers distant— and will almost surely be from the La Mancha DO, which produces more wine than any other denomination in Spain. In direct contrast to Mentrida, ninety per cent of production is white wine from the Airén grape, which produces a fairly neutral white wine, used a great deal in blending in other areas of Spain, and for brandy production in the *soleras* of Jerez.

✢~✢

Summer, especially July and August, is a season that many avoid spending in Madrid—especially the natives, who flee to the nearby mountains. There is absolutely no cooling breeze. The air hangs hot and heavy right through the night, with perhaps some slight relief at five or six in the morning, before the newspaper kiosks are open. Madrid is ringed by mountains and the high plains of La Mancha. The summer rains that sweep in from the Atlantic to the north are blocked by the Sierra de Guadarrama, only a few dozen kilometers away.

Having noted that, we must say that there are few things in life more pleasant around midnight of a typically hot Madrid summer day, than a coffee with brandy (called, inexplicably, *carijillo*, or small penis) in an outdoor café with lights splashing on a nearby fountain discussing that night's dinner, planning the next night's dinner, and watching people pass back and forth. These post-midnight *paseos* are excellent for the digestion and also prepare the feet for a few hours of dancing to follow. Yes, it is late, but there is always the next day to sleep, or try to, in the summer heat.

The best plan is to meet the next afternoon about 5 or 6 PM in one of the small cafés off the Plaza Major. In this older part of the city, the walls of the buildings are thick to keep out the heat, the infidel or the

French. Inside the café it will be dim, cooling to the eyes, at least. Do not move too fast. Take a cue from the *madrileños*. This is not Paris or New York, remember. It is only 6 PM. There is the whole night ahead.

One of the most popular meeting places is the Posada de la Villa, an old coaching inn established in 1642, which has been comfortably remodeled without at all overwhelming the spirit of the original. It is at 9 Cava Baja, one of the little streets opening out in a maze south of the Plaza Mayor. In the seventeenth century, Cava Baja was one of the major routes into the city, just off the Puerta Cerrada and the road to Toledo.

The restaurant upstairs is, to be honest, a bit too filled with the tourists who arrive in noisy buses from Germany, Italy or maybe even Barcelona. But at the moment, we need not be concerned with them. Up the stairs they go for a dish of roast suckling pig and we are left at the street level bar—still moving slowly, don't raise a sweat—which as it happens is one of the best all-purpose tapas bars in Madrid. There are other places that might have better this or better that, but at Posada de la Villa, everything will be of high quality.

A plate of olives will come with the first glass of wine. Order a light, slightly-chilled red wine from La Mancha. It is a wine that need not be fussed over. Not for one moment is it necessary to hold it to the light and admire the color, to swirl it in the glass and admire the nose, to hold it in the mouth, rolling it back and forth like an all-purpose mouthwash. None of the above is necessary. The only job at hand is to enjoy it. It is a pity that in the US, wine appreciation has become an arcane ritual, having nothing to do with the sheer pleasure of the wine itself.

Soon one of the locals will introduce him or herself, recognizing a stranger. A curious manifestation of Madrid culture is the effusiveness of introductions. 'You must meet Señor López. He is my tailor. He is the best tailor in all of Madrid.' By the third glass of wine, he has become the best tailor in all of Spain—possibly the world, for if one is the best in Spain, there is little else to compare.

At first, being a too-cynical, too-cautious American, the tendency is to draw back a bit. Why are these people being so friendly? What are they going to try and sell me? Are they planning on stealing my purse? Not to worry. Most everywhere in Spain, but especially in Madrid, you will meet with honestly friendly folks who will want to talk to you. First of all because they just like to talk, second because you are not Spanish and they are fascinated by anyone who has the great misfortune not to be a Spaniard.

The friendliness, the eagerness to meet and talk to strangers, borders on the naive, but *madrileños* are not naive. They are quite sophisticated people who live in an alternate universe where the greatest joy imaginable is to eat, drink and talk.

Before very long, someone will suggest a change of scene, perhaps to the bar of the Restaurant Neru on the Calle del Bordabores, only a few streets away from the Posada de la Villa, for an absolutely delicious blue cheese from Asturias. It is a sharp, acidic cheese, made from an exotic blend of sheep, goat and cow milk, mixed with Asturian cider to a spreadable consistency, and served on bread with a glass of cider at hand. The cider is spectacularly poured by the barman from a bottle held high above his head so that a small amount splashes into the glass, only a mouthful really. The aeration gives the cider an instant sparkle, and you must drink it before you lose the foam and sparkle, or throw it out and the barman will pour another.

About this time, a running discussion will begin about where to eat dinner. It is now past 9 PM. The last three hours have been filled with eating and drinking, but it is possible that a small dinner might be in order. There are those who worry about having too much to drink, but most generally, a careful recounting (and a careful recounting would not be possible if there had been too much) confirms that it has been, so far, a fairly moderate evening. The tumblers of wine have been small and, following the Spanish lead, it is easy to make them last.

That is the great secret of a long evening of eating and drinking in Madrid, without facing bankruptcy or temporary physical disability. Move slowly, nibble, sip. The evening is long and there are miles to go and, it could be, you are yourself walking the edge of that alternate universe.

❧

We found ourselves one memorable evening at the Posada de la Villa deep in conversation with a man and his wife. He was the minister of tourism in the previous administration but one. His father had been in Franco's government, although he himself was a child when Franco came to power.

Be careful here. Yes, of course, Franco was a dictator. Many terrible things were done by him, or in his name, during the civil war. But the Spanish are pragmatists. Many who are quite liberal have found a few good words to say about Franco, although they have learned to be cautious in saying them to Americans. To other Spaniards, the civil war is like an abscessed tooth that will not quite be cured. They are constantly probing it, touching it—'Yes, the pain is still there'—and inviting you to share the pain, or at least to look at it.

At any rate, this man, this rather funny looking little man whose name we do not propose to reveal, is offering to buy us dinner at a nearby Galician restaurant called Casa Gallega. It is, he assures us, the best Galician restaurant in all of Spain. Yes, of course it is, but why should he want to buy dinner for two Americans? Because he wants our advice, is the quick answer.

His wife interrupts. She will only go to Casa Gallega, she insists, if afterwards we can go for *callos* at Maxi's, a tapas bar on the Cava Alto, also nearby. Of course, yes, that is no problem. Certainly not, since Madrid is famous for this stewed tripe dish, which everywhere else in the world is called *callos a la madrileño*, but in Madrid, just *callos*. The true *callos* of Madrid is made from veal tripe, and Maxi's is said to have the best.

His wife disappears briefly to find recruits for the grueling two-block march to Casa Gallega and dinner and our new friend outlines his problem. It seems that he is a bit short of ready cash—here it comes, we think, he is getting ready to try and sell us the family silver—but he has some paintings that he believes might interest an American museum. He is thinking particularly of the Getty Museum in Los Angeles. Later, he says, he will show us the paintings but he doesn't want to bore us with them just now. The question is, should he try and deal directly with the museum, or should he work through an agent, who will take a large commission?

We asked, naturally, what are the paintings?

Picasso, Miró, some minor turn-of-the-century portraits. The paintings, we are told, are in his late mother-in-law's apartment and after dinner we can have a look. Yes, and we are guessing we will be stuck with the dinner check.

As it turns out, we are not stuck with the check, and the paintings, viewed after the callos at Maxi's, are as described. And the next morning we receive a call at the hotel from our host, inviting us to lunch.

Of course, he is not on hand, I assume, to meet every American who wanders into the Posada de la Villa, but it isn't difficult to meet and talk to people in Madrid. Perhaps more than most places, it is necessary to be a bit open, a bit trusting in Madrid. Yes, the crime rate is up, but it's up everywhere, isn't it? And it's still much lower in Madrid than most any other world capital. Think of Washington, DC.

Mountain climbers, downhill skiers, hang gliders and the like understand the joys of taking risks. It is necessary to put oneself at risk, to reap the heart-stopping rush of pleasure. Perhaps the same principle should be applied to visiting a strange land. Stick to the American-style hotels, the American-style restaurants, clutch your purse tightly at all times, avoid any place that doesn't accept American Express and count your change carefully. Doubtless, you will lower the odds of anything unpleasant happening to you. Likewise, of anything pleasant. Perhaps you should have stayed in Denver.

In short, Madrid, like most great cities, is a state of mind. You cannot be in Madrid and act like you are in Chicago.

⌇

In a small bar just off the Plaza Mayor it is after Mass, a late Sunday morning. Escaping the already hot sun for a few moments of coolness, a glass of chilled wine.

A few moments before there had been only three or four people at the bar. One man read a newspaper at a bench in the corner. The bar is called Las Cuevas de Luis Candelas. The caves of Luis Candelas. He was a seventeenth century Spanish Robin Hood who shared his booty with the poor. The bar was the entrance to a series of caves where he would hide from the king's soldiers.

That Sunday, it looked very respectable, perhaps even a bit dull. But within minutes it was filled with well-dressed families, from an infant in a carriage to an old grandmother who set herself firmly at the bar, turning her back on her grandchildren, who were arranged by the mother around one of the few tables in the bar. Coloring books, notebooks and reading books were spread out. Large glasses of fruit juice were handed about, along with bowls of nuts and olives.

The children were fairly quiet, though active; an older boy trod on the newspaper reader's toes as he went for more juice. The parents stood at the bar, eating, sipping wine, exchanging news of the week. Occasionally the mother or the father would take a look at the baby, sleeping in a carriage, blocking most of the narrow aisle. No one seemed concerned. People edged past the baby, smiling at it, taking care not to awaken it.

If it had been a thieves' den three centuries before, the old bandit was nowhere in sight. The wine was only thirty pesetas a glass. No robbery there. A television set was tuned to a soccer game, the volume very low.

A young couple—perhaps sixteen or eighteen—came in, hand in hand. They stopped and smiled at the sleeping baby, the young woman greeting some of the adults, some of the children at the table. Perhaps she was an older sister, a cousin or an aunt.

Her soft 'holas' were like a blessing.

✦✧✦

Inevitability, we were in a bar along the Plaza Mayor. Almost inevitability, we were having grilled prawns, looking out the window at not much of anything. It was a slow day. A tourist asked to use the bathroom and the barman waved him up the stairs, adding, 'If it is still there.' A little joke, we thought and went back to our prawns.

Moments later, the tourist returned, assuring the barman that it was, indeed, still there. 'No, no,' the barman explained. 'It wasn't a joke.'

It seems that a few weeks before, during a very busy evening, two Gypsies who had been drinking at the bar, created a bit of a disturbance. Eventually, it was all sorted out peacefully, but in the meantime there had been, of course, much shouting and to-ing and fro-ing.

In a short time, someone went upstairs to use the bathroom. They found that most of the essentials were missing. Sawed right off at the wall and hauled away. The barman could only guess that during the disturbance, other Gypsies, friends of the two at the bar, had slipped upstairs and taken away the toilet and the sink.

He shook his head in disbelief. 'And there is no other way in or out except right through that door,' he said, indicating the front door.

In Spain, Gypsies are blamed for everything, but I had never before heard them blamed for stealing the bathroom.

✦✧✦

The wall of water at the marvelous, cooling fountain in the Plaza Colón. On a hot afternoon, it cools the eyes.

The New Life

We had to be in Jerez de la Frontera in five days for the beginning of the *Vendimia,* the harvest festival. This was a true 'had to be' since José Ignacio Domecq was taking the time to have lunch with us and show us around the Domecq bodegas. We hadn't yet decided whether to turn in our rental car and fly, or take the coast-hugging autopista from Catalonia to Murcia, then cut across the bottom of Andalusia to Jerez.

We had a late lunch with friends in Tarragona, and in the first cool breeze of late afternoon had walked out to the partially-restored ruins of the Roman arena. The setting of the arena could not have been lovelier. It's high up a steep hillside above the sea, in a flower-splashed park area above the Playa del Milagro.

From our perch high in the upper reaches of the arena, it was obvious that the origins of Tarragona go far back in antiquity—to at least 2000 BC. Rome took the city from Carthage in 218 BC, and for a time it was the Roman capital of all Spain and one of the major cities in the empire. In fact, the citizens of Tarragona possessed imperial rights granted only to citizens of Rome.

Today, it has a slightly decayed air of forgotten power. It knows its best days are in the past, but no regrets. Standing on the steps of the cathedral, looking down through the medieval section of town toward the Rambla, one imagines it as just the right-sized city to live in. With a population of about 125,000, it is outside the bustling Barcelona zone where perpetual hurry is the rule.

Perhaps because its archeological past is so evident, Tarragona seems a step back in time, to a slower, more thoughtful Mediterranean world. In a few blocks, it is possible to walk past the ruins of thirty centuries, from the Iberians to nineteenth century fortifications. In contrast, only about one hundred kilometers north, Barcelona, even though it is on the Mediterranean, has a northern spirit. It is restless, part bravado, part adventure, ready to take on new projects, to accept new ideas, to embrace new philosophies. Which is quite wonderful and no complaints. But there are times one would simply like to sit in the sun.

Or better yet, in late August, in the shade, high on the west rim of this arena. Hundreds of sailboats dotted the Mediterranean, tacking and turning slowly, trying to catch the light wind from the north. Below, Playa del Milagro was crowded, although the real beach scene in Tarragona is a few kilometers south at La Pineda and Salou. A group of Japanese tourists, managing to look fresh and interested despite the late afternoon heat, filed onto the floor of the amphitheater, staring up at our group as if we were imperial judges, ready to give thumbs up or thumbs down. Far out on the Mediterranean, a few puffs of white cloud drifted slowly south, toward Africa.

We were with old friends who lived in L'Arboc, a few kilometers north of Tarragona. There was that contented feeling one gets after good food, a few glasses of wine and good company. We were idly discussing lunch, trying to settle on what our favorite dish had been. Had it been the snails sautéed with sausage, or perhaps the lamb chops in a stew of baby onions, carrots and fried morels?

While sitting in the arena, gazing out over the Mediterranean, searching our palate memories for the best of lunch (and occasionally straying back to dinner the night before—deer in red wine sauce) we made up our minds. We did not want to forsake the coast for an airplane. We wanted to drive, even though it would take longer. We wanted to soak ourselves in Spain. Most of all, we wanted to plunge back into the Mediterranean south.

+〜+

Three days later, on a mountain side above Málaga at the edge of an old vineyard, looking south toward Africa, we were visiting a man whose hands were as gnarly and twisted as the vines in the field he had worked for half a century. It was an old Moscatel vineyard that was alleged to have first been planted in the early days of the Arab conquest. The harvest would begin early next week. We all sampled some of the grapes. That intensely sweet Moscatel taste filled the mouth and the perfume of the grapes permeated the afternoon.

This whole hillside had been vines one hundred years ago, when Málaga was one of the most popular wines in the world. Now Don Diego's vines were the only ones in sight. The man, Don Diego Rodríguez, was patiently laying a bed of vine cuttings from the winter before inside a framework of fire-scorched loose brick, stacked three bricks high, with one side open. The frame was just the right size for a *paella* pan to set on.

'No one wants good wine anymore,' he said, as he carefully broke sticks into the right length to fit inside the brick fireplace he had constructed on a flat blackened gravelly area, where many fires had clearly been made in the past.

'Now it is all beer—beer and gin—that the young people drink,' he shook his head and spat.

'I see them drunk now in the streets of Málaga, standing outside those beer clubs. I knew their fathers, too. I worked this hillside with some of them. But they sold their oceanfront land to the English for those great ugly buildings and abandoned the land. You should not abandon the land.' He spat again. 'If you take care of the land, the land will take care of you.'

There is no ready explanation why the young people of Spain, or at least some of the young people, have taken so to beer and certain spirits. Spanish-made gin and rum are cheap, but so is wine. Beer is much the same price as wine. It isn't a matter of price.

Some blame television. Beer and spirits look more glamorous, especially in the American, German and English shows. Many teenagers believe that wine is the old way. It's what their parents and grandparents drink and by the trendy teen set, wine is considered old-fashioned. The beer drinking set is most evident along the coasts, in areas where there are a lot of foreigners. It seems that it is connected with the desire of a lot of younger people to reject their 'Spanishness' in favor of an indefinite, ambiguous 'European' attitude.

On the other hand, it seems to fade when school is finished and regular work begins. We would hate to offer any pretended universal insight into trends about Spanish youth, based on their switch from wine to beer, gin and rum. It quite possibly means only that Spanish teenagers, like teenagers all over Europe and the US, have become more affluent. And with money to spend, they prefer to spend it with their peers, rather than stay at home with Mom and Dad, watching the telly and sipping a little wine with dinner. At any rate, teenage drinking patterns had nothing to do with the decline of the great vineyards of Málaga, whatever Don Diego believed.

The sweet wines of Málaga drew high praise from the Romans. Pliny, Vergil and other Roman writers wrote in glowing terms about them. The Moors, who were not the strict prohibitionists that many believe, made at least two wines from Málaga, both sweet: the Xarab al Maqui and the Zebibi, which, according to Jan Read in *The Wines of Spain* was made from sun-dried grapes. Málaga wine was very popular in Victorian England and it has been written that Catherine the Great of Russia kept a good store of Málaga on hand.

The best Málaga is made from Moscatel vines that grow on the steep mountain slopes inland from the city. In the nineteenth century, it was called 'mountain wine' and was most highly regarded.

What killed the market for Málaga was the decline in the fashion for sweet wines. Yet, curiously enough, one of the most popular wines in the world today is the light-bodied, sweet lambrusco from Italy. And certainly the sweet wines of Oporto and Madeira have held their own in the modern age, perhaps even advanced a bit. I'm afraid that Málaga somehow simply missed the boat when it took the wines to market.

Don Diego had laid the fire to his satisfaction. He waved away all offers of help. There were six of us gathered on the hillside for a country *paella*. In the house behind, Don Diego's daughter was lighting the oil lamps, which he insisted on in the evening, even though electricity had been laid on a few years before. The oil lamps fit well with the house, which was stone and tile. Don Diego didn't know how old it was. He had been born there, but he thought the house was 'not very old. Perhaps three hundred years.' The interior was all dark wood, worn and cracked tile and odd little hidden corners where a tiny shelf supported a few wine glasses or an image of the Virgin.

A winery representative had introduced us to Don Diego only a few hours before. For some reason, he had taken an instant liking and had insisted when he learned that we had no dinner plans that he make a real 'mountain *paella*' for us, his daughter and son-in-law and a young granddaughter who was visiting from Madrid.

'I must do it, you see, because I know you have been to Valencia and they have made you *paella* there. The whole world thinks that Valencian *paella* is true *paella*. Well, that's nonsense. I've been to Valencia and had the *paella*.' Don Diego paused, struggled briefly with his good intentions and decided to be polite in front of the visitors. 'It is quite good *paella*, you understand, and they are very good with rice, the *valencianos*, but they don't know how to make *paella* from the *país*, the country. *Paella* with rabbit, chicken and sausage, like you will have tonight.'

Don Diego explained that the vine cuttings gave just enough heat. 'You mustn't cook the *paella* too fast or too slow. This way, over a wood fire, that is the best way,' he said.

It was a beautiful dish, finished by lamplight as darkness fell over the mountain side. Don Diego carried the *paella* carefully inside and set it on the table 'to rest' for ten minutes or so. He opened a bottle of dry Málaga and we went back outside, into the cool night, to drink it. A truly dry Málaga is seldom found and almost never exported. It has the quality of a very nutty *amontillado* or a dry Madeira but with a bit more bite.

The coast was lit up by miles of lights, the brick and concrete apartments of retired British civil servants or army officers, or the vacation villas of the rich—Spanish, English and maybe German. Beyond the glaring slash of the coast there was blackness all the way to Africa. That night there was not even the light of a fishing boat.

Behind us, over the ridge of the mountain top, there was a faint glow where the moon would be rising soon. But before it broke above the ridge line, we were enjoying an outstanding *paella*—perfectly done rice, tender, juicy rabbit and chicken, with a slight spiciness from the sausages echoing through the dish.

And, most delightful, a taste of the burnt rice for everyone—the *quemada*—which Spaniards consider to be the mark of a perfectly made *paella* or any other rice dish. It sounds a bit odd to talk about burnt rice as a special taste treat, but it does add a remarkable flavor. Don Diego had got it just right by throwing on an extra double handful of cuttings at the last minute, creating a burst of heat and blackening a section of rice in the center of the pan.

We quickly polished off a bottle of light, fruity Valdepeñas with the first plate of *paella*. The granddaughter murmured something in her grandfather's ear, went to the kitchen and came back in a moment with a carafe of red wine. I saw Don Diego frown slightly, but Carmen, his granddaughter, simply smiled and passed the carafe around, paying no attention to him. She was a doctor, just starting with a family practice in one of the poorer areas of Madrid, and like many late twentieth century Spanish women, was thoroughly liberated.

Don Diego said gruffly that the wine his granddaughter had bought was not a true Málaga. 'It is something some French people have made. A few years ago they came from Algeria and bought an old vineyard further up the mountain. They pulled out the old vines, good Moscatel it was, and planted some other stuff. I don't know what it is, I don't know why Carmen wants to bring it here.'

Carmen shot me a quick smile. 'I'm sure you know the grape and so do you grandpapa,' she said. 'It is Cabernet Sauvignon. They have built a small winery. Two brothers. The younger one is unmarried.' She blushed and saw that we had noticed. She smiled a quick secret smile again and shrugged slightly.

'Grandfather likes to say they are crazy to plant anything here but Moscatel. But many of the English people like what they make. They have sold some to the local restaurants. They do not even put it in bottle yet. You have to bring your own jugs and they take it straight from the barrel. I stopped on my way to get a big jug of it for tonight. I am curious to know what you think.'

By the time she had finished speaking she had got over her blush and looked defiantly at her grandfather. This was going to be a bit tricky, so I stalled a bit, sniffing the wine, rolling it in the glass and holding to the lamp to get the color, which was a lovely, rich purple.

'Surely, this is a very warm climate for Cabernet,' I said, expecting to get an answer from Carmen, but to my surprise it was Don Diego who answered.

'That is what the foreigners say, but they do not know Málaga. We can grow anything here. The Moors knew that. That is why they fought so hard to keep Málaga. They say in the old days, Tamerlane the Great sent to Málaga for his wine. There is nothing wrong with this wine.'

He too held it to the light. 'You see the color? That is the soil of Málaga. And they had the good sense to go high up the mountain, where the nights are cold. My father himself knew that. And his father. That is why we planted up here. The grapes like to get cold at night. We can grow anything we want in Málaga.'

Don Diego set the glass down carefully. He seemed to realize that he had been tricked out of his curmudgeon role. 'At least,' he said, 'it is something to keep the English happy. And where there are vines, there cannot be concrete.'

I tasted the wine. It was lovely, partaking much more of the character that Cabernet Sauvignon develops in California than in France. It had an intense, brambly fruitiness typical of a young California Cabernet from Mendocino or Lake county, north of San Francisco.

'It is quite nice,' I said at last. 'Certainly goes well with your *paella*, Don Diego.'

He nodded and asked for another plate of *paella* and another glass of wine.

Later, as we sat around the fireplace with a small fire lit against the post-midnight chill, Don Diego agreed that he knew a bit more about the Algerian grape growers than he had admitted earlier.

'They have worked hard and if the wine they make is not the wine I would make, well, it is their day not mine. I wish them well,' he said.

Later his granddaughter Carmen took me aside and offered to take us to see the Algerians' winery the next day. I quickly agreed. She said that both brothers had been trained in France, but when they left Algiers, they decided they wanted to go to Spain, not France, because they felt they had more freedom to experiment, to try something new in Spain.

'I am very proud of my grandfather, you know. He tries to be hard, but he has actually helped them. He gave them some old barrels and talked to them about the local weather conditions of which they were ignorant. In the end, I believe he is simply happy to see the possibility of wine making a return to Málaga. He said it is not his life and that is true, but he welcomes the new life.'

We raised a glass of sweet Málaga, an old bottle from a small store Don Diego kept in his cellar:

'*¡Viva España!*' I said.

'*¡Viva!*' she answered.

RECIPES FROM
THE HEART OF SPAIN

About the Recipes

Cookery books, as I have so often said, are not very good guides to good cooking, but they do at least spur the imagination and encourage us to alter our little ways.
—Nicholas Freeling, *The Cook Book*

The recipes in this book are authentic Spanish recipes adapted for the American kitchen. Most are almost identical to an original Spanish version, but others have been changed in order to simplify, to adjust for ingredients available in the US or, in the case of country dishes, to lighten them up a bit.

Part of the adaptation was done to encourage American cooks to make these everyday dishes on the family menu, not special occasion dishes. Spanish food is very much rooted in the home kitchen. This is reflected in the large number of Spanish women chefs, such as Montse Gillian, who have become well-known in Spain and abroad. It is home-cooking, refined over centuries of isolation, not only from the rest of Europe, but from other regions within the Iberian peninsula. Regional Spanish cuisines with strong local roots are maintained to this day.

A number of these recipes can easily become part of the standard repertory of the inquisitive, imaginative cook who wants to try new techniques and ingredients. In short, this is not exotic terrain to be entered on rare occasions with compass and map. It is standard Mediterranean territory where most of the usual culinary road signs apply—with just a touch of Africa and the Mideast contributed by Moors.

Treat these recipes as a Spanish cook would, as a base to work from. There is nothing sacred about the text. It exists only as a guide to what your own imagination can produce. Perhaps the best thing to do is to take the approach that is used in translating poetry. Word for word is obviously impossible. What one is after is the feeling of the poem, the emotion, the 'wholeness' of the verse. It is the same in trying to duplicate a dish from another cuisine.

So as the best translator regards the text of the poem as an indication of the direction the translation should take, a good cook will use a recipe from another cuisine simply as a series of signs pointing toward the finished dish.

Even the most simple recipe is there only to serve the cook's needs. It should be interpreted within your kitchen so that when the dish reaches the table, it has become your own creation, or at least a variation on a theme.

Edward Espe Brown, the Zen chef who created *The Tassajara Bread Book* wrote: 'A recipe doesn't belong to anyone. Given to me, I give it back to you. Only a guide, only a skeletal framework. You must fill in the flesh according to your nature and desire. Your life, your love will bring these words into full creation. This cannot be taught. You already know. So please cook, love, feel, create.'

The recipes here have been gathered from various sources—restaurants, the home kitchens of friends, winery kitchens, even a monastery. Although there are a number of regional Spanish cuisines, there is a great deal of overlap from region to region, the same dish appearing in a slightly different version. An example is *menestra*, a vegetable stew found everywhere in Spain, with the major differences being the seasonal variations and regional food specialties. In these cases, the recipe presented in this book may be a synthesis of several regional recipes.

What You Need in the Kitchen

As a caterer and cooking teacher, I have worked in a lot of kitchens. Sometimes, I have had to create them on the spot from a closet without running water, or in an outdoor courtyard with a garden hose. So, when people tell me how much space and how many things they have in their kitchens, it doesn't impress me. All of the gadgets you can buy will not necessarily add up to a good meal.

Granted, it is nice to have ample counter and cabinet space and, most importantly, good, sharp carbon steel knives and a sharpening steel. But Spanish cooking requires very little in the way of special equipment. Following are a few items that would be helpful, in addition to normal kitchen supplies.

- Ceramic casseroles, called *cazuelas* in Spain. They are available in many shopping areas that cater to the Hispanic community in the

US and, generally, through good kitchen supply catalogs such as Williams-Sonoma. They can be used on top of the stove as well as in the oven, and can be taken directly to the table.

- *Paella* pan. There is really no substitute for a *paella* pan. It's a flat-bottomed, shallow metal pan with two handles. *Paella* pans should always be oiled before storage.
- A citrus zester. This handy little device allows you to remove just the colored part of the citrus rind in fine strips.
- Ceramic mortar and pestle. This should be of at least a three to four cup capacity. Any smaller is useless. It is important that it be a glazed ceramic mortar. The rough stone mortars used in Mexico or Southeast Asia absorb odors and don't produce a fine consistency.
- A large fine-mesh strainer or *chinoise.*
- Heavy duty food processor with a chopping blade, and a blade for mixing dough.
- Blender.
- Easy-to-use pepper grinder.
- At least one 12-inch pizza pan.

And that's it, unless you are really just starting to put your kitchen together. In that case, buy as you need and buy good quality. Think carefully before buying too many gadgets. Storage can be a problem.

As for food sources, most of these recipes can be made with food from your local supermarket or butcher. We have also noted substitutes when certain items may be hard to find.

For many years, pork products from Spain, such as hams and sausages, have not been available in the US for various bureaucratic reasons. The claim has been that since hoof-and-mouth disease is present in Spain, importing a Spanish sausage might lead to an outbreak of that swine disease in the US. We find it unlikely that many people would buy an Iberico ham from Spain (more expensive than prosciutto) and feed it to the pigs. The good news is that in the very near future the ban is reportedly going to be lifted, and Spanish hams and sausages will be available here.

Sauces

CATALAN GARLIC SAUCE
Allioli

All i oli, garlic and oil, that's it. The original sauce was no more than these two ingredients. Now, more often, you will find an egg added to make it easier to hold the sauce together. Of the two methods presented here I prefer the handmade. The consistency is much nicer and it really is very easy to make. The sauce is delicious with rice, grilled meats and fish, as a dip for vegetables, and a spread for bread. Just put it on the table and your guests will find a way of using it.

Note: We prefer to use half extra virgin and half virgin olive oil.

HANDMADE

MAKES 2 CUPS
4 medium-large cloves of garlic, peeled
2 egg yolks
1½ cups olive oil
Salt

Put the garlic in a mortar and mash it with pestle until a rough paste is formed. Using the pestle, stir in the egg yolks. Always stir in the same direction so that the surface tension of the forming emulsion is not broken. Continue stirring slowly and steadily with the pestle while very gradually adding the oil—a drop at a time at first—until a thick sauce is formed. Sprinkle in a little salt and taste, adding more salt if desired.

Variations: A handful or a pinch of fresh herbs, or a pinch of saffron, can be pounded with the garlic for a flavored *allioli.*

MACHINE MADE

MAKES 2½ CUPS
6 medium-large cloves of garlic, peeled
1 whole egg

1 egg yolk
2 cups of olive oil
Salt to taste

Put the garlic, whole egg and yolk into a blender or food processor. Whirl until the garlic is well minced with the egg. With the motor running slowly add the oil in a thin stream. Sprinkle in a little salt and taste for seasoning. Add more salt if desired.

Variation: Add one cup of basil leaves with the garlic, a teaspoon of lemon juice and proceed as directed.

SWEET RED PEPPER AND ALMOND SAUCE
Salsa de romesco

Romesco is one of the great Catalan sauces. It can be served with grilled meats, fish or vegetables, or be the base for a wonderful fish stew (See *Romesco de peix,* page 202).

MAKES 2½ CUPS
½ cup whole almonds
One 1½-inch slice white bread
3 cloves garlic, unpeeled
1 red bell pepper, stemmed, seeded and chopped
3 ripe tomatoes, quartered
2 Tablespoons paprika
½ teaspoon salt
½ teaspoon freshly ground black pepper
2 teaspoons hot red pepper flakes
1 cup olive oil
½ cup red wine vinegar

Preheat the oven to 400°. Put the almonds, bread and garlic on a baking sheet. Bake in the oven for 15 minutes or until the almonds and bread are toasted. Put the almonds and the bread, cut into cubes, into a food processor and whirl until very finely ground.

Peel the garlic and add to the processor along with the bell pepper, tomatoes, paprika, salt, black pepper, and pepper flakes. Whirl until the mixture is smooth. With the motor running, gradually add the oil and then the vinegar until the sauce is thick and smooth.

GREEN OLIVE SAUCE
Salsa de Aceitunas

This is a quickly prepared sauce that is really delicious and colorful with grilled fish or chicken.

MAKES 2 CUPS
1 cup of pimiento stuffed olives, finely-minced
2 cloves garlic, minced
3 tomatoes, seeded and cut into small dice
3 Tablespoons olive oil
1 Tablespoon sherry wine vinegar
Salt and freshly ground black pepper

Combine the olives, garlic, tomatoes, olive oil, vinegar. Add salt and pepper to taste. Allow to rest for 1 to 2 hours before serving.

SPICY DIPPING SAUCE
Mojo-Picón

This is a slightly *picante* salsa we first had with skewers of grilled pork at a tapas bar in Seville. Later we tasted *mojo* sauces in their home territory, the Canary Islands. They range from green and mild to red and fiery. All are good accompaniments to grilled meats and fish.

MAKES 1 CUP
1 dried ancho chili
¼ teaspoon cumin seeds
⅛ teaspoon cayenne
1 teaspoon paprika
5 cloves garlic, peeled and minced

¼ teaspoon dried thyme
¼ teaspoon dried oregano
½ teaspoon salt
3 Tablespoons red wine vinegar
½ cup olive oil

Stem and seed the ancho chili. Heat skillet hot and dry over medium heat. Toast the chili in the skillet until the color changes but do not let it scorch. In a mortar, grind the ancho and cumin seeds until powdered. Put the cayenne, paprika, garlic, thyme, oregano and salt in a blender with the ground mixture. Add the vinegar and with the motor running slowly add the olive oil.

Tapas and First Courses

POTATO AND ONION OMELET
Tortilla española

The recipe here is less fluffy and more dense than some Spanish *tortillas*, and has a wonderful caramelized flavor from the slow-cooked onions.

SERVES 6
½ cup, plus 2 Tablespoons, olive oil
4 medium onions, peeled and thinly sliced
3 medium Idaho potatoes, peeled, quartered and sliced ⅛-inch thick
6 extra large eggs, lightly beaten
Salt and white pepper to taste

Heat the oil in a 8-inch non-reactive skillet. Sauté the onions over medium heat, sprinkled lightly with salt and pepper, until meltingly soft and golden, about 30 minutes. Pour onions into a colander and drain the oil into a bowl. Return the drained oil to the skillet, and add the 2 Tablespoons of additional oil.

Reheat the oil, and add the potatoes, sprinkling with salt and pepper. Cook the potatoes, tossing occasionally, until they are soft and starting to take on a golden color. Drain the potatoes, reserving the oil.

Combine the onions, potatoes and eggs. Return the oil to the skillet and reheat. Pour in the egg mixture and cook over medium heat. As the tortilla cooks, lift the edges with a spatula, allowing the liquids to flow under. Cook for about 10 minutes, until the *tortilla* sets on the bottom and the top is still rather runny.

Cover the top of the skillet with a large plate or pizza pan. Quickly invert the skillet and turn the *tortilla* out, then slide it back into the skillet. Scrape any liquid remaining on the plate onto the top of the *tortilla*. Cook the *tortilla* until it is almost set through, about 10 minutes. Cover the skillet once again with a plate, invert the skillet to turn out the *tortilla* and slide it back into the pan. Cook briefly, until the *tortilla* is cooked through. The *tortilla* should have a rounded, firm texture, moist in the center. Serve at once, or at room temperature, sliced into wedges.

TRIPLE-LAYERED VEGETABLE OMELET
Tortilla bandera

This *tortilla* is a real architectural feat. Don't be overwhelmed by all the steps. It is not difficult to make and is so delicious and beautiful that you will want to add it to your kitchen book.

We had known this *tortilla* before as three separate omelets stacked one on top of the other. Antonio Buendia, the talented Catalan chef at Cafe Barcelona in Coral Gables, Florida, introduced me to this version and it is so much more interesting. The colors are supposed to represent the Spanish flag, by the way.

SERVES 8 TO 12
3 small heads broccoli
1 large head cauliflower
Olive oil
3 large red peppers
Salt and white pepper
12 eggs

Remove the florets from the broccoli and cauliflower and cook in separate pots in lightly salted, boiling water. Drain and keep the vegetables separate.

Stem and seed the peppers and cut into 1-inch squares. Heat one Tablespoon of oil in a skillet. Cook the peppers, lightly sprinkled with salt and white pepper, until soft.

Heat 1 Tablespoon of oil in a 10-inch heavy skillet over low to moderate heat. For best result use a well-tempered cast-iron skillet.

Beat 4 of the eggs with salt and white pepper to taste; combine with the red peppers and pour into the hot oil. Cook until set on the bottom. Put a plate or pizza pan over the top of the pan and turn the omelet out onto the pan and then slide it back into the skillet. Use a spatula to tuck the edges under. Cook until just set.

Beat 4 more eggs and combine with the broccoli. It will seem as if there are not enough eggs but don't worry. Season with salt and white pepper to taste. Pour the egg-coated broccoli on top of the red pepper omelet leveling it with the back of the spatula. Cook for about 8 minutes. Turn the whole omelet over using the pizza pan method again.

Combine the cauliflower with the remaining 4 eggs and add salt and white pepper to taste. Again there will not seem to be enough egg. Pour the cauliflower mixture over the omelet and flatten it with the back of the spatula. Cook for about 10 minutes occasionally running a spatula around the edge of the omelet. Turn the whole *tortilla* over using the pizza pan again. Cook until the tortilla is firm. It may be necessary to turn it over again. It will be golden and beautiful.

Serve immediately, cut into wedges, or serve at room temperature.

SCRAMBLED EGGS WITH
SALMON AND RAISINS
Revueltos de salmón con pasas

The Spanish are fond of scrambled egg dishes as first courses or as part of their light, late supper. The combination of raisins and salmon is unusual and very delicious.

SERVES 4 TO 5
2 Tablespoons butter
¼ cup black raisins
3 cloves garlic, minced
4 ounces of fresh salmon filet, shredded
8 whole eggs, beaten
2 Tablespoons milk or cream
Salt and white pepper to taste

Heat the butter and sauté the raisins and garlic until golden. Add the salmon and sauté until barely done. Combine the eggs with the milk or cream and stir into the salmon. Sprinkle with a little salt and pepper and stir and cook until fluffy and barely set.

Serve immediately.

HARD-COOKED EGGS WITH SAUSAGES
Huevos duros con chorizo

Every Spanish tapas bar is sure to have at least a couple of egg tapas. The most famous, of course, is the *Tortilla española* (page 205). This particular egg tapa varies from area to area, and is sometimes served cold, sometimes hot. I prefer it warm as a tapa, or as a light supper dish.

SERVES 6 TO 12 AS A TAPA
6 whole eggs
2 Tablespoons olive oil
5 cloves garlic, sliced
1 onion, minced
¾ pound mild, dry chorizo or linguiça, thinly sliced
1 cup dry white wine or chicken stock
1 Tablespoon tomato paste
Salt and freshly ground pepper to taste

Put eggs in a sauce pan and cover with cold water. Bring to a boil, remove from the heat and let the eggs sit in the hot water for 15 minutes.

Heat the olive oil in a skillet. Cook the garlic over medium heat until golden. Add the onions and cook until soft. Add the chorizo and cook for 3 minutes. Stir in the wine or chicken stock, and the tomato paste. Cook until the sauce begins to thicken.

Peel the eggs and add to the sauce. Cook for about 5 minutes. Cut the eggs in half and baste with the sauce. Serve immediately with the sauce.

NEW POTATOES WITH ALLIOLI
Patatas fritas con allioli

Hot and crisp on the outside and the creamy essence of potato on the inside, topped with a cool dollop of garlic mayonnaise, these potatoes are one of our favorite tapas.

SERVES 4 TO 8
2 pounds red new potatoes
Olive oil for deep frying (not extra virgin)
Salt
Allioli, hand or machine made (page 201)

Bring a large pot of salted water to a boil and cook the potatoes, whole, until tender when pierced with a fork. Drain the potatoes and when cool enough to handle cut into quarters or eighths depending on their size. The potatoes can be precooked and fried much later, but do not cut them until it is time to fry.

Heat the oil, preferably in a deep fryer, to 365°. If using a regular pan, check the temperature with a deep fat thermometer and carefully maintain that temperature.

Fry the potatoes until golden. Drain on paper towels. Toss with salt and heap on a platter. Serve the *allioli* on the side or put a big dollop on the top. Serve immediately.

SNAILS AND SAUSAGES IN VINAIGRETTE
Caracoles con salchichón y vinagreta

Snails are a favorite treat at Easter time. The snails have been sealed in their shells for the winter and poke out their heads in the spring to feed on all the new little shoots. They are at their tastiest then. There is a famous Spring festival in Lérida in Catalonia, where snails are the center of the feast. This recipe is from a nearby village.

You can use canned snails without shells for this recipe, or gather them from your garden. If you do collect snails from the garden, they will need preparation. I refer you to *Joy of Cooking*, which contains complete information on preparing snails. The Spanish say the best snails come from cemeteries.

SERVES 6 TO 8

Vinaigrette: 1 Tablespoon balsamic vinegar
2 teaspoons red wine vinegar
1 clove garlic, peeled

1 teaspoon Dijon-style prepared mustard
2 Tablespoons olive oil
Salt
Freshly ground black pepper

Snails and
Sausages: 1 pound breakfast sausage links, cut into ¾-inch pieces
3 cloves garlic
1 large onion, minced
¼ cup hot water
24-30 snails

To prepare the dressing:

Combine the ingredients for the dressing and let rest while the snails and sausages cook.

To prepare the snails and sausages:

In a non-reactive skillet, cook the sausages until done. Remove sausages from pan and set aside. Pour off all but 1 Tablespoon of oil.

In the same pan cook the garlic and onions slowly until the onions begin to caramelize, about 15 minutes. Pour in the water and stir. Return the sausages to the pan and add the snails. Cook to heat through and until the liquid is evaporated. Remove from heat, stir in the dressing and toss well.

Serve hot in the same pan or in a preheated small casserole. Serve with small plates and tiny forks or toothpicks. Spear a pieces of sausage and a snail for each bite.

CHICKEN LIVER PATÉ WITH OLIVES
Pâté de higados de pollo con aceitunas

Spanish tapas bars are lined with fish, vegetable and meat pâtés. Some are intricately decorated, others a simple slice on bread. In San Sebastián, we were served a creamy chicken liver pâté studded with green olives, presented in a little bowl with toasted bread—one of the best.

SERVES 10 AS A TAPA
8 Tablespoons butter

½ cup chopped onion
2 cloves garlic, minced
½ pound chicken livers
⅓ cup dry sherry
½ teaspoon salt
Pinch of ground cloves
⅓ cup chopped green olives

Heat 2 Tablespoons of the butter in a skillet and cook the onions and garlic over medium heat until they soften. Add the livers and cook for 5 minutes. Pour in the sherry and cook over high heat until dry.

Transfer the liver mixture to a blender or food processor and blend with the remaining butter and salt and cloves until smooth. Stir in the olives and pour into a small bowl or crock.

Refrigerate until firm.

Serve directly from the bowl or unmold onto a platter and garnish with more olives. Serve with fresh or toasted sliced baguettes.

MARINATED PORK TENDERLOIN
Probar de cerdo Trujillo

'Taste of the pork' is the name of this recipe, which refers to the custom of seasoning a little of the freshly butchered pork and cooking it to see if that particular pig should be made into ham and sausages or eaten fresh. Or so the story goes. It makes a great tapa.

SERVES 6 TO 8
1 pound pork tenderloin
3 cloves garlic
2 teaspoons paprika
1 teaspoon oregano
1 teaspoon salt
1 teaspoon freshly ground black pepper
1 Tablespoon red wine vinegar

Begin preparation 2 days ahead.

Cut the pork tenderloin into 4-inch pieces. In a mortar, crush the garlic and grind into a paste with the remaining ingredients: paprika, oregano, salt, pepper and wine vinegar. Rub this paste into the pork tenderloins. Put the pork into a glass or stainless steel container, cover and refrigerate for 2 days.

Remove the pork from the refrigerator and let it come to room temperature. Preheat the oven to 400°. Bake the pork for about 25 minutes or until it registers an internal temperature of 145°. Let rest 10 minutes. Slice and serve with, or on top of, a slice of good bread. The pork is also very good cold. In that case, refrigerate it before slicing.

CLAMS IN GREEN SAUCE
Almejas en salsa verde

All over Spain you will find variations on this clam tapa. A favorite of ours was served in a tiny restaurant in Sanlúcar near Jerez, where the clams were tiny, plump and juicy, the *Manzanilla* well chilled, and the night warm and full of the earthy scent of geraniums.

SERVES 10 AS A TAPA, 6 AS A FIRST COURSE
2 pounds small clams in shell
1 cup dry white wine
2 Tablespoons olive oil
6 cloves garlic, minced
¼ cup minced onion
¼ cup minced fresh parsley
1 teaspoon all-purpose flour
Salt and freshly ground black pepper to taste

Clean the clams thoroughly. Bring the wine to a boil in a sauce pan, add the clams. Remove them from the pan as soon as they steam open. Discard any that do not open. Reduce the steaming liquid to one cup.

Remove and discard the top shells of the clams, leaving the meat attached to the bottom shell. Heat the olive oil in a skillet and cook the garlic and onion until soft. Stir in the parsley and cook 1 minute. Stir in the flour and cook 1 minute. Strain the reduced steaming liquid into the skillet. Cook until the sauce begins to thicken. Taste for salt and pepper.

Add the clams to the sauce and simmer for 5 minutes.

Serve on individual plates, or in a ceramic casserole for everyone to share. Serve lots of good bread for dunking into the sauce.

SALT COD PUFFS
Buñuelos de bacalao

Salt cod puffs and croquettes are popular all over Spain. Often in restaurants they are presented as a little plate to sustain you until your first course has arrived. Usually they are fried light, lovely and greaseless.

We tasted these baked puffs in Madrid and the flavor was wonderful. I thought that baking would be a lot easier for the home cook who would like to be a part of the party and not in the kitchen doing last minute frying. However, if you would like to fry them, this same recipe works perfectly.

SERVES 6
½ pound salt cod
2 Tablespoons olive oil
1 medium onion, minced
1 Tablespoon parsley, minced
²/₃ cup water
¼ cup butter
²/₃ cup flour
4 eggs
Salt and white pepper

Soak the cod in cold water for 24 hours, changing the water several times. Drain the cod, squeeze dry and chop medium fine.

Preheat the oven to 400°.

Heat the oil in a skillet. Add the onion and sauté over medium heat until golden. Stir in the cod and parsley. Stir and cook for 2 minutes. Drain off any liquid. Put the cod mixture into a bowl.

Bring the water and butter to a boil in a medium-sized sauce pan.

When the butter is melted, stir in the flour and continue to stir until it pulls away from the sides of the pan and forms a ball. Remove pan from the heat. Put dough mixture into the bowl of a food processor and, with the motor running, add the eggs and whirl until the eggs are fully incorporated into the dough. Add salt and pepper to taste.

Stir the dough into the cod mixture and combine well. Drop by teaspoons onto greased baking sheets. Leave about an inch between them. Bake in the preheated oven for 15-20 minutes, or until golden and puffed. Serve immediately.

STUFFED MUSSELS
Mejillones rellenos

We have had these in San Sebastián at several of the wonderful tapas bars in the old quarter. There they are deep fried. Frying does keep you in the kitchen, so if you want to be with your guests while these are cooking, bake them as we do here. They are just as delicious.

SERVES 6 OR MORE
2 pounds mussels (about 30)
I cup dry white wine
Olive oil
I onion, minced
2 cloves garlic, minced
Pinch of hot red pepper flakes
Pinch of dried or fresh thyme
I Tablespoon flour
Salt and freshly ground black pepper
I red pepper, roasted and peeled. See instructions for Pepper
        Stuffed with Crab (page 263)
$^{1}/_{3}$ cup fine, dry bread crumbs

Wash the mussels and debeard, if necessary. Bring the wine to a boil in a pot, preferably a spaghetti cooker with an insert to make it easy to remove the mussels. Steam open the mussels—it takes only a few minutes. Remove the mussels. Reduce cooking liquid to ½ cup. Pour the reduced liquid through a fine strainer or through cheesecloth to remove any grit. Set aside.

Remove the mussels from the shells, reserving half of the shells. Heat the olive oil in a small pot and cook onions and garlic until golden. Stir in the red pepper flakes, thyme and flour. Cook one minute. Add the reduced cooking liquid and stir until smooth and thickened. Taste for salt and pepper.

Coarsely chop the red pepper and mussels and stir them into the sauce. Fill the reserved mussel shells with the mussel mixture. Refrigerate until firm.

Preheat the oven to 400°. Pour the bread crumbs onto a plate. Coat the filled side of the mussels with the crumbs and place them on a baking sheet filled side up. Sprinkle the tops with olive oil. Put the mussels in the oven and bake for 5 minutes. Remove from the oven, then put them briefly under the broiler until golden. Serve immediately.

If serving as an appetizer, serve with tiny appetizer forks. As a first course, divide them among 6 plates.

MARINATED ARTICHOKES
Alcachofas en escabeche

These are nothing like the canned, marinated artichoke hearts most of us know. The fresh herbs, especially the mint, give these a light feeling with an explosion of flavors that excite the palate. Mint is called *hierba buena* in Castilian, the good herb. It's a favorite homegrown herb, though it can almost always be found fresh in the market. It turns up in a lot of soups, sometimes even in gazpacho.

SERVES 6
1 Tablespoon salt
2 lemons
6 medium artichokes
$\frac{1}{3}$ cup olive oil
2 cloves garlic, whole
Pinch each of fresh sage, marjoram, parsley and mint

Begin preparation several hours ahead of serving. Bring a large, non-reactive pan of water to a boil with the salt. Cut one lemon in half and squeeze the juice into the water. Toss in the squeezed lemon halves, too.

Cut off and discard the stems at the base of the artichokes. Cut off the top 1/3 of the artichokes and discard. Remove any tough outer leaves.

Put the prepared artichokes in the boiling water and cook until the bottoms feel tender when pierced with a fork. Drain and, when cool enough to handle, cut into quarters using a very sharp knife. With a small knife, remove the furry choke and discard. Put the artichokes in a glass bowl or pan.

Squeeze the juice from the remaining lemon into another bowl, and combine with the oil, garlic and fresh herbs. Season with additional salt if necessary.

Pour over the artichokes and toss. Leave at room temperature, covered, for several hours before serving. This dish can be refrigerated, but bring to room temperature before serving.

STUFFED BABY ARTICHOKES
Alcachofas rebozadas rellenas

These artichokes are a great tapa or, if served in a pool of the fresh tomato sauce, an interesting first course. Remember when planning your menu that artichokes really alter the taste of other foods, especially wine. They make the other foods taste sweet and the wine slightly metallic. A dry fino sherry, I've found, is the best wine to drink with them.

SERVES 6 AS A FIRST COURSE, 8 AS A TAPA
1 lemon
16-20 very small baby artichokes
½ Tablespoon unsalted butter
½ cup minced shallots
⅔ cup, about 3 ounces, minced ham
All-purpose flour
½ cup milk
2 Tablespoons grated Parmesan cheese
Salt and white pepper to taste

2 eggs
1½ cups fine dry bread crumbs
Olive oil for frying

Bring a pot of salted water to a boil with the lemon. Cut the stems and about ½-inch from the bottoms of the artichokes. Cut one third off the tops and remove the tough outer leaves. Immediately plunge the artichokes into the water and cook over medium heat until tender, about 20 minutes. Drain well and cool.

In a small pan melt the butter and sauté the shallots until golden. Stir in the ham and cook 2 minutes. Sprinkle 2 teaspoons of the flour over the ham and stir it in and cook for a minute. Pour the cold milk in all at once and stir until thickened. Add the parmesan and salt and white pepper to taste.

Barely open the artichokes gently removing a few of the inner leaves to form a cavity. Divide the ham mixture among the artichokes.

Beat the eggs with a Tablespoon of water. Put the bread crumbs and some flour into separate bowls. Dip the filled tops of the artichokes first into the flour then the egg and then the bread crumbs. (This can all be done ahead and refrigerated until time to cook them.) Note that the whole artichoke is not breaded, just the tops.

Heat two inches of oil to 380°. Drop in a few of the artichokes and fry until golden. Drain on paper towels.

The artichokes stay very hot so can be done a little ahead of serving, or even reheated briefly in the oven.

MARINATED MUSHROOMS
Champiñones en escabeche

These mushrooms are a great tapa—deep flavored, sharp and addictive. They are ubiquitous in Spain, often served in the south as a free nibble when you order a glass of sherry, which matches well with this dish.

SERVES 6 TO 10 AS A TAPA
2 pounds small white or brown mushrooms
¼ cup olive oil

8 cloves garlic, peeled and minced
1 teaspoon dried oregano
1 teaspoon dried thyme
3 Tablespoons fresh parsley leaves, minced
1 teaspoon hot red pepper flakes
1 Tablespoon paprika
½ cup red wine vinegar
1 cup dry red wine
1 teaspoon salt
½ teaspoon freshly ground black pepper

Clean the mushrooms and trim the stems even with the cap. Do not remove the stem entirely.

Heat the oil in a large non-reactive skillet. Cook the garlic until golden. Add the oregano, thyme, parsley and pepper flakes. Cook for 2 minutes. Stir in the paprika until dissolved. Add the mushrooms and turn to coat. Pour in the vinegar and red wine and season with the salt and pepper. Bring to a boil. Reduce heat and cook for 15 minutes. Pour into a non-reactive bowl, cool and refrigerate for 24 hours before serving. Serve in a bowl with toothpicks on the side.

LEEK FLAN WITH SPINACH SAUCE
Flan de puerros con salsa de espinacas

Alboronia, a beautifully decorated restaurant in El Puerto de Santa Maria near Jerez, has a delightful patio where, on a warm summer's evening we enjoyed this *flan* as a first course.

SERVES 6
2 pounds leeks, well-cleaned
¼ cup butter
4 eggs
1 cup half and half
½ teaspoon salt
1 teaspoon white pepper
1 bunch of spinach, washed

I teaspoon sherry vinegar
¾ cup milk
Salt and white pepper

Preheat oven to 350°. Roughly chop the white part of the leeks and ¹/₃ of the green part. Heat the butter in a skillet and cook leeks slowly, stirring occasionally, until soft and slightly golden. Reserve one half cup of the leeks. Puree the remaining leeks in a blender or food processor with the eggs, half and half, salt and white pepper.

Oil six ½-cup *flan* molds. Divide the leek mixture among the molds. Put the molds into a pan and pour hot water into the pan so that it comes half way up the sides of the molds. Cover the entire pan with foil. Bake for 30 minutes.

While the *flans* are cooking prepare the sauce. Clean the spinach well. Reserve 6 small, perfect leaves. Put the remaining spinach into a sauce pan, cover and cook until wilted. There will be enough water adhering to the leaves to cook it properly.

Put the cooked spinach and reserved leek in the blender or food processor and puree with the sherry vinegar, milk, salt and white pepper to taste. Return the sauce to the pan and heat through.

Remove the *flan* molds from the oven, uncover and remove the individual molds from the water bath. To serve, pour a puddle of the sauce onto 6 individual plates and unmold the *flans* on top of the sauce. Garnish with a small spinach leaf. The *flans* and sauce may also be served cold.

BLACK-EYED PEAS WITH ONIONS AND ANCHOVIES
Chícharos con cebolla carmelizada

Black-eyed peas, a favorite of the southern United States and a dish traditionally served every New Year's day to insure a prosperous and healthy year, are also very popular in Spain, especially in Catalonia. We were never particularly fond of this legume until we tasted them at L'Olivé, a splendid and unassuming little restaurant in Barcelona. Absolutely do not leave out the anchovies.

SERVES 6

1 pound dry black-eyed peas
1 small onion
3 medium onions, peeled, sliced into ¼-inch rings
6 whole cloves
1 bay leaf
2½ teaspoons salt
2 Tablespoons butter
½ teaspoon freshly ground black pepper
1 cup dry white wine
Two 2 ounce cans anchovy filets

Begin preparation one day ahead. Clean the beans, removing any bits of gravel or stone. Rinse under cold running water, then soak overnight in 4 cups of cold water.

Drain and rinse the beans, and combine with the whole small onion studded with the cloves, and the bay leaf, in a stock pot. Pour in cold water to cover by 2 inches. Bring to a boil. Reduce heat and cook for 40 minutes. Add 2 teaspoons of the salt. Cook until the peas are tender, about another 10 minutes. Drain and discard the clove-studded onion, bay leaf and cooking liquid.

Meanwhile heat the butter in a skillet. Cook the medium onions slowly for 15 minutes, sprinkled with the remaining ½ teaspoon salt and the pepper. Pour in the wine and cook over moderate heat until the pan is dry and onions have begun to caramelize. Remove from the heat.

To serve, arrange the peas at one end of a large platter. Heap the onions beside the peas. Drain the anchovy fillets of excess oil and arrange at the end of the platter beside the onions. Encourage your guests to take some of each and mix together with each bite.

SPINACH WITH PINE NUTS, RAISINS AND APRICOTS
Espinacas catalanas

Simple, colorful and bursting with flavors. The combination of a vegetable with pine nuts and raisins make this a Catalan classic.

SERVES 6
3 bunches spinach
2 Tablespoons butter
$\frac{1}{3}$ cup pine nuts
$\frac{1}{3}$ cup raisins
$\frac{1}{3}$ cup dried apricots, diced same size as the pine nuts

Clean the spinach very well. Put the cleaned spinach in a large pan, cover and cook until wilted, about 5 minutes. There is enough water clinging to the leaves to cook the spinach without any additional liquid.

Drain the spinach and when cool enough to handle, squeeze dry with your hands. Chop the spinach and set aside. This can be done early in the day.

Heat a skillet with the butter. Add the pine nuts, raisins and apricots and cook over a medium heat until golden and plumped. Stir in the spinach and toss to combine. Cook until it is heated through. Serve immediately. We do not usually add any salt or pepper, but we do use salted butter.

BAKED EGGPLANT WITH
TOMATOES AND ANCHOVIES
Berenjenas rellenas con anchoas l'Empordá

Ampurdán, an excellent restaurant in Figueres, has an unassuming interior but with an open, friendly feeling. They serve a wonderful mix of classic dishes from the L'Empordá region (north of Barcelona on the Mediterranean coast) and some modern adaptations. We return to it again and again, especially since one of our favorite museums in Spain is the nearby Dali Museum, one of the most successful museums in the world at bringing a single artist to life. On one recent visit we had the following dish. Its satisfying flavor can stand alone as a first course, or can accompany a simple grilled fish or meat course.

SERVES 4 TO 8
Two 1 pound eggplants
3 Tablespoons olive oil

5 anchovy filets

3 large tomatoes, peeled and seeded

Preheat the oven to 375°. Do not peel the eggplants. Cut them into quarters lengthwise, place on a baking sheet with the eggplant skin resting on the baking sheet and the point of flesh facing upwards. Sprinkle the eggplant with two Tablespoons of the olive oil. Put into the oven and bake for 20 minutes.

Meanwhile, heat the remaining Tablespoon of oil in a small frying pan. Mince the anchovies and sauté them in the oil until they dissolve. Chop the tomato pulp and slowly cook with the anchovies until the sauce is thickened to a paste.

Remove the eggplant from the oven. With a thin-bladed knife, split open the flesh of the eggplant lengthwise along the center of the point, creating a gap that will hold the tomato sauce. Divide the sauce among the eggplants. Return them to the oven and bake for another 20 minutes, or until the eggplant is tender. Serve immediately with accumulated juices.

Soups and Stocks

There is nothing difficult about making meat or vegetable stocks, and a homemade stock can turn an everyday dish into something very special. Canned stocks simply don't compare and are often too salty.

Many of our recipes call for either stock or wine. If you prefer, you can substitute stock for wine, and water for the stock. But beware, the flavors will be very different, less intense and more flat.

POULTRY STOCK
Caldo de pavo, pato o pollo

For recipes using turkey, chicken or duck, do buy the whole bird instead of parts. It is cheaper, and you then have the backs and wing tips for stock. Just put the extra parts in a plastic bag and freeze until you have enough to make a good stock. I also bag the chicken and duck livers and freeze them until I have enough for a pâté.

For a good poultry stock, you'll need the following:

A turkey carcass with wings tips and neck; or several chicken or duck
    backs, wing tips and necks; or a chicken or duck carcass
Onion
Carrots
Leeks
Bay leaves
Peppercorns

Put the bones in a large stock pot and cover with cold water. Add an onion or two, carrots and leeks depending on the amount of bones, a couple of bay leaves and a few peppercorns.

Bring to a boil and skim off the foam that rises to the top. Reduce heat and cook over very low heat for at least 2 hours. Strain the stock and cool to room temperature. Refrigerate it, then take off the congealed fat. After the fat is removed, the stock can be boiled to reduce it further, which will intensify the flavor.

Use immediately or freeze the stock in small containers or in ice trays for easy use later. If you freeze it in ice trays, empty the cubes into plastic bags, close tightly and keep frozen. You can easily remove as much as you want whenever needed.

Variation: Roast the bones and vegetables in the oven at 400° until they are browned. Put the roasted bones and vegetables into a stock pot. Deglaze the roasting pan with water or white wine and pour into the stock pot. Continue as above.

VEAL STOCK
Caldo de ternera

You can find veal bones at a good butcher shop. If possible, have your butcher crack the bones. It will give your stock an extra boost of flavor.

10 pounds veal neck bones, cracked
2 leeks, split and washed
2 carrots, cut into quarters
1 onion, peeled and halved
1 cup of red wine
1 small stalk of celery with leaves
10 whole black peppercorns
2 bay leaves

Preheat oven to 400°. Put the bones, leeks, carrots and onion in a roasting pan and bake in the oven until well browned. Transfer the bones and vegetables to a stock pot. Pour off any fat. Deglaze the roasting pan with the red wine. Pour the wine over the bones and add the celery, peppercorns and bay leaves. Cover the bones with water.

Bring to a boil and remove the foamy bits that rises to the surface. Reduce the heat to low and cook, partially covered, for 3 hours. Skim the surface from time to time. Strain the stock and discard the solids. Pour the stock into a bowl, cool, cover and refrigerate.

When cold, remove the fat that covers the surface. The stock can now be reduced to intensify its flavor and then frozen in small containers for future use. Or use, as is, right away.

FISH STOCK
Caldo de pescado

Keep a supply of fish stock at the ready in your freezer. It's easy to make and adds greatly to the success of many fish dishes, or as a base for soups. Just order the bones from your fish market. Be sure to remove fish gills as they are often bitter.

3 Tablespoons olive oil
2 medium onions, minced
3 cloves garlic, minced
3 medium carrots, chopped
Leaves only of 2 stalks of celery
10 sprigs of parsley
2 bay leaves
10 peppercorns
5 pounds fish bones, rinsed

Heat the oil in a large stock pot. Cook the onions, garlic and carrots until soft but not browned. Add the remaining ingredients, plus water to cover the bones by one inch, and bring to a boil. Reduce heat and simmer for 30 minutes. Remove any foam that rises to the surface. Strain the stock and discard the solids.

When cool, refrigerate the stock. Several hours later or the next day, remove any fat from the surface. Gently reduce the stock by ¼ over low heat.

At this point use the stock in any of the recipes here calling for fish stock, or divide among several containers, cool and freeze for future use.

TOMATO SOUP WITH BREAD, EXTREMADURA-STYLE
Sopa de tomate extremeña

We were told that this is a 'very old recipe', but it can't be really ancient since tomatoes in Spain only date from the time of the European discovery of the Americas. When grapes or figs are in season they are served in a bowl beside the soup and you add them to each bite of the soup.

SERVES 4 TO 6
2 Tablespoons olive oil
1 large onion, minced
½ stalk celery, thinly sliced
3 tomatoes
3 cups of chicken stock (page 223)
1 bay leaf
2 cloves
Salt and pepper
1 cup of ½-inch cubed, day old bread

Heat the oil and slowly cook the onions and celery until very tender but not colored. Puree 2 of the tomatoes and stir them into the onions. Cook quickly until the tomatoes form a paste. Pour in the stock and add the bay leaf, cloves and salt and pepper to taste. Cook over a medium low heat for 30 minutes.

Peel, seed and cube the remaining tomato and add to the soup just before serving. Heat the soup through. Stir in the bread cubes and serve immediately in individual bowls.

SALT COD, LEEK AND GARBANZO SOUP
Sopa de bacalao, puerros y garbanzos

We first tasted this soup not in Spain, but at Bay Wolf restaurant in Oakland, California. Chef Carol Brendlinger prepared it as part of a Spanish week menu. We loved the soup and found it later on our travels in Spain. There it had the same great taste, but it had not been sieved and the stringy texture of the cod made the soup less appealing. So here it is the more elegant Bay Wolf version.

SERVES 6
½ pound boneless skinless salt cod
4 Tablespoons olive oil

1 medium onion, chopped
1 pound leeks, cleaned, white part chopped
2 medium carrots, chopped
1 Tablespoon parsley, minced
1 pound can of cooked garbanzos, liquid drained
1 pound potatoes, peeled and quartered
4 large garlic cloves, peeled and thinly sliced crosswise
2 thick slices white bread, crusts removed, cut into ½-inch dice
½ teaspoon white pepper
Salt to taste

Begin preparation a day in advance. Soak the cod in cold water for 24 hours, changing the water several times. Remove the cod from the water and squeeze dry. Cut the cod into chunks and set aside.

Heat 2 Tablespoons of the oil in a large pot and sauté the onion, leeks and carrots until they begin to color. Stir in the parsley, garbanzos, potatoes, cod and 6 cups of water. Bring to a boil, reduce heat and cook uncovered until the potatoes are very tender, about 45 minutes.

Puree the soup in a blender and return to the pot through a fine sieve. Push down the solids to extract as much of the liquid as possible. Heat the remaining 2 Tablespoons of the oil in a skillet and stir in the bread cubes and sliced garlic. Stir and cook until golden and drain on paper towels.

Heat the soup and season with the pepper and salt if necessary. Divide the soup among heated soup bowls, sprinkle with the bread cubes and garlic, and serve immediately.

COLD TOMATO AND VEGETABLE SOUP
Gazpacho

You will find *gazpacho* all over Spain, but it is most at home in Andalusia where there are dozens of variations. *Gazpacho* should be made at the height of the tomato growing season, using the best and the ripest fruit. Use a blender for this recipe rather than a food processor. It gives a much nicer texture.

SERVES 6

2 one-inch slices of good white bread, crusts removed

1 large clove garlic

½ cup extra virgin olive oil

¼ cup red wine vinegar

1 small onion, chopped

1 red or green bell pepper, stemmed, seeded and chopped

½ cucumber, peeled, seeded and chopped

3 pounds (about 9 medium-size) ripe tomatoes, cored and chopped.
　　　　You may want to peel and seed them for a smoother soup,
　　　　　but the peel adds a lot of flavor.

Salt and freshly ground black pepper to taste

Condiments:

½ cucumber, peeled, seeded and diced

½ large red pepper, peeled, seeded and diced

2 firm, ripe tomatoes, cored and diced

2 Tablespoons olive oil

2 one-inch slices white bread, crusts removed, cut into ½-inch cubes

Soak the bread in water to cover. Place the garlic in a blender and finely mince. Squeeze the bread dry and add to the garlic and whirl. Combine the olive oil and vinegar and, with motor running, gradually add to the bread. This will produce a thick, white sauce. Transfer to a bowl.

Put the onion, pepper, cucumber and tomatoes in the blender—in batches if you have a smaller work bowl—and blend until smooth. Pour into a large container, stir in the bread mixture and combine well. Season with the salt and pepper to taste. Cover and refrigerate several hours until very cold and the flavors have blended.

Arrange the vegetable condiments in an oval dish. Heat the olive oil and cook the bread cubes until golden. Drain and put into a small dish.

Serve the soup cold in chilled bowls and pass the condiments to be added to the individual bowls.

Variation: If you do not have access to flavorful, ripe tomatoes, substitute 2 cups of tomato juice for 1 pound of tomatoes.

MEATBALL AND PASTA SOUP
Sopa de pelotas

This soup is substantial enough to serve as a main course for lunch, or as a light supper, accompanied by a salad.

SERVES 4 TO 6

2 one-inch slices bread
½ medium onion, peeled
3 cloves garlic, peeled
3 Tablespoon fresh mint
½ teaspoon salt, plus salt to taste
¼ teaspoon freshly ground black pepper, plus pepper to taste
⅛ teaspoon cinnamon
1 egg
¼ pound ground veal or beef
¼ pound pork
⅓ cup all purpose flour
8 cups chicken stock (page 223)
3 ounces vermicelli broken into small pieces
White pepper to taste

In the food processor, puree the bread, onion, garlic, mint, salt, pepper, cinnamon and egg. Put into a large bowl, mix thoroughly with the ground meats.

Form into 18 to 24 one-inch meatballs. Dredge with the flour, shaking off excess flour, and discard leftover flour. Bring the stock to a boil. Drop the meatballs into the boiling broth, reduce heat to medium and cook for 10 minutes. Add the vermicelli and cook for another 10 minutes. Season with salt and pepper to taste and serve hot.

FISH SOUP, PASAGE DE SAN JUAN-STYLE
Sopa de mariscos al Pasaje de San Juan

Fish soups vary from region to region in Spain. Some have saffron, some have cream, some orange zest. We discovered this soup in an ancient fishing village outside San Sebastián in Basque Country. The shellfish were as fresh as the sea breeze blowing across our table.

SERVES 6
2 Tablespoons olive oil
2 onions, minced
4 garlic cloves, minced
5 medium tomatoes, chopped
1 cup dry white wine
8 cups fish stock (page 225)
Salt and white pepper
18 small clams, about 1½ pounds
12 mussels, about ½ pounds
12 prawns in shell, about ½ pound
6 lemon wedges

Heat the olive oil in a pot and cook the onions and garlic until they begin to color. Add the tomatoes and cook until most of the liquid is evaporated. Stir in the wine and cook until most of the liquid is again evaporated. Add the stock, bring to a boil, reduce heat to medium and cook for about 20 minutes. Strain the stock, discarding the solids.

Return the stock to the pot and cook to reduce to about 8 cups. Add the shellfish to the stock: first add the clams and cook 1 minute, then the mussels and prawns. Cook until the clams and mussels are open and the prawns are pink. Remove the shellfish with a slotted spoon to a serving bowl, discarding any clams or mussels that do not open. Garnish with the lemon wedges.

Pour the stock into a tureen through a fine strainer, to remove grit.

Serve at the table. Divide the shellfish among the soup bowls—preferably large flat ones—and pour the stock over the shellfish. Garnish each bowl with a lemon wedge and tell your guests to squeeze the lemon juice over the soup before eating.

Breads and Savory Pastries

SPANISH BREAD
Pan pueblo

¡ No hay pan. Dios mio! It is inconceivable to be served a meal in Spain without bread. The texture and quality of the Spanish breads vary from region to region with the quality of flour and water. And, of course, there are many different shapes. This recipe is typical of the kind of bread you will find in much of Spain.

1½ cups lukewarm water
1 Tablespoon dry active yeast (1 package or 1 cube)
5 cups unbleached white bread flour
2 teaspoons salt
3 Tablespoons olive oil, plus extra olive oil

Pour the water into a bowl. Add the yeast and let it dissolve. Stir in 1 cup of the flour. Cover the bowl and let the mixture rest for about one hour in a warm place.

Add the salt and oil and 2 more cups of flour and mix well. Add one more cup of flour and again mix well. Turn the dough out onto a floured surface and knead in the last cup of flour. You may not need all of the remaining cup.

Form the dough into a ball and put into an oiled bowl, turning the dough until all sides are oiled. Cover and let rise in a warm place until doubled in size. This may take 2 hours.

Punch the dough down and form into a large oval. Then shape the loaf to about 4 to 5 inches wide. Put the dough onto a baking sheet sprinkled with cornmeal. Brush the top of the loaf with olive oil. Cover the dough and let rise until doubled.

Preheat the oven to 400°. Put the risen dough into the oven and bake for 15 minutes. Reduce heat to 375° and cook for another 30 minutes or until puffed and golden.

Note: For a crusty bread, spray the loaf with water several times during the baking.

PORK TENDERLOIN PIE
Empanada de lomo

The *empanadas* of Galicia are large, flat, oval or round pies with rope-like edges and decorated crust on top. You'll find them filled with meat, vegetables, and fish, served as a snack in tapas bars, or as a takeout in bakeries. The edges of the pastry can be decorated in various ways, indicating what's inside.

SERVES 8 TO 10

Dough:
> 2 teaspoons yeast
> 2 cups all-purpose white flour
> 1 Tablespoon olive oil
> 1 teaspoon salt

Filling:
> ¾ pound pork tenderloin
> 2 cloves garlic
> 1 teaspoon paprika
> 1 teaspoon oregano
> ½ teaspoon salt
> ½ teaspoon freshly ground black pepper
> 2 Tablespoons olive oil
> 3 medium onions, chopped
> 2 red peppers, chopped
> 3 large tomatoes, chopped
> 2 eggs, hard-boiled, chopped
> 1 egg, beaten

To prepare the dough: Mix ¾ cup warm water, the yeast, and ¼ cup of the flour together and let stand in a warm place for 20 minutes. The mixture will become foamy.

Stir in the remaining flour, olive oil and salt. This can all be done in the food processor. Whirl until the mixture pulls away from the sides of the bowl. Gather into a ball and put the dough into an oiled bowl, turning the dough so all sides are coated with the oil. Cover with a cloth or plastic wrap and set in a warm place until the dough doubles in size.

Preheat oven to 450°.

Prepare the filling: Slice the pork loin into ¼-inch thick rounds and put it into a bowl. In a mortar, make a paste of the garlic, paprika, oregano, salt and pepper. Rub this mixture into the pork pieces.

Heat the oil in a pan and cook the pork just until it is no longer pink. Remove the pork. Add more oil to the pan if necessary and cook the onions and peppers until soft. Add the tomatoes and cook to reduce to a thick paste. Cool this mixture slightly before filling dough.

Punch the dough down and divide in half. Lightly oil a 12-inch pizza pan. Stretch one of dough halves over the bottom of the pan. Spread half of the tomato mixture over the dough, top with the pork slices, sprinkle the pork with the chopped eggs and cover the eggs with the remaining tomato mixture.

Roll out the remaining dough half to a size that will cover the filling. Put the dough in place on top of the filling and trim off any excess dough. This trim can be rolled into a rope to decorate the top of the empanada. Roll the edges of the bottom dough up over the top dough forming a neat seal around the edge of the empanada. Decorate with the remaining dough. Brush the top of the empanada with beaten egg. Bake for 20 minutes. Serve immediately or cool on a rack to serve later at room temperature.

SALT COD PIE
Empanada de bacalao

SERVES 6

Dough:
    1⅓ cups lukewarm water
    1 Tablespoon dry active yeast (1 package or 1 cube)
    2 teaspoons sugar
    ½ cup yellow cornmeal
    ½ Tablespoon salt
    2 Tablespoons olive oil
    2½ to 3 cups all-purpose flour

Filling:
    1 pound boneless salt cod
    3 Tablespoons olive oil

2 large onions, thinly sliced
2 large sweet red peppers, stemmed and
     seeded, cut into thin strips
3 large tomatoes, chopped
½ teaspoon freshly ground black pepper

Begin preparation two days in advance. Soak cod in cold water for 48 hours, changing the water several times. Drain, squeeze dry and shred the cod.

To prepare the dough: Pour the warm water into a food processor. Add the yeast and sugar and allow to sit until the yeast activates, about 5 minutes. The top of the water will be foamy with yeast. Add cornmeal, salt, olive oil and one cup of flour.

Whirl for 30 seconds. Add 1½ cups flour and whirl to form a ball. If the dough is not forming a ball or is very sticky add more flour until the dough is smooth and soft. Oil a bowl and put dough into the bowl, turning to coat the top of the dough with oil. Cover with a towel and put in a warm place until doubled in volume, about 1 hour.

To prepare the filling: Heat the oil in a skillet, add onions and cook over a moderate heat until golden. Add the pepper strips and cook and stir for 5 minutes. Add tomatoes and cook briskly until the sauce is thick. Stir in the cod and cook over a low heat for 5 minutes. Add the black pepper and taste for salt. You may need a little salt since most of the salt in the cod has been soaked out. Drain excess liquid.

Putting it all together: Preheat the oven to 400°. Punch the dough down and divide in half. Use a 12-inch pizza pan and push and pull half the dough to cover the pan allowing a ½-inch overlap on the edge of the pan. Pour filling onto dough. Pinch a small ball of dough off the remaining dough and set aside. On a floured surface, roll out remaining dough so it will cover the filling. Put dough on top of the filling. Pull the edges of the bottom dough up and over the top dough, rolling and pinching the doughs together to seal in the filling. Roll the little ball of dough into a long coil and form a decorative E or B or whatever on the top of the *empanada*. This is just a fun decoration that breaks up the great expanse of dough and one you often see on the *empanadas* of Galicia.

Put the pie into the oven and bake for about 20 minutes. Brush the pie with milk and return to the oven until golden, another 5 to 10 minutes. Serve the *empanada* hot from the oven or at room temperature, cutting it into pie shaped wedges.

FLATBREAD WITH ASSORTED TOPPINGS
Coca Lérida

We visited a bakery in Lérida that produced no fewer than 28 different *cocas*. They kept popping out of the giant ovens about every 15 minutes. The toppings are limited only by your imagination. However, avoid putting too much stuff on top.

You needn't bake all four *cocas* the same day. Half the dough can be punched down after the first rising and put in a plastic bag and refrigerated until the next day. Then bring the dough to room temperature, form into *cocas* or a small loaf of bread, let rise and bake. This dough can also be used for pizza crust.

MAKES 4 *COCAS*
1½ cups warm water
1 Tablespoon yeast
2 Tablespoons olive oil
1½ teaspoons salt
4 cups flour
Corn meal

Place water in the food processor bowl and add yeast. After about 5 minutes the yeast will have dissolved and begin to foam. Add the olive oil, salt and 1 cup of flour. Whirl for one minute. Add the remaining flour and whirl until a ball forms. The dough may be a little sticky. Do not add more flour.

Turn the dough out into an oiled bowl. Roll the dough over so all its surface is covered with oil. Cover the bowl, put in a warm place and let the dough rise to double its size. Punch the dough down and divide into quarters.

Preheat the oven to 450°. Have ready 4 baking sheets lightly sprinkled with cornmeal. Roll the dough out into long oval shapes about 11-inches long and 6-inches wide and put onto the baking sheets. Top with any of the toppings described below, or make up your own. Let rest 10 minutes, then bake for about 15 minutes or until the *coca* is golden underneath and cooked through.

Can be served immediately or at room temperature.

EGGPLANT AND OLIVE TOPPING

FOR I *COCA*
4 Tablespoons olive oil
1 large eggplant, about 1 pound, cut into small cubes
Salt and freshly ground black pepper to taste
½ cup pitted black olives, halved

Heat 3 Tablespoons of the oil in a medium skillet and cook the eggplant sprinkled with the salt and pepper until very tender. Cover one of
the *cocas* with some of this topping. Sprinkle with the olives and the
remaining olive oil. Let rest and bake as directed above.

ONION, TOMATO AND ANCHOVY TOPPING

FOR I COCA
3 Tablespoons olive oil
2 medium onions, peeled and thinly sliced
Salt and freshly ground black pepper to taste
2 large, ripe tomatoes, thinly sliced
6 anchovy filets, drained of excess oil and cut in half lengthwise
Paprika

Heat 2 Tablespoons of oil in a medium skill and cook the onions,
sprinkled with salt and pepper, until soft and golden. Arrange the tomato slices over the surface of the *coca*. Strew the onions over the tomatoes and arrange the anchovy strips in a pattern over the onions. Let rest
and bake as directed above. Remove from the oven and sprinkle with
olive oil and a light dusting of paprika.

RED PEPPER, CHORIZO AND TOMATO TOPPING

FOR I *COCA*
1 Tablespoon olive oil
1 red bell pepper, seeded and sliced into thin strips
3 ounces firm chorizo, sliced into thin rounds
2 large ripe tomatoes, thinly sliced

Heat I Tablespoon of olive oil in a medium skillet and cook the peppers until soft but not browned. Add the chorizo and cook for 2 minutes. Drain excess oil. Arrange the tomatoes on top of the *coca*. Scatter the pepper and chorizo over the tomatoes. Bake.

May be sprinkled with extra virgin olive oil after baking, if desired.

Salads

ASPARAGUS AND PRAWN SALAD
WITH HAM DRESSING
Ensalada templada de gambas y esparragos
con vinagreta de jamón

A warm salad can sometimes be intimidating since you want to be with your guests and not in the kitchen. Don't let this put you off with this recipe. Much of the salad can be done ahead and the last minute cooking just takes a couple of minutes if you plan your timing.

SERVES 6
18 prawns, about ¾ pound
½ onion, sliced
Sprig of parsley
1 stalk celery, cut in 4 pieces
10 peppercorns
2 teaspoons salt
2 pounds asparagus, pencil thin, ends trimmed, sliced diagonally into
        1 to 2-inch sections
2 Tablespoons olive oil
2 ounces ham or prosciutto, thinly sliced and shredded
3 cloves garlic, peeled and thinly sliced
½ teaspoon freshly ground black pepper
1 Tablespoon vinegar

Shell and de-vein the prawns and set aside, reserving the shells. Bring 3 cups of water to a boil. Add the onion, parsley, celery, peppercorns and salt. Cook for 5 minutes. Add the prawn shells and cook for 10 minutes over a medium heat. Strain this stock into another sauce pan and discard the shells and vegetables. Bring stock to a boil. Taste for salt; it should taste a little salty. (The recipe to this point can be done ahead. Refrigerate the stock and prawns if kept more than a couple of hours. Return stock to a boil and proceed.)

    Boil the prawns in the stock until pink. Remove the prawns to a bowl and keep warm. Meanwhile, steam the asparagus over boiling water until just tender—this will depend on their size. Combine the asparagus in the bowl with the prawns.

Heat the olive oil in a small skillet and cook the ham with the garlic until the ham begins to crisp and the garlic is golden. Stir in the pepper and the vinegar. Heat through and pour the ham and sauce over the prawns and asparagus. Toss well. Divide the salad among 6 heated plates and serve immediately.

SALT COD SALAD
Esqueixada de bacalao

Bacalao, dried salted cod, is ubiquitous in Spain and Portugal. However, this salad version seems to be found only in Catalonia where it is often served as a first course. Salt cod may have been first brought to Spain by the Basques, who ranged right across the Atlantic and were fishing off Newfoundland centuries before Columbus was even born.

SERVES 6
1 pound boneless dried salt cod
1 red or green pepper, stemmed, seeded and cut into strips
1 medium red onion, peeled and thinly sliced
1 ripe tomato, cut in quarters
½ cup extra virgin olive oil
¼ cup red wine vinegar
4 large cloves garlic, peeled and chopped
Salt and pepper to taste
12 black olives
2 hard-boiled eggs, quartered

Begin preparation a day in advance. Soak the cod in cold water for at least 24 hours (longer is better), changing the water several times. Drain and shred the cod by hand. Do not use a knife as that will cause the flesh to compact and stick together.

Toss the cod with the pepper, onion and tomato. Combine the oil, vinegar and garlic in a bowl, blend well and pour over the cod. Toss the mixture and season to taste with salt and pepper. Garnish with olives and hard-boiled egg.

CHICKEN VEGETABLE SALAD WITH SAFFRON-ALMOND DRESSING
Ensalada de pollo en pepitoria

This dish, usually presented as a chicken and vegetable stew flavored with saffron, is found on menus all over Spain, and sometimes turns up in Provence as well. *Pepitoria* refers to a sauce or dressing based on seeds or nuts. We enjoyed this version presented as a salad at a friend's house in Arcos de la Frontera, near Jerez. Try using the saffron and almond dressing for other dishes or as a vegetable dip.

SERVES 6

Dressing:
2 eggs
5 large cloves of garlic, unpeeled
20 whole almonds
I Tablespoon fresh parsley
Small pinch of saffron threads
½ teaspoon salt
I cup extra virgin olive oil
Juice of one lemon

Salad:
I quart of chicken stock (page 223)
I pound tiny new potatoes, about 12
I pound boiling onions, about 12, skinned
½ pound thin carrots, peeled and sliced
¼-inch thick on the diagonal
2 pounds boneless, skinless chicken breasts

Prepare the dressing several hours ahead, or the night before, to let its flavors mingle. To make the dressing, hard boil I of the eggs and set aside to cool. Put the garlic and almonds on a baking sheet and bake for 10 to 12 minutes or until the almonds are toasted. Let cool. Meanwhile, peel the hard-boiled egg and separate the white from the yolk.

Finely chop the egg white, cover, and set aside. Cover and set aside the egg yolk.

Peel the toasted garlic and put into a blender or food processor with the almonds. Turn the motor on and whirl to a paste. Add the parsley, saffron and salt, plus the uncooked egg and the cooled yolk of the hard-boiled egg. Whirl to mix well. Combine the olive oil and lemon juice, and, with the food processor motor running, gradually add this mixture to the paste. Scrape down the sides of the food processor bowl and whirl once more until creamy. Pour into a bowl, cover and refrigerate for several hours or overnight.

(Occasionally, the dressing will break and not thicken properly. In that case, remove the broken dressing to a container with a pouring spout. Place I Tablespoon tepid water in the bowl of a blender or food processor with ¼ cup of the broken dressing. Whirl, and with the motor running, gradually add the remainder of the broken sauce. It should set up immediately. You can use this same technique to salvage mayonnaise or other mayonnaise-based sauces.)

To make the salad: Preheat the oven to 400°. Heat the stock in a large pot. Add the potatoes and onions and cook until tender. Remove from the stock and set aside. Add the carrots and cook until tender. Remove from the stock and set aside. Add the chicken and poach for about 10 minutes or until cooked through. Remove from the stock and set aside to cool slightly. Strain the remaining stock and reserve for future use. Shred the chicken.

To serve, arrange the chicken, potatoes, onions and carrots on a large platter. Stir and pour I cup of the dressing over the chicken and vegetables and sprinkle with the chopped egg white. Pass the remaining sauce separately.

EGGPLANT SALAD
Ensalada de berenjenas

Eggplant salad is wonderful as a tapa served with slices of toasted baguette. It also works as a first course served with grilled meat or fish.

SERVES 12
¼ cup olive oil, plus more if necessary
2 pounds eggplant, unpeeled, diced into ½-inch pieces
Salt and freshly ground black pepper to taste
1 medium onion, chopped
2 red or green bell peppers, seeded and diced into ½-inch pieces
3 tomatoes, peeled and chopped
¼ cup sugar
2 Tablespoons red wine vinegar
2 Tablespoons capers

Heat the oil in a large non-reactive skillet and when very hot add the eggplant and toss to coat with the oil. Reduce heat to medium. Sprinkle lightly with salt and pepper. Cook quickly until the eggplant begins to color. Remove and drain on paper towels.

Add a little more oil if necessary and cook the onions and peppers until soft. Stir in the tomatoes and cook to a paste. Return the eggplant to the pan and stir in the sugar, vinegar and capers. Cook over low heat until the eggplant is soft but still holds its shape. Taste for salt and pepper and add if necessary.

The salad can be served hot, but it is really better after it cools and the flavors mingle for a while. If refrigerated, let warm to room temperature before serving.

ESCAROLE SALAD WITH
TUNA AND ALMOND SAUCE
Xato

The *Xato* festival, held in Vilanova i la Geltrú, takes its name and purpose from this simple salad and its incredibly delicious sauce. *Xato* sauce
is, in fact, a type of *romesco*, so it is not surprising that the Catalans
celebrate it, as they do many other *romesco*-related dishes.

SERVES 6 TO 8

Sauce:
I dried ancho chili
¼ cup of hazelnuts
¼ cup almonds
6 cloves garlic, unpeeled
2 small tomatoes, quartered
8 sprigs parsley
⅓ cup olive oil
2 Tablespoon red wine vinegar
¾ teaspoon salt
½ teaspoon freshly ground black pepper

Salad:
I head of escarole, washed and drained
I head of chicory, washed and drained
One 12½-ounce can of albacore tuna, flaked
½ medium onion, cut in rings
12 black olives
2 ripe tomatoes, quartered

To make the dressing: Preheat oven to 400°. Bring a small pot of water
to a boil. Add the ancho chili and remove from the heat. Let stand until
needed. Put the nuts and garlic cloves on a baking sheet and bake for
12-15 minutes, or until the nuts are toasted. Transfer the nuts to a food
processor or blender and finely chop. Peel the garlic and combine with
the nuts. Add the tomatoes and parsley and whirl to form a paste. Drain
the ancho, stem and seed it and add to the food processor. Puree. With
the motor running add the oil, vinegar, salt and pepper.

To make the salad: Tear the cleaned escarole and chicory into pieces and arrange on a platter. Scatter the tuna, onions, olives and tomatoes over the greens. Half an hour before serving, toss with the dressing and arrange attractively. Leave at room temperature until serving. The greens should wilt a little from the dressing.

FIG AND ANCHOVY SALAD
Ensalada de brevas y anchoas

This is one of the best salads I've ever eaten. Its success simply depends on the very best ingredients. *Brevas* is the name given to the first crop of Spanish figs, plump and black, the figs that ripen at the end of June. You oh so lucky ones with your own fig trees, just pluck them from the tree, slice and serve them still warm from the sun.

SERVES 6
1 large head of curly endive, finely shredded
12 fresh figs, stemmed
1 two-ounce can of anchovies, drained and rinsed
3 ripe but firm, medium tomatoes, peeled, seeded and diced
Extra virgin olive oil
Freshly ground black pepper

Divide the endive among 6 plates. Cut the figs in quarters lengthwise and arrange in the center of the plates. Crisscross 2 filets of anchovies over the figs and scatter the tomatoes over all. Now drizzle the olive oil over the tops, sprinkle with pepper and serve immediately.

SQUID AND FAVA BEAN SALAD
Ensalada de habas con cochos

We had this combination as a tapa in northern Spain, but I have also served it as a salad on a bed of mixed greens. Either way it has a refreshing flavor and very interesting texture.

SERVES 6 AS A SALAD, 10 AS A TAPA

Dressing: 3 cloves of garlic

3 anchovy fillets

½ cup minced parsley

½ cup olive oil

1 teaspoon salt

½ teaspoon freshly ground black pepper

¼ teaspoon hot red pepper flakes

3 Tablespoons fresh lemon juice

3 Tablespoons wine vinegar

Salad: 2½ pounds fava beans in the shell

1 bay leaf

3 whole cloves

1½ pounds cleaned squid, tentacles left whole,
tubes cut into ½-inch rings

Begin preparation 5 or more hours in advance.

To prepare the dressing: In the blender or food processor combine the garlic, anchovies and parsley and blend to a paste. Add the olive oil, salt, pepper, pepper flakes, lemon juice and vinegar and whirl to combine well. Set the dressing aside.

To prepare the salad: Shell the fava beans. Put the shelled beans, bay leaf and cloves in a pan and cover with water. Bring to a boil and cook the beans until tender. The time for this will vary with the age of the beans. Young ones will only take about 7 to 10 minutes. Drain the cooked beans and remove the bay leaf and cloves. Combine the beans with the dressing.

Bring another pot of salted water to a boil. When the water is at a furious boil, add the squid, cook for 30 seconds and drain. Toss the squid with the beans and coat well with the dressing. Allow to cool and refrigerate for at least 5 hours before serving.

Rice Dishes

RICE COOKED IN FISH STOCK
Arroz abanda

This version is billed as 'the best *Arroz abanda* in all of Spain', at the restaurant La Pegola in Denia, on the coast south of Valencia. No argument here. It was the highlight of a superb lunch on a day of brilliant Mediterranean sunlight. The rice glistened in the pan golden brown from the *sofrito* and the fish stock. You could dig your fork into the rice and find the *quemada*, the crusty rice at the bottom of the pan—sign of a perfectly done rice dish. *Abanda* simply means 'apart' indicating that the rice is served apart from the fish.

Equally famous is *fideuà abanda*, the same recipe and preparation, but with short pieces of thin noodles, *fideos*, substituted for the rice. It's quite delicious with a unique melting texture.

SERVES 6
4 Tablespoons olive oil
1 medium onion, minced
3 garlic cloves, minced
2 pounds tomatoes, chopped
8 cups of fish stock (page 225)
½ teaspoon saffron threads
3 cups short grained rice, Valencian or arborio
3 teaspoons salt
2 cups allioli (page 201)

Heat 2 Tablespoons of the oil in a large non-reactive skillet, and cook the onions and garlic over medium heat until soft. Stir in the tomatoes and cook slowly to a paste. Pour in the stock and cook until reduced by ¼, to about 6 cups. Strain the stock into another pan, discarding the solids, and bring to the boiling point.

Heat a paella or other flat pan and toast the saffron, crushing it with the back of a spoon, taking care not to burn it. Add the remaining 2 Tablespoons of oil to the saffron and stir in the rice. Stir and cook until the rice is coated with the oil and begins to take color. Add the salt. Gradually add the stock one cup at a time, without stirring the rice, adding more stock only when the rice has absorbed the previous stock. Ideally a nice crunch, the *quemada*, will form on the bottom of the pan and the rice will be tender but not mushy.

When all the stock has been absorbed, remove rice from the heat, and allow it to rest covered with a towel for 5 minutes before presenting it at the table. Pass the allioli for guests to stir into the rice if they wish.

Note: Some purists say the allioli should only be served with the rice if you are serving the fish that went into the stock as well. Since at this point the fish would have given all its flavor to the stock it would need some *allioli* for taste. I find the allioli stirred into the rice punctuates its already creamy texture and makes it even more appealing.

BLACK RICE
Arroz negro sin tinta

This is a variation on a well-known Catalan dish of rice tinted black with squid ink. I kept hearing of a black rice made without the ink and finally tasted it at the home of a wonderful waiter we met in Lérida. We had such a good time talking about all the foods at the restaurant that he invited us to his home to taste his rice. It is delicious and while not quite black, it is at least a decent dark gray.

We use a 12-inch *paella* pan to prepare and serve this dish. It can be done in a non-reactive skillet.

SERVES 6

7 cups fish stock or water (page 225)

1/3 cup olive oil

1 large onion, minced

3 cloves garlic, minced

2 medium artichokes, hearts only, minced

1 pound cleaned squid tubes, cut into 1/4-inch rings

3 cups short grain rice, preferably Valencian or Italian arborio

2 teaspoons salt

2 cups allioli (page 201)

Heat the stock or water to a boil in a large sauce pan. Heat the oil in the *paella* pan or skillet. Add the onions, garlic and artichokes to the skillet and cook over medium heat for 10 minutes, stirring often. Add the squid and cook 5 minutes.

Pour in 1 cup of the boiling stock or water and cook over medium heat until very little liquid remains in the pan. Stir in the rice and salt.

Pour in the remaining 6 cups of stock or water. Bring to a boil, reduce heat and cook for 20 minutes. Do not stir. (You can slide the pan around on the burner so the heat source reaches all areas of the pan.) Remove the pan from the stove. Cover with a cloth and let rest for 10 minutes or longer.

The Spanish, in general, don't care if a rice dish is piping hot. It certainly makes it easier to assemble the rest of your menu if you can have the Black rice done a bit in advance. I love the rice served with allioli so you can stir some of it right into the rice.

Variation: If you want to make the traditional black rice, eliminate the artichokes from this recipe and tint your rice with squid ink. You can do so using fresh or packaged ink. If you start with uncleaned squid, you will find a little ink pouch under the tentacles when you pull them from the body tube. It's an awfully little bit of ink and you need a lot of squid to get enough of it, but it is possible get your ink this way. A few fish markets are also willing to get fresh squid ink for you if requested in advance. Packaged, dried squid ink is available in specialty stores and many Latin markets. You will need to dissolve two packages of it in ½ cup hot water. Substitute this ½ cup for ½ cup of the stock.

DUCK AND CHICKEN PAELLA
Paella de Montaña

Most people think of *paella* as the quintessential dish of Spain. In fact, it was originally served only along the Mediterranean coast and the mountains bordering it. It has since spread everywhere in Spain. Practically everyone has at some time tasted *paella*, usually made with shellfish and chicken. But there are many variations, as we discovered in Valencia one evening when our host prepared no fewer than six. This one, from the mountains outside Tarragona, sometimes contains snails.

SERVES 6

2 Tablespoons olive oil

6 ounces boneless pork, cut into small cubes

6 chicken thighs

One 4 to 5 pound duck

1 medium onion, minced

3 cloves garlic, minced

3 large tomatoes, chopped

Sprig of fresh rosemary

½ pound fresh green beans, ends removed and cut in half

1 cup of cooked, large white lima or Great Northern beans

5 cups unsalted chicken or duck stock (page 223)

½ teaspoon saffron threads

2 cups short grained rice, preferably Valencian or arborio

1½ teaspoons salt, plus other salt for flavoring

Heat the *paella* pan or other wide, flat-bottomed pan and add the olive oil. Sauté the pork until golden, remove from the pan and set aside. Using a heavy knife or cleaver, cut each of the chicken thighs in half. Sprinkle the halves lightly with salt and cook them quickly until golden but still underdone. Remove and set aside.

Cut the duck into serving pieces, and reserve the backs, wings and neck for stock. Remove excess fat from remaining pieces and cut them into smaller chunks with the cleaver. Remove all the fat from the paella pan. Sprinkle the duck lightly with salt and sauté it in the pan until golden. Remove and set aside. Pour off from the pan all but 3 Tablespoons of the fat.

Cook the onions and garlic in the fat over medium heat until soft. Add the tomatoes and rosemary leaves and cook over medium high heat until all liquid is gone. Meanwhile in another pan, bring the stock to a boil.

Scatter the cooked meats and green beans over the tomato mixture (which would now be called a *sofrito*) and stir into it 1 cup of the stock. Cook quickly over medium high heat until all the liquid has cooked away.

Toast the saffron threads for one minute in a hot, dry pan, then pulverize them in a mortar and pestle or with the back of a spoon.

Stir the rice, 1½ teaspoons salt and toasted saffron into the meat and tomato mixture. Pour in the remaining stock and bring to a boil. Reduce heat to medium and cook, moving the pan around on the burner from time to time so that all parts of the bottom of the pan receive heat. Do not stir the rice. Cook until the rice has absorbed almost all the liquid and is tender but still a little firm, about 20 minutes.

Alternately, after bringing the *paella* to a boil, place it on the floor of a preheated 400° gas oven or on the lowest shelf of an electric oven and cook for 20 minutes.

Remove the *paella* from the heat and drape a clean, dry cloth over it. Allow the *paella* to rest for 5 to 10 minutes. *Paella*, traditionally, is not served piping hot from the oven. It really does taste better after it has cooled slightly.

Variation: The instructions for this *paella* can be followed when using other ingredients, such as shellfish. Unshelled prawns are sprinkled with salt and cooked in hot oil for 1 minute at the start of the recipe. Then when 10 minutes of cooking time remain, the prawns and other shellfish, such as fresh mussels and clams, are arranged on top of the paella and cooked with it. Sprinkle the juice of one lemon over a shellfish *paella* just before serving.

SEAFOOD AND MEAT PAELLA
FOR COVERED BARBECUE
Paella al Weber

The proper making of *paella* is an art form in Spain. Each region has a preferred fuel for the outdoor fire over which the *paella* is cooked. In Valencia, it's said, the wood must be trimmings from the orange groves. In other parts of Spain, vine prunings are usually preferred. Cooking *paella* on a covered barbecue would bring howls of outrage from some Spanish purists, but it works quite well, and many of us haven't easy access to vineyards or orange groves to stoke our cooking fires.

SERVES 8
3 Tablespoons olive oil
1 medium onion, minced

3 cloves garlic, minced
½ pound tomatoes, chopped
½ pound squid tubes, cleaned and sliced into rings
1½ pound meaty chicken pieces cut with a cleaver into
        chunks (use all dark meat for more flavor)
¼ pound boneless pork or linguiça, chopped
2 teaspoons salt or more to taste
6 cups of chicken or fish stock or water (page 223, 225)
½ teaspoon saffron threads
3 cups of short grain rice, preferably Valencian or arborio
1 pound cleaned mussels in shell
1 pound prawns in shell
1 cup of fresh peas or 1 pound of asparagus tips (optional)
2 lemons cut into wedges

Light the coals in a covered barbecue. When the coals are white hot, heap them in the center of the barbecue. Put the *paella* pan on the grill above the hot coals. Pour in the oil and, when hot, add the onions and garlic and cook until limp. Stir in the tomatoes and cook until all the liquid is evaporated.

Push the vegetables to the side of the pan. Add the squid, chicken, and pork or linguiça. Sprinkle with the salt . Grind the saffron threads to a powder in a mortar and add, or simply rub the threads between your palms and sprinkle over the pan. Cook, turning the pieces over, until the chicken begins to color, about 5 minutes. Add the stock or water.

At this time you may need to stoke the fire with a few sticks of kindling to bring to a boil. Taste for salt. It should taste slightly salty. Cook at a rapid boil for about 5 minutes. Stir in the rice, turning the chunks of chicken over so all the rice is submerged. Now cook the paella for about 10 minutes.

Arrange the prawns over the top of the paella, and the mussels, hinge side down, around the edge of the paella. If you wish, add the peas or asparagus now. Cook for another 5 minutes. Cover the grill with the lid. Cook another 5 minutes.

Remove the paella to the table and cover with a cloth. Allow to rest for about 5 minutes. Decorate the top of the paella with lemon wedges.

Serve each portion with a lemon wedge and direct your guests to first squeeze the lemon juice over their servings.

Note: The onion, garlic and tomato base for the *paella,* the *sofrito,* is as important as the saffron or the stock for making your *paella.* When you order a *paella* in a restaurant in Spain, the sofrito has likely been cooking all day or is part of a *sofrito* that has been going as long as the restaurant has been in operation. It is a dark rust color and has deep, rich flavors. The chef just dips into the pot any time he has need for a *sofrito,* the base for so many dishes.

When making the *sofrito* at home, it is important to use the very best tomatoes available and to cook them until there is no liquid left so that the flavor is very concentrated.

Main Courses

TROUT, NAVARRE-STYLE
Truchas a la Navarra

The river Ebro flows along the southeastern border of the Navarre region. The rich farm lands that border the river are the source of abundant produce, which shapes much of the cuisine of this area. The river itself is the source of delicious trout, which are used in this recipe.

SERVES 6
1 Tablespoon lemon juice
½ pound button mushrooms, stems cut off and discarded, sliced
4 ounces prosciutto, in 1 piece
1 large clove of garlic, peeled
2 Tablespoons of parsley
2 Tablespoons olive oil
6 cleaned trout, 8 to 12 ounces each
1 onion, peeled and thinly sliced
½ teaspoon salt
Parsley and garlic for garnish

Toss the mushrooms with the lemon juice and set aside. Cut the prosciutto into thin strips. Finely chop the garlic and parsley together.

Heat the oil in a large skillet and sauté the trout quickly on each side until golden but still underdone. Remove the trout. Put the onion into the skillet and sauté until soft. Add the mushrooms and cook until most of their liquid has evaporated. Stir in the prosciutto. Lay the trout on top of the mushroom mixture, sprinkle with salt, cover and cook for 5 minutes. Test the trout by poking it with your finger. If the flesh is firm, the fish is done.

To serve, place the trout on serving plates, divide the vegetables and juices among the plates and sprinkle with parsley and garlic.

CHICKEN STUFFED WITH OLIVES
Pollo relleno con aceitunas

When you pot roast a whole chicken in this fashion, it stays very moist and creates its own sauce. Try serving this with New Potatoes with Allioli (page 208).

SERVES 4 TO 6
I 3½ to 4 pound chicken
4 Tablespoons olive oil
I medium onion, peeled and minced
2 cups of day old-bread cubes
½ cup pimiento stuffed green olives, sliced
2 Tablespoons parsley, chopped
2 cloves garlic, minced
I teaspoon fresh oregano or ¼ teaspoon dry
¼ teaspoon salt
½ teaspoon pepper
I egg
I Tablespoon brandy
I cup dry white wine

Thoroughly clean the chicken, removing the giblets and freezing them for other use. Heat 2 Tablespoons of the olive oil and sauté the onion until golden.

Put the bread, olives, parsley, garlic, oregano, salt and pepper, in a bowl. Add the sautéed onions and egg and toss well. Pour in the brandy and toss. Stuff the bird with this mixture and truss it closed.

Heat the remaining olive oil in a large pot. Put the chicken in the pot, breast side down. Pour in the wine. Bring to a boil, reduce heat, cover and simmer for 30 minutes. Turn the bird over. Cover and simmer for 20 minutes. Remove lid and continue to cook for 15 minutes.

Remove the chicken to a platter. Increase the heat and cook the remaining liquid quickly to reduce to desired consistency for sauce. To serve, carve the chicken into serving pieces and pass the sauce separately.

CHICKEN WITH PRAWNS
Mar y montaña

The Costa Brava north of Barcelona is spectacular country, with mountains dropping dramatically into the Mediterranean. The area along the sea harbors many resorts and several splendid restaurants—a combination not often found. Chicken and prawns are an unusual combination but one that is very popular in this region. You will also find here dishes of rabbit and shellfish.

SERVES 6

¼ cup whole almonds
21 prawns, about 1 pound
1 bay leaf
5 cups water
¼ cup all-purpose flour
1 teaspoon salt
¼ teaspoon freshly ground black pepper
½ teaspoon cinnamon
6 boneless skinless chicken breasts
1 Tablespoon unsalted butter
3 Tablespoons olive oil
1 medium onion, minced
¾ pound tomatoes, peeled, seeded, and chopped
2 Tablespoons Spanish anise, or other anise liqueur
        such as Ricard or Pernod
1 cup dry white wine
1 ounce unsweetened chocolate, minced or grated
3 garlic cloves, peeled and chopped
1 Tablespoon fresh parsley leaves
Pinch of thyme
Pinch of oregano

Preheat the oven to 400°. Toast the almonds on a baking sheet for 12 to 15 minutes and set aside. Peel the prawns and set aside. Put the prawn shells in a small sauce pan with the bay leaf and cover with 5 cups of water. Bring to a boil, reduce heat and cook for 15 minutes. Drain, reserving the stock, and discarding the shells and bay leaf.

Put the flour, salt, pepper and cinnamon in a bowl. Dip the chicken breasts into the flour mixture, coating the breasts on both sides.

Heat the butter and 1 Tablespoon of the oil in a ceramic casserole or skillet. Cook the chicken until golden on both sides and remove to a platter. Add the prawns to the skillet, cook half a minute on each side, and remove to another platter.

Heat the remaining 2 Tablespoons of oil in the skillet and cook the onion until golden. Add the tomatoes and cook down to a paste. Stir in the liqueur, wine, and reserved stock from the prawns, and cook until reduced by half.

Meanwhile, in a mortar, grind together the chocolate, garlic, toasted almonds, parsley, thyme and oregano. Add a little of the stock and grind the mixture to a paste. Set aside.

Return the chicken to the skillet and cook for 5 minutes. Stir in the prawns. Taste for salt and pepper and add if necessary. Cook for another 5 minutes or until the chicken and prawns are cooked through and the sauce is thickened. Serve directly from the casserole or skillet.

CHICKEN WITH ONIONS AND MUSHROOMS
Pollo con cebollitas y champiñones

Chicken as a common dinner dish is fairly new in Spain. Until the end of Franco's regime, when most Spaniards lived in the country or in very small villages, chickens would rarely be killed until they had ceased to be good egg layers. As a result many of Spain's traditional chicken dishes are for larger hens—what we would call stewing hens. This dish, which calls for a smaller bird, was quite likely made originally with rabbit

SERVES 6
3 Tablespoons olive oil
One 3½ pound chicken, cut into 8 pieces (Reserve back for stock.)
Salt and pepper to taste
12 small boiling onions, peeled
18 medium mushrooms, stems cut off at base and discarded
¼ cup of fresh sage leaves

¼ cup fresh rosemary leaves
I cup of dry sherry—Amontillado or Fino

This dish may be partially prepared up to 2 hours ahead. Heat the oil in a large, ovenproof skillet. Sprinkle the chicken pieces with salt and pepper and cook until they begin to color. Remove the chicken to a platter. Add the onions and cook until golden and remove them to the platter with the chicken.

Cook the mushroom in the same oil. Remove the mushrooms and set aside. Pour off any excess oil and add the sage and rosemary to the skillet and cook to wilt. Pour in the sherry, stir and scrape the bottom of the skillet. Return the chicken and the onions to the skillet. (At this point, if you wish, you can set the dish aside—covered and unrefrigerated—for later cooking.)

Put the skillet in the oven and cook for 25 minutes. Stir in the mushrooms and cook for another 10 minutes. The chicken and the onions should be tender when pierced with a fork. Reduce the sauce further if desired and season with salt and pepper if necessary.

Put the chicken and vegetables on a serving platter, and pass the sauce separately.

CHICKEN WITH VEGETABLES, CATALAN-STYLE
Pollo en samfaina

This is hardly a recipe, just an outline map leading to a very enjoyable dish. Although it calls for a full recipe of *samfaina* it can work with less. You can add a little broth or wine and some herbs, too.

SERVES 4 TO 6
I recipe *samfaina* (page 268)
2 Tablespoons olive oil
One 3½ pound chicken, cut into serving pieces
Salt and freshly ground black pepper to taste

Prepare the *samfaina*, preferably using the variation suggested at the end of the recipe. Set aside.

Heat the olive oil in a ceramic casserole or deep skillet. Add the chicken, sprinkle with salt and pepper and cook over medium heat until golden on the outside and about half cooked on the inside. Pour off excess oil and stir in the *samfaina*. Cook the chicken for another 30 minutes, stirring the mixture several times while it cooks so that it does not scorch. Taste for seasoning and serve immediately.

CHICKEN WITH GARLIC
Pollo al ajillo

This is a dish often found in small country restaurants in Spain, the kind called *comida casera*, which simply means home cooking—food of the *casa*. It's a warming, friendly dish with whole nuggets of golden garlic nestling among chicken pieces in a wine and herb sauce.

SERVES 4 TO 6
½ cup olive oil
15 large cloves of garlic, peeled, left whole
One 3½ to 4 pound chicken, cut into 8 serving pieces
I teaspoon salt
½ teaspoon freshly ground black pepper
½ teaspoon dried thyme
½ teaspoon dried oregano
I cup dry white wine

Heat the oil in a large, heavy non-reactive skillet. Add the garlic cloves and cook until golden, turning them gently and often. Remove the garlic and set aside.

Add the chicken to the hot oil and sprinkle with the salt and pepper. Cook until lightly browned. Pour off excess oil and return the garlic to the pan. Add the thyme, oregano and wine and bring to a boil. Cover the pan and simmer for 30 minutes. Remove the chicken and garlic cloves to a platter and keep warm.

Turn the heat to high and boil the juices in the skillet until they are thick. Pour over the chicken and serve immediately.

VEGETABLE STEW
Menestra de verduras

Every region of Spain has a version of *menestra* for every season of the year. I've tasted it flavored with salt pork, with lamb, with clams, and with vegetables only. It can be found served as a first course, a side dish or a light main dish. This is hardly a recipe because a fixed recipe for this stew would be impossible. Use it as a rough guide. Play with it. Try lots of different combinations.

SERVES 6 TO 8

¾ pounds each of 4 or 5 seasonal vegetables, such as green
        beans, artichoke hearts, carrots, turnips and zucchini
2 Tablespoons olive oil
1 large onion, minced
¼ pound slivered ham or prosciutto
Salt and freshly ground black pepper to taste

Prepare the vegetables for cooking, peeling those that need to be peeled. Keep the different vegetables separated. Cut the larger ones into easy to eat pieces. Bring a large pot of lightly salted water to a boil. If you have a spaghetti cooker with an insert, use it. It makes it a lot easier to remove the vegetables after cooking.

Cook one vegetable at a time in the water until tender but not mushy. Set aside. Once the vegetables are cooked they can be combined. Reserve the cooking liquid.

Heat the olive oil in a large pan and cook the onions and ham until golden. Stir in the vegetables and 1 to 2 cups of the reserved cooking liquid. Season to taste with salt and pepper. Cook the stew over a medium heat for about 10 minutes. Serve immediately.

SWORDFISH WITH
PINE NUTS AND RAISINS
Pez espada con piñones y pasas

L'Olivé, a bustling restaurant in Barcelona is always full of locals—not the kind of restaurant to turn up in many tourist guides. The food, which is very good and not overly sophisticated, is the draw. This dish is a good example.

SERVES 4 TO 6
3 Tablespoons olive oil
½ cup minced onion
⅓ cup pine nuts
⅓ cup golden raisins
2 pounds swordfish filets, cut into 4 or 6 pieces
¼ teaspoon salt
¼ teaspoon white pepper
2 teaspoons fresh rosemary leaves, chopped
¾ cup dry white wine
3 Tablespoons cold butter, cut into pieces

Heat 2 Tablespoons of the oil in a large, non-reactive skillet and cook the onions until they begin to color. Add the pine nuts and raisins and cook until the nuts are golden. Remove the onions, pine nuts and raisins and set aside.

Add the remaining Tablepoon of oil to the skillet if it is dry. Cook the fish, sprinkling it with the salt, pepper, and rosemary, and turning it until it begins to color on both sides. Add the wine and bring to a boil. Reduce the heat to medium, add the raisin mixture and cook until the fish is tender, about 5 minutes depending on the thickness of the fillets. Remove the fish to a platter. Increase the heat under the cooking liquid and boil for 2 minutes. Gradually stir in the cold butter until a thick sauce is formed. Pour over the fish and serve immediately.

FAVA BEAN STEW WITH CLAMS
Habas con almejas

Probably the most famous dish of Asturias is the traditional bean dish, *Fabada asturiana*. Here is another wonderful bean dish, but much lighter, with clams substituted for sausages.

SERVES 6 TO 8

2 pounds dried fava beans
1 pound small clams in the shell
2 bay leaves
1 large onion, minced
1 clove of garlic, peeled
1 Tablespoon olive oil
1 cup dry white wine
1 teaspoon salt
1 teaspoon freshly ground black pepper

Begin preparation 12 hours ahead. Cover the beans with cold water and soak overnight. The next day, clean the clams, put them into cold water and set aside. Drain the beans and put into a large pot. Add the bay leaves, onion, garlic and olive oil. Cover with cold water and bring to a boil, remove the surface scum, reduce heat and cook beans until tender. Test the beans after 45 minutes by removing one bean and blowing on it. If the skin cracks the beans are done.

While the beans are cooking prepare the clams. Put the clams in a pot with the wine, cover and steam until the shells open. Remove clams and reserve the cooking liquid, discarding any clams that do not open.

Preheat the oven to 350°. When the beans are tender, drain them, reserving the liquid. Put the beans in an ovenproof casserole and top with the clams. Put the reserved bean liquid in a separate pot and pour the clam liquid through a fine sieve into the pot. Over medium heat, cook down the liquid and reduce it by half. Season with the salt and pepper. Pour liquid over the beans and clams and heat in the oven just until hot. Serve immediately in flat soup plates.

GRILLED FISH WITH OLIVE AND
SWEET RED PEPPER SAUCE
Pez de San Pedro a la Parilla
con salsa de aceitunas y pimiento dulce

This resembles a popular dish from Andalusia, where the green olive sauce given on page 203 is served cold on the side.

This particular grilled fish with a warm olive sauce is a variation on one we had at Ampurdán, an outstanding restaurant in Figueres, the home of the Dali museum, about an hour north of Barcelona. If you can, grill the fish over a fire or in your backyard barbecue. The smoky flavor of fire-grilled fish is really wonderful with the sauce.

SERVES 6 TO 8
2 red bell peppers
3 pounds swordfish or sea bass filets, or other firm white fish
2 Tablespoons olive oil
Salt
½ teaspoon white pepper
1 medium onion, minced
6 cloves of garlic, minced
½ pound tomatoes, chopped
½ cup minced green olives
Salt and freshly ground black pepper to taste

Roast the red peppers under the broiler or over the flame of a gas stove until the skin is charred all the way around. Withdraw the peppers from the heat and put them into a paper bag and close tightly. Let rest for 15 minutes. Remove the peppers from the bag, peel them (the skins will slip off readily), remove their stems and seeds. Chop them into large chunks and set aside.

Prepare an outdoor charcoal fire and allow it to burn until the coals are evenly white, or preheat an oven broiler. Place the fish filets on a platter and rub with 1 Tablespoon of the olive oil, a little salt and white pepper. Set aside to come to room temperature before cooking.

Heat the remaining Tablespoon of olive oil in a pan. Add the onions and garlic and cook until they begin to color. Stir in the tomatoes and prepared red peppers and cook until thick and pasty. Place the mixture in a food processor or blender and puree. Stir in the minced olives. Taste for seasoning. Keep warm or reheat before serving.

Put the fish on an oiled grill over a fire or cook under the broiler of your oven until done. Serve the grilled fish topped with the warm olive and red pepper sauce.

PEPPERS STUFFED WITH CRAB
Pimientos rellenos de txangurro

The classic presentation of this delicious crab dish is to serve it in the crab shell, with one shell served to each guest. I find it is too much for one person to eat. Juan Marí Arzak, at his restaurant in San Sebastián, presents the dish as described here and, to my mind, it's better.

SERVES 6
2 fresh Dungeness crabs, cooked, or ¾ pound crab meat
7 medium-size red bell peppers
2 Tablespoons olive oil
I small leek, white part only, cleaned and chopped
I small onion, peeled and minced
I carrot, minced
I½ pounds tomatoes, peeled, seeded and pureed
¾ cup fish stock (page 225)
I cup cream
Salt and white pepper

Preheat the oven to 400°. If using fresh crabs, crack them and remove the meat from the legs and body. Carefully pick over the crab meat to remove any shell or cartilage. Set aside.

Roast the red peppers under the broiler or over the flame of a gas stove until the skin is charred all the way around. Withdraw peppers from the heat, put them into a paper bag and close it tightly. Remove the peppers after I5 minutes. While keeping their shells intact, carefully peel the peppers, and remove their stems and seeds. Set aside.

Heat the olive oil and cook the leek, onion and carrot slowly until very tender. Stir in the tomatoes and cook to a paste. Pour in ½ cup of the stock and ½ cup of the cream. Cook until reduced and thick. Stir in the crab meat and season with the salt and white pepper.

Stuff 6 of the peppers with the crab mixture and arrange them in a circle with the open ends pointing out in a round ceramic or other baking pan. Heap any excess filling in the center where the peppers meet.

Puree the remaining red pepper with the remaining ¼ cup stock and the ½ cup of cream. Season to taste with salt and white pepper. Pour over the peppers and bake for 25 minutes or until hot through and bubbling. Serve immediately.

MONKFISH WITH LEEKS AND ZUCCHINI
Rape con puerros y calabacines

Juan Marí Arzak is generally considered one of the best chefs in Spain. And rightly so. Even with so many good and great restaurants in the Basque country his Arzak stands out as the best. He is very inventive, while staying true to the fundamentals of Basque cooking.

This is a very simple dish that allows all the flavors to come through—distinct, uncluttered. Arzak wraps each scallop of fish in a large slice of zucchini. You might want to prepare it that way when you have large zucchini. I feel the following adaptation is easier for home preparation.

SERVES 6
2 medium leeks
4 small zucchini
3 Tablespoons unsalted butter
1 teaspoon salt
½ teaspoon white pepper
1 cup fish stock (page 225)
½ cup cream
2 pounds monkfish

Preheat oven to 400°. Cut off the green shoots of the leeks and discard, leaving about 2 inches of leaves above the whitish bulb. Cut the leeks in half lengthwise and wash thoroughly. Peel off several layers of the leek and roll them together into a cylinder. Then slice into thin circles. Unrolling these circles you will have thin, long curls of leek. Slice the remainder of the leeks in this way. Set the leek curls aside.

Remove the ends of the zucchini. Slice each zucchini lengthwise into four strips. Then thinly slice each strip on a diagonal. You will have many little slivers of white with green tips at each end. Set aside.

Heat the butter in an ovenproof skillet. Braise the leek curls and zucchini in the butter until they begin to soften. Sprinkle with the salt and pepper. Pour in the fish stock and cream. Increase the heat and cook until the vegetables are soft and the sauce begins to thicken.

Meanwhile, prepare the monkfish. Remove any traces of the thin gray membrane and cut the fish into 18 round scallops. Add the fish to the sauce and put the skillet in the oven. Cook for 10 minutes. Remove from the oven. Remove the fish and vegetables to a serving platter and keep warm. Reduce sauce over a high heat to a medium thickness. The sauce should not be overly thick or it will take away from the fresh flavor of this dish. Pour the sauce over the fish and serve immediately.

BASQUE TUNA WITH POTATOES
Marmitako

Marmitako is a very simple fishermen's dish from the Basque country. Before the discovery of the Americas, fishermen prepared their 'catch of the day' with bread, onions and water—pretty basic!

Later they added the potatoes, tomatoes and green pepper, which were brought from the New World. Still a simple dish, but a very satisfying one.

SERVES 6

3 Tablespoons olive oil
1 large onion, minced
1 green pepper, stemmed, seeded and cut into chunks
2 pound white potatoes, peeled and quartered
3 pounds fresh tuna or bonita, cut into six servings

1 teaspoon salt
½ teaspoon white pepper

Preheat the oven to 400°. Heat the olive oil in a large sauté pan or ceramic casserole, large enough to hold all the ingredients. (I like to use a ceramic casserole that I can cook and serve in.) Add the onion and the green pepper, and cook over medium heat until soft but not golden.

Add the potatoes to the casserole, season with the salt and pepper, and pour in enough water to just cover the ingredients. Put the casserole in the oven and cook until the potatoes are tender but not falling apart, about 20 minutes. Place the fish pieces on top of the potatoes and cook in the oven for 10 minutes. Taste for seasoning. Serve hot, placing the fish on a plate and pouring the potatoes and sauce over the fish.

CATALAN FISHERMAN'S FISH STEW
Romesco de peix

A son and grandson of Catalan fishermen explained to us that fishermen would take *romesco* sauce (page 202) out on their boats to be eaten as an accompaniment to their fish dinner. Sometimes the sauce, which contains spices and vinegar, would be poured over raw fish to preserve it for a future meal. Thus was born *romesco*, the stew.

SERVES 6 TO 8
2 dried ancho chilies
6 Tablespoons olive oil
26 prawns, about 1 pound, in their shells
Salt
6 garlic cloves
2 one-inch thick slices white bread
½ cup almonds or hazelnuts, or a combination of the two
1 medium whole tomato
1 sprig of parsley
1 teaspoon paprika
½ teaspoon freshly ground pepper
3 cups fish stock (page 225)

I medium onion, peeled and minced
½ pound small clams in shell, scrubbed clean
½ pound mussels in shell, beards removed and scrubbed clean
2 pounds mixed firm fish—monkfish, snapper, and sea bass—
      cut into 2- to 3-inch pieces

Put the chilies in a bowl and cover with boiling water. Leave in the water for 15 minutes. Drain and discard the water. Remove the stems and seeds from the chilies, chop them and set aside.

Heat 3 Tablespoons of the oil in a ceramic casserole or wide skillet about 3 inches deep. Add the prawns and sprinkle lightly with salt. Sauté 1 minute and remove. The prawns should not be fully cooked.

Add 2 Tablespoons more oil to the pan and sauté the garlic, bread and nuts until golden. Add the whole tomato and the chilies and cook 2 minutes more over medium high heat.

Put this mixture, the *picada*, into a food processor; add the parsley, paprika and black pepper and whirl to form a paste. Pour in 1 cup of the fish stock and continue to whirl until smooth.

Heat the remaining 1 Tablespoon of oil in the pan and sauté the onion until soft. Stir in the puree, pour in the remaining 2 cups of fish stock and add ½ teaspoon salt. Cook to thicken and reduce by half. (The dish can be prepared ahead to this point. Allow to come to room temperature, then refrigerate. Reheat before continuing.)

Taste sauce for salt and add if needed—keep in mind that fish and shellfish have a certain amount of saltiness, so don't overdo it. Arrange the clams, mussels and fish in the sauce and cook for 5 minutes. Scatter the prawns over the fish and shellfish. Cook another 5 minutes, or until the clams and mussels have opened and the fish is cooked.

Serve the stew on large dinner plates or in flat soup plates with plenty of bread for soaking up the sauce.

CATALAN VEGETABLE STEW
Samfaina

Samfaina is one of the basics of Catalan cooking, related to the *ratatouille* of France and *caponata* of Italy. The Catalans do a lot more with their version though, making it into a sauce by pureeing it and adding cream, serving it as a vegetable side dish, or using it as a base for other dishes such as *Pollo en samfaina* (page 257).

SERVES 5

¼ cup olive oil

2 medium onions, thinly-sliced

2 garlic cloves, sliced

2 red peppers, seeded and cut into ½-inch cubes

1 pound eggplant, peeled and cut into ½-inch cubes

5 ounces zucchini, cut into ½-inch cubes

½ pound tomatoes, peeled, seeded and chopped

1 teaspoon salt

1 teaspoon freshly ground black pepper

2 sprigs of fresh parsley, chopped

1 sprig of fresh thyme, chopped

Heat the olive oil in a large skillet. Cook the onions and garlic over low heat until very soft, about 20 minutes. Add the red peppers and cook for another 10 minutes. Add the eggplant and zucchini and stir to coat with the oil. Cover and cook for 15 minutes. Uncover and stir in the tomatoes, salt, pepper, parsley and thyme. Cook uncovered over low heat until the eggplant is soft. Taste for seasoning.

Variation: Do not peel the eggplant, and do not cover the pan at any time. Increase the amount of tomato by ½ pound. This will produce a stew with firm and distinct chunks of vegetable that works very well in the recipe for *Pollo en samfaina.*

DUCK WITH PEARS
Pato con peras

This recipe is a variation on a Catalan classic, often made more like a stew with the pears cut into cubes. It is a perfect party dish. So much can be done ahead and the presentation is really spectacular.

Arrange individual plates in the kitchen, each with a whole leg, a breast and an upright pear. If you prefer smaller portions, cut the pears in half and arrange a half pear and one piece of duck on each of 8 plates.

SERVES 4 TO 8

Stock:
- Two 4-pound ducks
- 1 carrot, cut into 1-inch pieces
- 1 medium onion, peeled and quartered
- 1 cup dry white or red wine

Pear Sauce:
- 6 pears, small Bosc or other, peeled, leaving stem attached
- 1 carrot, minced
- 1 medium onion, minced
- 3 cloves garlic, peeled and minced
- ¼ cup grape or pear brandy
- 1 teaspoon salt
- ½ teaspoon white pepper

Begin preparation 24 hours ahead. To prepare the stock: Preheat the oven to 400°. Cut ducks into 4 whole legs and 4 breasts, cover and refrigerate. Freeze duck liver and save for a pâté or *picada*.

Put duck backs, wings and necks in a baking pan with the carrot and onion and brown in the oven for one hour. Remove the duck parts and vegetables to a stock pot. Pour off any grease from the baking pan and add the wine. Scrape to loosen any particles and pour liquid into the stock pot with the duck parts and vegetables. Cover with cold water, bring to a boil, reduce heat and cook, partially covered, for 2 to 3 hours. Strain, discarding bones and vegetables, cool and refrigerate overnight.

On the following day: Remove the congealed fat formed at the top of the stock. Bring the stock to a boil, reduce the heat to medium high.

Poach the pears in the stock until tender, about 20 minutes. Remove the pears and slice a piece from the bottom of each so they will stand upright. Cook the stock rapidly to reduce to 3 cups.

Preheat oven to 400°. Heat a dry skillet on the stove until it is very hot. Put the duck legs into the pan skin side down and cook until golden, about 15 minutes. Remove the legs to a large baking pan or ceramic casserole. Pour the fat from the skillet and save for cooking another time.

Reheat the skillet and put in the breasts, skin side down and cook until golden, about 20 minutes. Remove the breasts and arrange around the duck legs. Pour off all but 1 Tablespoon of the fat from the skillet. Add the carrot, onion and garlic, and sauté until golden, about 10 minutes. Add the brandy and cook until brandy is evaporated. Pour in the reduced duck stock and season with salt and pepper.

Pour the sauce over the duck legs and breasts. Place in the oven until the duck is tender, about 1 hour. Near the end of the cooking time, reheat the pears in the oven or microwave.

Remove the legs and breasts to a platter, surround with the pears and keep warm. Cook the sauce quickly to reduce by $1/3$, then strain it over the duck and pears and serve immediately.

DUCK SEVILLE
Pato a la sevillana

This classic from Seville should be made with the bitter Seville oranges—the kind that Nell Gwyn, the dashing red-haired mistress of Charles II once sold in the theaters of Restoration London. 'Pretty witty Nellie' would have a hard time finding the Seville orange at her local supermarket today, so we have added lemon juice to this recipe to compensate for our sweeter oranges.

SERVES 4 TO 6
Two 4-pound ducks
1 large onion, minced
Zest and juice of 2 oranges
Juice of one lemon

1 cup dry sherry, such as an amontillado
1 cup duck or chicken stock (page 223)
Salt and white pepper to taste

Separate the ducks into 4 breasts and 4 whole legs. Remove excess fat. Reserve the backs, wings and necks for stock.

Heat a large dry skillet to medium hot. Cook duck breasts skin side down for about 20 minutes, until golden. Remove breasts from pan and set aside. Pour off fat. Place the whole legs in the pan and sauté until golden on all sides, about 15 minutes. Set aside.

Pour off all but 1 Tablespoon of the duck fat. Over medium heat sauté the onion in the fat until golden. Add the zest, and orange and lemon juices, and reduce until the liquid evaporates, about 5 minutes. Pour in the sherry and stock. Return the duck legs to the pan and cook for 30 minutes. Add the breasts to the pan and cook for 20 minutes longer. The duck breasts and legs should be tender. Cook longer if needed.

Remove the duck pieces to a platter and keep warm. Carefully skim off all the fat from the surface of the sauce and increase heat to medium high. Quickly cook the sauce to reduce to desired consistency. Season with the salt and pepper. Pour sauce over the duck pieces and serve.

DUCK CONFIT
Confit de pato

Duck *confit* may be French in origin, but cooks pay no attention to political borders and the Spanish Basques have made it their own—at home, and at the simplest and grandest restaurants. With *confit*, the main concern is to preserve the meat without refrigeration. This method not only does that, but also creates a new and wonderful flavor called *confitado* in Spain.

This recipe might look a bit intimidating, but it goes together easily and the flavors at the end justify the effort.

To get together enough duck fat, ask your butcher to order it for you from his duck supplier. Otherwise, just pull off as much fat as possible from the ducks you cook, heat it over a medium-low heat until it liquefies, then strain it and save it refrigerated. Add good quality lard to the duck fat to arrive at enough to cook the duck pieces. The best lard can be found at food stores serving the Mexican community. The fat can be used several times within a year for preparing *confit*.

2 whole ducks
1/3 cup Kosher salt
3 bay leaves
Several sprigs of fresh thyme or 2 teaspoons dried thyme leaves
12 black peppercorns
2 pounds duck fat, or a combination of duck fat and good quality lard
1 medium onion studded with 12 whole cloves

Begin preparation 24 hours in advance. Remove fat from the ducks. Put this duck fat in a pan and cook over medium low heat to liquefy it. Cut the ducks into pieces, keeping the legs and thighs whole, and reserving the backs, wings and necks for the stock pot.

Put the whole legs and breasts in layers in an enamel or glass pan and sprinkle each layer with salt, bay leaves, thyme and peppercorns. Refrigerate, covered, for 24 hours. You could use only the legs for the *confit* and keep the breasts for other recipes. But breasts are delicious *confitado*, particularly in salads.

Preheat the oven to 300°. Heat a large non-reactive pan over medium low heat and add enough fat to cover all the duck pieces. Slowly melt the fat. Add the clove-studded onion. The fat should be only about 200°. You do not want to fry the duck. A quick read oven or meat thermometer is useful here.

Wipe off the traces of seasoning from the duck pieces and slide them into fat so that they are entirely covered. Reheat the fat to 200°. Put the uncovered pan into the oven. Cook the duck until it exudes no juice when pierced. This usually takes 1½ to 2 hours.

Meanwhile thoroughly clean a non-porous container that can hold all the duck and the fat. Now you want to cover the bottom of the container with something to raise the duck off the bottom so it will be completely encased in the fat. You can use sterilized sticks, cooked duck bones or simply marbles, sterilized by boiling—they are inexpensive and reusable.

Gently lift the duck pieces from the fat and put them in layers in the prepared container. Pour the fat through a strainer over the duck pieces, completely covering them. Leave behind any meat juices at the bottom of the pan.

When the fat has set, cover the top with foil, closely fitting it to the top of the fat. Keep in a cool place. Since our homes are usually much warmer than the kitchen larder or pantry of many years ago, I keep my *confit* in the refrigerator just for safety. If you are lucky enough to have a basement or wine cellar, it should keep well there for several months. It will keep covered in fat and refrigerated for at least six months.

To use the *confit*, bring to room temperature so the fat liquefies and gently lift out as many pieces as you wish. Remove any fat adhering to the pieces. Use the pieces whole or shredded as you wish or follow one of the following recipes. Cover the unused duck with fat and return to the refrigerator.

DISHES USING DUCK CONFIT

Once you have begun to make *confit*, your imagination will guide you to all sorts of wonderful presentations. Duck *confit* can be substituted, for example, for regular duck in any of the recipes in this book. Simply bring the *confit* to room temperature so the fat liquefies and take out as many pieces of duck as you wish. Brown the duck and set aside. Then prepare the sauces and heat the duck in the sauce before serving.

Here are a couple of ideas to get you started with *confit*.

DUCK CONFIT SALAD WITH WALNUT OIL DRESSING
Ensalada de confit de pato con vinagreta de nueces

Many supermarkets have a selection of mixed salad greens using several different types of lettuce, all washed and ready to use. While it may seem expensive, remember there is no waste. How many times have you discarded lettuce while trying to get the best leaves for a salad?

SERVES 6
3 Tablespoons walnut oil
1 Tablespoon olive oil
1 teaspoon Dijon-style mustard

1 clove of garlic, crushed
1 Tablespoon lemon juice
1 Tablespoon sherry wine vinegar
1 teaspoon salt
¼ teaspoon freshly ground black pepper
2 legs duck *confit*
2 half breasts duck *confit*
Mixed salad greens—lettuces, spinach, escarole, radicchio, endive
3 Tablespoons mixed fresh herbs, chopped, such as
        parsley, marjoram and sage

Prepare the dressing by combining the oils, mustard, garlic, lemon juice, vinegar, salt and pepper. Set aside.

Skin and shred the duck leg meat and put into a bowl. Skin the half breasts and cut into 3 diagonal slices each. Put into a separate bowl.

Attractively arrange the greens on individual dinner plates, strewing the leaves over a large part of each plate and using the endive spears as a decorative flourish.

Add the chopped herbs to the dressing. Immediately divide the dressing between the two bowls of meat and toss with the meat.

Arrange the shredded leg meat on top of the greens and garnish the edge of each plate with 1 slice of the reserved breast.
Serve immediately.

DUCK CONFIT WITH OLIVE SAUCE
Confit de pato con salsa de aceitunas

This is a favorite lunch dish in Andalusia, where you might dine in the shade of the tree that produced the olives.

SERVES 4
1 Tablespoon duck fat
2 half breasts and 4 legs of duck *confit*
1 medium onion, finely minced
3 tomatoes, peeled and grated
½ cup dry white wine
2 cups duck, chicken or veal stock (page 223, 224)

1 cup Spanish green olives
Salt
Black pepper, freshly ground

Heat the fat in a large skillet and cook the duck *confit* over medium heat, skin side down, until brown, about 3 to 5 minutes. Remove duck from the skillet, pour off all but 1 Tablespoon of duck fat, and in the same skillet, cook the onions until they begin to color. Add the tomatoes and cook to a paste. Stir in the wine and the stock and cook over high heat to reduce to 1 cup, about 7 minutes. Add the olives and taste for seasoning, adding salt and pepper as needed. Return the duck to the pan and heat through in the sauce. Serve immediately.

VENISON STEAKS WITH SHALLOT SAUCE
Ciervo con salsa de escaloñas

Venison, wild boar, hare and other game are often found on Spanish menus in the fall and winter. Preparations range from simple grills to warming stews. These steaks, with their delicious sauce, are a wonderful match with one of the great red wines from Rioja.

SERVES 6
Six 5-ounce venison steaks
1 bottle of good red wine
2 bay leaves
6 juniper berries
1 teaspoon coarsely ground black pepper, plus additional to taste
Salt to taste
1 pound shallots, peeled and finely chopped
2 cups veal stock (page 224)
8 ounces cold, unsalted butter

Begin preparation 24 hours ahead. Put the venison in a flat, non-reactive pan and add the wine, bay leaves, juniper and black pepper. Cover and refrigerate for 24 hours.

Bring the steaks and marinade to room temperature. Remove the steaks from the marinade and pat dry. Strain the marinade and reserve the liquid. Discard the bay and juniper.

Heat a large dry skillet very hot and sprinkle with a very little salt. Cook the steaks 2 minutes on each side and remove from the pan.

Add the shallots to the pan and pour in the reserved marinade and veal stock. Bring to a boil and cook over a high heat until reduced to about 1½ cups of liquid. Return the steaks to the skillet and cook for 2 minutes on each side. Remove steaks and keep warm.

Take the butter from the refrigerator and cut into small pieces. Lower the heat under the skillet to medium and gradually whisk in the butter, a piece or two at a time. You don't want the butter to melt quickly or it will not combine with the sauce to thicken it. Taste for salt and pepper.

Serve the steaks on individual plates with the sauce poured over the steaks. Delicious with a simple potato dish and seasonal vegetable.

PARTRIDGE WITH APPLES
Perdiz con manzanas

Partridge are a great prize of hunters in Spain, especially in Andalusia and La Mancha. Avid British hunters often take hunting cottages during the season around Jerez de la Frontera—hunting by day, sherry by night. The birds are also grown commercially, but good restaurants will have a few wild birds for their best customers. Many US restaurants now feature game on their menus, and partridge can be found in specialty shops in larger cities. Check with your local butcher or a restaurant meat supplier. You may also substitute game hen.

SERVES 6
6 partridge or 6 game hens
¼ pound pancetta, thinly sliced
6 sprigs of fresh rosemary
12 cloves of garlic, peeled
3 pippin apples, peeled, cored and cubed
¼ cup brandy
I cup chicken stock (page 223)
Salt and pepper

Preheat oven to 375°. Thoroughly clean the birds, removing the giblets and discarding or freezing them for other use. Stuff each bird with a sprig of rosemary and 2 cloves of garlic. Wrap the birds in strips of pancetta and arrange them in a roasting pan. Roast for 30 minutes. Remove from the oven and take off the pancetta, setting it aside, then roast the birds for another 10 minutes.

Remove the birds from the oven. Heat the accumulated juices in a sauté pan. Add the apples and sauté quickly. Pour in the brandy and stock and cook over high heat until the sauce begins to thicken. Add salt and pepper to taste.

Put the birds in the pan and coat with the sauce. Chop the pancetta and sprinkle over the birds. Serve immediately.

PARTRIDGE IN CHOCOLATE SAUCE
Perdiz con chocolate

This dish was obviously devised after the introduction of chocolate to Spain from the New World. The cinnamon spicing gives an unusual medieval taste to the birds. Since cinnamon was quickly taken up by Mexican cooks, this dish may have originated in Mexico (perhaps using quail rather than partridge) and brought back to Spain. Check with specialty game suppliers for partridge, or substitute game hen.

SERVES 6
6 partridge or 6 game hens
4 Tablespoons olive oil
1 medium onion, peeled and minced
5 cloves garlic, peeled and minced
1 cup dry white wine
¼ cup sherry wine vinegar
1 cup chicken stock (page 223)
1 teaspoon salt
½ teaspoon pepper
2 whole cloves
1 teaspoon thyme
1 bay leaf

¼ teaspoon ground cinnamon
2 ounces unsweetened chocolate

Preheat oven to 375°. Thoroughly clean the birds, removing the giblets and discarding or freezing them for other use. Rub the birds with 2 Tablespoons of the olive oil and put them in a roasting pan. If using game hens, cut them in half. Bake for 30 minutes.

Meanwhile, heat the remaining 2 Tablespoons of oil in an oven-proof sauté pan or, preferably, a ceramic casserole large enough to hold all the birds. Sauté the onion and garlic in the oil until golden. Add the wine and cook over a high heat until it evaporates, about 5 minutes.

Pour in the vinegar and stock. Add the salt, pepper, cloves, thyme, bay leaf, cinnamon and chocolate, and simmer for 30 minutes. Remove the birds from the oven. Place the birds in the sauce and bake for an additional 15 minutes. Serve with the sauce spooned over them.

PARTRIDGE IN CABBAGE ROLLS
Perdiz en col

There is something homey and rustic about the smell and taste of cabbage, yet, as in this dish, it also lends itself to sophisticated cooking. We first encountered this variation on the classic Catalan dish, Perdiu amb farcellets de col, at Celler del Penedés just outside of Vilafranca del Penedés, the bustling wine capital of Catalonia. The classic dish is partridge served with little balls of cabbage.

At first glance, there seem to be a lot of steps in the preparation, but just break them up and it really becomes a do-ahead party dish.

SERVES 6
2 partridges or game hens
3 Tablespoons olive oil
¼ pound pancetta, chopped
2 leeks, white parts only, cleaned and chopped
3 carrots, coarsely chopped
1 medium onion, coarsely chopped
3 cloves garlic, minced

Salt and pepper to taste
3 cups of chicken stock (page 223)
I large head savoy cabbage

Preheat oven to 450°. Thoroughly clean the birds, removing the giblets and discarding or freezing them for other use. Rub the birds with 1 Tablespoon of the olive oil. Put them in the oven and immediately reduce the heat to 350°. Begin to test them for doneness after 45 minutes by jiggling the leg. The leg should move freely and, when pricked with a fork, the juices should run clear. When done remove the birds from the oven and allow to cool before handling.

Heat the remaining 2 Tablespoons of olive oil in a large ovenproof pan and sauté the pancetta until golden. Add the leeks, carrots, onion and garlic, and cook slowly over medium heat until tender. Season with salt and pepper to taste. Remove half of the vegetable and pancetta mixture from the pan and set aside. Pour the chicken stock into the pan and continue cooking the mixture slowly for 30 minutes.

Meanwhile bring a large pot of salted water to a boil. Core the cabbage and gently separate the leaves leaving them whole. Cook the leaves briefly, until tender, in the boiling water. Remove the leaves; drain and dry them.

Lay out 6 of the largest cabbage leaves, patching any holes with smaller leaves. Reserve the remaining leaves. Remove the skin from the birds and separate the meat from the bones, leaving the meat in fairly large chunks. Combine the meat with the reserved vegetable mixture and pancetta.

Divide the meat and vegetable mixture into 6 equal portions and place them on top of the selected leaves. Top with the remaining cabbage leaves and roll each into a large bundle.

In a blender or food processor, puree the vegetables and stock mixture. Return the puree to the pan or casserole. Put the cabbage rolls on top of the pureed sauce, spooning some of it over them. Cook in the oven for 20 to 30 minutes until hot through and the sauce has thickened. Serve directly from the pan or, more formally, arrange on individual plates with the sauce and garnish with steamed baby carrots and steamed leek curls (see Monkfish with leeks and zucchini, page 264).

RABBIT WITH TURNIPS AND PEARS
Conejo con peras y nabos

Turnips were a much more popular vegetable in the Middle Ages before the potato was brought to Europe, so this recipe probably goes back several centuries. It is also typical of medieval cooking to mix fruit and game. The Catalan kitchen, which is the source of this recipe, has retained many dishes from the Middle Ages.

SERVES 6

2 Tablespoons olive oil
One 2½ pound rabbit, cut in 6 serving pieces
1 medium onion, peeled and minced
2 leeks, white part only, cleaned and finely chopped
2 cloves garlic, peeled and minced
1 carrot, peeled and chopped
1 tomato, peeled, seeded and chopped
1 bay leaf
Sprig each of fresh thyme, marjoram and oregano
Salt and freshly ground black pepper
6 small pears, peeled
2 cups chicken stock (page 223)
1 cup white wine
2 pounds turnips, peeled and cut into strips

Heat the olive oil in a large skillet and sauté the rabbit until golden. Remove the rabbit. Add more oil if necessary and sauté onion, leeks, garlic and carrot until soft. Add tomato, bay leaf, herbs, salt and pepper to taste and cook over high heat until reduced to a paste.

Return the rabbit to the sauce, and arrange the pears around the rabbit. Pour one cup of the stock and the wine over the rabbit and cook, covered, over medium low heat for 30 to 45 minutes or until the rabbit is tender when pierced with a fork .

Meanwhile bring the remaining cup of stock to a boil in a medium sauce pan and add the turnips. Cook covered until tender but not falling apart, 5 to 10 minutes. Drain, reserving the stock, and set the turnips aside on a heated platter.

Remove the rabbit and pears from the skillet and set them with the turnips to keep warm. Puree the sauce from the skillet in a blender or food processor, pour it through a fine sieve back into the skillet and add the reserved turnip stock. Cook over high heat to reduce and thicken the sauce. Taste for seasoning. Pour sauce over the rabbit and serve.

RABBIT IN ALMOND SAUCE
Conejo en salsa de almendras

At first glance this recipe and the recipe for *Conejo al salmorejo* that follows seem to be very alike. Although they both use a *picada* to thicken and flavor, the *picada* is used differently in each and the resulting flavors are different. These two dishes demonstrate the variety of styles that can be achieved using a *picada*.

SERVES 4 TO 6
¼ cup olive oil
1 medium onion, chopped
6 garlic cloves
20 whole almonds
One 2½ pound rabbit, cut into 6 serving pieces, plus the liver
½ teaspoon cinnamon
1 Tablespoon chopped parsley
10 black peppercorns
2 whole cloves, peeled
Pinch of saffron
1 teaspoon salt
2 cups dry white wine
2 bay leaves

Heat 2 Tablespoons of the oil in a skillet or ceramic casserole. Cook the onion, garlic and almonds until the onions are limp and begin to color. Add the rabbit liver and cook until firm.

Put these ingredients into a blender or food processor with the cinnamon, parsley, peppercorns, cloves, saffron and salt. Puree with ½ cup of the wine to a paste (a *picada*).

Add the remaining oil to the pan and cook the rabbit pieces until golden. Stir in the paste, remaining wine and the bay leaves. Bring to a boil and cook for 30 minutes or until the rabbit is tender and the sauce has reduced and thickened. Discard the bay leaf. Serve directly from the ceramic casserole.

RABBIT WITH WINE, VINEGAR AND HERBS
Conejo al salmorejo

This recipe involves a lot of steps, none of which takes much time. Once you start making and using *picada* to flavor and thicken, you'll find the process very simple and rewarding.

SERVES 4 TO 6
One 2½ pound rabbit, cut into 6 serving pieces, liver reserved
1 bay leaf
1 sprig oregano
1 sprig thyme
6 whole black peppercorns
8 cloves of garlic, peeled
⅓ cup wine vinegar
3 cups dry white wine
¼ cup olive oil
¼ cup whole almonds
1 one-inch slice of white bread, crust removed
1 teaspoon salt
½ teaspoon freshly ground black pepper

Begin preparation 24 hours ahead. Preheat oven to 350°. Put the rabbit in a non-metallic bowl. Add the bay leaf, oregano, thyme, peppercorns, garlic, vinegar and wine. Cover the bowl and marinate the rabbit, refrigerated, overnight.

Remove the rabbit from the marinade and pat dry. Set the marinade aside. Heat the olive oil in a large, ovenproof skillet or ceramic casserole. Add the rabbit pieces and cook until golden, about 20 minutes. Remove the rabbit and set aside.

Remove the cloves of garlic from the marinade. In the oil remaining in the skillet, sauté the garlic until golden. Remove the garlic to a blender or food processor. In the remaining oil, sauté the almonds, bread and the rabbit liver until golden. Remove the liver as soon as it firms. Add the sautéed almonds, bread and liver to the garlic in the blender or food processor and blend to a paste (the *picada*). Set aside.

Pour off any remaining oil from the skillet. Strain the marinade into the skillet and bring to a boil. Add the rabbit. Place the skillet in the oven and bake for 30 minutes.

Take the skillet from the oven and, with a slotted spoon, remove the rabbit pieces and keep them warm. Put the skillet over high heat and bring liquid to a boil. Cook quickly to thicken. As the liquid starts to thicken add the *picada.* This will thicken the sauce more. Season with salt and pepper. Cook to desired consistency. Return the rabbit to the sauce and turn it to coat with the sauce. Serve the rabbit at the table in the skillet or casserole.

RABBIT OR CHICKEN WITH SNAILS
Fritada de conejo o pollo con caracoles

This combination is found in northern Spain, from Catalonia to Rioja. There you can buy small tasty snails at the market in their shells. In the US, you can use canned snails without shells, or better, get revenge on the garden snails that have been nibbling your herbs. Eat them—they will be nicely pre-seasoned. If you collect snails from the garden, they will need preparation. I refer you to *Joy of Cooking*, which contains complete information on preparing snails.

SERVES 4 TO 6
3 Tablespoons olive oil
1 rabbit, cut into 6 pieces, or one 3½ pound chicken cut into 8 pieces
Salt
Freshly ground black pepper
24 to 30 snails
6 cloves garlic, peeled and thinly sliced
2 medium onions, peeled and minced

2 small red bell peppers, stemmed, seeded and chopped
1 pound tomatoes, peeled, seeded and pureed
2 sprigs of fresh thyme or ½ teaspoon dried thyme
I cup chicken stock (page 223)

Preheat oven to 350°. Heat the oil in a skillet. Add the rabbit or chicken, lightly sprinkled with salt and pepper, and cook until golden, about 20 minutes.

Meanwhile, if using canned snails, refresh them under cold running water, removing any grit. Set aside. Remove the rabbit or chicken from the skillet and set aside.

Add the garlic to the skillet and cook over moderate heat until browned. Add the onions and cook until soft. Stir in the peppers and cook 1 minute. Add the tomatoes and cook to a paste. Add the thyme and stock and cook until the liquid is reduced to about ½ cup. Mix sauce with the meat in an ovenproof casserole. Add the snails. Cook in the oven for 30 minutes. Serve immediately, directly from the casserole.

GRILLED PORK LOIN WITH
SWEET AND SOUR SAUCE
Lomo de cerdo con salsa agridulce

The Moors brought oranges and sugar to Spain, and these flavors form the basis for this sweet and sour sauce. It is nothing like the industrial tasting sweet and sour sauce of American-Chinese restaurants. The original recipe would have used the bitter Seville orange, so we have added lemon juice to reduce the sweetness of the modern Valencia-style orange.

SERVES 6 TO 8
Two 1½ pound boneless pork loin roasts
Zest of one orange
Zest of one lemon
I teaspoon fresh lemon sage, chopped
3 cloves garlic, minced

1 cup fresh orange juice
½ cup fresh lemon juice
½ cup sugar
Salt and freshly ground black pepper to taste

Lay the pork loins fat side down and sprinkle the top of each with the citrus zests, sage and garlic. Press the pork loins together, enclosing the spices between them. Tie the roasts together securely at 1-inch intervals.

Pour the orange and lemon juices into a glass pan and marinate the pork for 1 hour at room temperature. Remove the meat from the marinade and reserve the marinade.

Heat charcoal in a covered barbecue grill. Bank the coals to one side and put a drip pan on the other side. You can easily fashion a drip pan for the purpose using aluminum foil. When the coals are uniformly hot, put the loin on the side opposite the coals, above the drip pan, cover the barbecue, and cook for about 45 minutes to an hour, or until the pork reaches an internal temperature of 145°. It is not necessary to turn the pork during cooking.

Baste the pork several times during the cooking with the marinade. Remove the pork to a platter and let rest for 10 minutes. Heat the sugar in a heavy non-reactive skillet, and melt and cook to a deep golden. Pour in the remaining marinade and any juices that have accumulated under the resting pork. Do not use any of the drippings from the drip pan. Cook the sauce for 5 minutes over moderate heat. Add the salt and pepper to taste. To serve, slice the pork and arrange on a platter. Pass the sauce separately.

LAMB SHANKS WITH WHITE BEANS
Pierna de cordero guisada con judías blancas

An abundance of lamb and cold nights have helped create some wonderful stews in the north of Spain. You will find this combination of white beans and lamb on the Spanish and French slopes of the Pyrenees. If possible, have your butcher crack the bones of the lamb shanks. This will bring out rich flavors otherwise sealed inside them.

SERVES 6

1 pound dry Great Northern beans
¼ cup olive oil
4 pounds lamb shanks, cracked by your butcher
2 teaspoons salt
1 teaspoon freshly ground black pepper
6 cloves garlic, minced
1 large onion, minced
2 carrots, chopped
3 cups dry white wine
4 bay leaves
1 sprig fresh rosemary
1 sprig fresh thyme
1 small onion studded with 8 whole cloves

Begin preparation the day before by soaking the beans overnight.

Heat the olive oil in a large, deep skillet or heavy soup pot. Brown the lamb shanks in the oil, sprinkling with 1 teaspoon of salt and the pepper while they cook. Remove the shanks. Pour off all but 1 Tablespoon of the oil. Cook the garlic, minced onion and carrots in the remaining oil until tender. Return the lamb shanks to the pan. Pour in the wine. Add 2 of the bay leaves, the rosemary and thyme. Bring to a boil, reduce heat, cover and simmer for 1½ hours.

Meanwhile, drain the beans and put into a pot, cover with cold water to 2 inches above the beans, and add the clove-studded onion and the remaining 2 bay leaves. Bring to a boil. Skim off the foam. Reduce the heat and cook the beans, uncovered, for 45 minutes. Add the remaining teaspoon of salt to the beans and continue to cook until tender. Remove the cloved onion and bay leaves. Drain the beans, reserving the liquid.

Preheat oven to 375°. Remove lamb from cooking liquid. Remove bay leaf, thyme and rosemary from the cooking liquid and discard. With a slotted spoon remove the remaining solids from the cooking liquid and puree in a blender or food processor. Return the puree to the pot and boil quickly to reduce by half.

Pour half of the beans into a ceramic casserole or other ovenproof casserole and arrange the lamb on top of the beans. Cover with the remaining beans. Pour reduced cooking liquid over the beans and put in the oven to bake for 30 minutes. Check after 15 minutes. If the beans have become too dry, add some of the reserved bean cooking liquid.

Remove stew from the oven and allow to rest for 10 minutes before serving in flat soup plates.

LAMB WITH PEPPERS, NAVARRE-STYLE
Cordero al chilidrón

Hemingway made Pamplona famous for its running of the bulls, but Pamplona has charms beyond that madness. And some very good food as well—after all, the Basque influence is strong here. Walk down the narrow streets, for example, look up and you are likely to see strings of peppers drying outside all the windows. This lamb stew is a specialty of the region.

SERVES 6
3 dried ancho chilies
3 large red bell peppers
2 Tablespoons olive oil
2½ pounds boneless leg of lamb, cut into 2-inch cubes
Salt and freshly ground black pepper to taste
2 medium onions, minced
3 cloves garlic, minced
¼ pound prosciutto, or Spanish ham if available, cut into thin strips
6 large tomatoes, peeled, seeded and chopped
1½ cups dry white wine, or veal or chicken stock (page 223, 225)

Preheat oven to 350°. Bring a pot of water to the boil, add the ancho chilies, remove from the heat and allow to rest for 15 minutes, then stem, seed and peel them and set aside.

Roast the red peppers under the broiler or over the flame of a gas stove until the skin is charred all the way around. Withdraw the peppers from the heat and put them into a paper bag and close tightly. Let rest for 15 minutes. Remove the peppers, stem, seed and peel them. Cut into large chunks and set aside.

Heat the oil in a large skillet. Sprinkle the lamb cubes with salt and pepper and cook in small batches until they start to color. Remove the lamb to a platter.

In the same skillet, cook the onion, garlic and prosciutto or ham until limp. Return the lamb to the skillet, add the tomatoes, peppers, chilies and wine or stock. Bring to a boil, reduce heat and cook for about 45 minutes or until the lamb is tender and the sauce thick.

The lamb should be tender and the sauce sufficiently reduced at this point. If, however, the cooking gods have not been with you, remove the lamb and vegetables and keep them warm. Increase the heat and reduce the sauce to desired consistency.

Taste for salt and pepper. Pour sauce over the lamb and serve.

LAMB CASSEROLE, MÉRIDA-STYLE
Caldereta de cordero Mérida

One night in Mérida we ate this lamb stew twice. The dish is worthy of two helpings, but we didn't really do it on purpose. We had arranged to meet friends at a restaurant for dinner. When they didn't appear we went ahead and ordered. The lamb arrived and was good, but not as wonderful as we had been led to expect. In walked our friends, who had been waiting in the restaurant next door. We hastily paid our perplexed waiter, and went on to another, and better, caldereta at Bar Nicolas, a short walk from the excellent parador in Mérida.

SERVES 6
2 Tablespoons olive oil
3 pounds boneless leg of lamb, cut into 2-inch cubes
2 medium onions, peeled and sliced
3 tomatoes, chopped
1 green pepper, stemmed, seeded and quartered
4 cloves of garlic
2 bay leaves
10 springs of parsley
2 sprigs of thyme
1 cup dry white wine
1 one-inch slice of white bread

1 Tablespoon white wine vinegar
8 peppercorns
2 teaspoons paprika
1 whole clove
1 teaspoon salt

Heat the olive oil in a large pot with a cover. When hot, cook the lamb pieces in small batches until golden. Discard excess fat. Return all the lamb to the pot. Add the onion, tomatoes, green pepper, garlic, bay leaves, parsley, thyme and white wine. Bring to a boil, reduce heat, cover and simmer for about 45 minutes or until the meat is tender.

Meanwhile soak the bread in the vinegar, with water to cover, until soft. Squeeze the bread dry and puree it in a blender or food processor with the peppercorns, paprika, clove and salt. Add some of the cooking juices to obtain a smooth puree.

Remove meat to a platter. Puree the cooked vegetables and cooking liquid in a blender or food processor and pour back into the pot through a sieve, pushing down on the solids to extract as much juice as possible. Stir in the bread mixture. Cook to reduce and thicken. Return the lamb to the pot and heat through. Taste for salt. Serve immediately.

LAMB, SHEPHERD-STYLE
Cordero pastoril

Wild rosemary and mint, gathered near the shepherd's campfire, season this simple stew. The flavors are so pure you can almost smell the smoke.

SERVES 6
3 pounds boneless leg of lamb, cut into 2-inch cubes
4 cloves garlic
2 Tablespoons fresh rosemary
3 Tablespoons fresh mint leaves
Freshly ground black pepper
3 Tablespoons wine vinegar
12 medium-sized red new potatoes
1 Tablespoon olive oil

2 cups dry white wine
Salt

Begin preparation 3 to 12 hours in advance. Put the lamb cubes into a non-reactive pan. Grind together the garlic, rosemary, mint and pepper. Stir in the vinegar to form a paste. Rub this into the lamb. Cover and refrigerate for several hours, or overnight.

Parboil the potatoes in boiling salted water for about 10 minutes. Drain them and discard the water. Cut the potatoes in halves or quarters according to your preference and the size of the potatoes.

Heat the oil in a ceramic casserole or skillet. Add the lamb, potatoes and wine. Bring to a boil, reduce heat to medium low and cook until the lamb is tender and the potatoes have browned, about 45 to 60 minutes. There will be little or no liquid remaining. Season to taste with salt and pepper and serve immediately.

STEAK IN BLUE CHEESE SAUCE
Entrecot al queso de Cabrales, Cabo Mayor

The foundation for this dish is *Cabrales,* a blue cheese from Asturias that is truly one of the world's noble blue cheeses and is at last available in the US. We would rank it right up there with Stilton, Roquefort and Gorgonzola. If you can't find *Cabrales* in your area, substitute one of those.

SERVES 6
½ teaspoon salt
6 five-ounce steaks
1 cup good dry red wine
1 cup stock, preferably veal stock (page 224)
4 ounces *Cabrales*, or other fine blue cheese
¼ cup cream

Heat a heavy-bottomed skillet until very hot and add the salt. Brown the steaks for about 5 minutes on each side, but do not cook all the way through. Remove the steaks from the skillet and add the wine, reducing it to about 2 Tablespoons. Stir in the stock and reduce by half.

Crumble in the cheese and pour in the cream. Stir to combine. When the cheese has melted and the sauce has bubbles all over the surface, return the meat and any juices accumulated with them to the pan. Turn the meat to coat with the sauce, and cook to desired doneness. Remove the steaks to a platter and taste the sauce for seasoning, adding more salt if necessary. The sauce should not be thick, but about the consistency of heavy cream. Pour the sauce over the steaks and serve immediately.

OXTAILS, JEREZ-STYLE
Rabo de buey jerezana

Tendida 6 is a restaurant in Jerez situated just across the street from the bull ring—facing Gate 6, in fact. There is a great tapas bar at the front of the restaurant, jammed with bullfight trivia and well worth a visit on its own. The restaurant itself serves a good range of Andaluz food, from the basic to the more ornate, ceremonial dinners. This is a version of an oxtail stew served there. It is a full-flavored dish, with the vegetables, meat and red wine slowly coming together during the cooking.

SERVES 6
¼ cup olive oil
Salt
Freshly ground black pepper
3 oxtails, cut into joints
2 leeks, white part only, cleaned and chopped
1 medium onion, peeled and chopped
3 carrots, chopped
2 celery stalks, chopped
3 cloves garlic, minced
2 cups red wine
2 cups stock, preferably veal stock (page 224)
2 bay leaves
3 sprigs parsley
3 sprigs thyme or ½ teaspoon dried thyme

Heat the oil in a large skillet with a lid. Sprinkle salt and pepper over the oxtails, brown them in the oil, remove with a slotted spoon and set aside.

Cook the leeks, onion, carrots, celery and garlic in the same skillet over medium heat until very soft. Stir in the wine, stock, bay, parsley and thyme. Bring to a boil, reduce heat and return the oxtails to the pan. Cover and simmer until very tender, 2 hours or more.

Remove the oxtails to a serving platter and keep warm. Pour the contents of the pan through a fine sieve into a bowl pushing down on the solids to extract as much sauce as possible. Pour sauce over the oxtails and serve immediately.

This dish can be made ahead. Cool the oxtails and the sauce separately. Refrigerate for up to 2 days, then reheat the oxtails in the sauce.

BEEF STEW, SEVILLE-STYLE
Estofado de buey a la sevillana

A definite Moorish influence here, almost like a Morrocan *tagine*. A beef stew that is exotic and, at the same time comforting and homey. Serve this with boiled rice or potatoes and a bottle of red Rioja.

SERVES 6
2 cups dry sherry
3 pounds stewing beef, cut into 2-inch cubes
4 Tablespoons olive oil
Salt
Freshly ground black pepper to taste
4 cloves garlic, sliced
2 one-inch pieces cinnamon stick
Zest of one orange
24 small pitted green olives, or green olives stuffed with pimiento

Begin preparation one day ahead. Combine the sherry and the beef in a glass or stainless steel bowl and refrigerate over night.

Remove the beef from the refrigerator, bring to room temperature and pat dry. Reserve the marinade. Heat the oil in a deep skillet. Brown the beef cubes in small batches. Season with small amounts of salt and pepper as they cook. Remove beef cubes when seared and set aside.

Cook the garlic in the remaining oil until golden. Pour in the reserved marinade and bring to a boil. Return the beef to the skillet. Add the cinnamon stick and orange zest. Reduce heat, cover and cook until tender, about 2 hours. Discard the cinnamon stick after the first hour.

Remove the meat with a slotted spoon to a deep serving platter and keep warm. Increase the heat under the sauce and add the olives. Cook the sauce to reduce to desired consistency. The sauce should be rather thin. Taste for seasoning. Pour the sauce and olives over the beef and serve at once.

TRIPE, MAXI'S-STYLE
Callos al Maxi's

Tripe has the reputation of being a restorative. Mexican restaurants feature it on Sunday morning to help dispel the effects of the night before. The French want their tripe at the end of a market day to refresh them for the evening to come. And in Madrid, a bowl of tripe stew is just the thing to revive you before going off to the discos until dawn. Maxi's, a bustling tapas bar near the Plaza Mayor, is an excellent place to find it.

SERVES 6 TO 8
2 pounds tripe
2 medium onions
2 heads of garlic, plus 2 garlic cloves, peeled
2 bay leaves
2 small serrano chilies
3 Tablespoons olive oil
5 ounces ham, cubed
5 ounces chorizo, cut into rounds
1 Tablespoon paprika
5 ounces blood sausage
2 cups of cooked garbanzo beans
Salt and freshly ground black pepper to taste

Begin preparation 24 hours ahead. Peel and halve 1 of the onions. Cut the tripe into 1-inch squares and put it into a large pot with the halved onion, 2 heads of garlic, bay leaves and 1 of the chilies. Cover with cold water and bring to a boil. Reduce heat and partially cover. Cook for four hours. Remove from the heat and allow to cool in the cooking liquid. Refrigerate overnight.

The next day, remove the tripe from the pot, reserving the liquid. Discard the onion, garlic, bay leaves and chili.

Heat the oil in a large skillet or ceramic casserole. Mince the remaining onion and garlic cloves and cook until golden. Mince the remaining chili, and add it to the skillet with the ham, chorizo and the tripe. Stir in the paprika, blood sausage and garbanzos. Pour enough of the reserved cooking liquid over to cover all ingredients. Season very lightly with salt and pepper, because the liquid is going to reduce a great deal during the cooking and the sausages will give off more of their flavor. Cook, uncovered, for 1½ hours.

Remove the blood sausage, slice into rounds and return to the pot. Taste again for salt and pepper. Add more liquid if necessary or, if there is too much liquid, increase heat to further reduce to reach the consistency of a thick stew. Serve directly from the skillet or ceramic casserole.

VEAL SHANKS, ARAGON-STYLE
Ternera asada a la aragonesa

Veal is eaten more often than beef in Spain. Spanish veal is butchered older and has a richer flavor than the usual American veal. The Spanish don't confine the calves to small stalls but allow them to feed in the field. These braised veal shanks are economical, but fancy enough for any dinner party.

SERVES 6

All-purpose flour

3 whole veal shanks (have butcher cut each into several pieces)

½ cup olive oil

Salt

Freshly ground black pepper
1 medium onion, minced
3 cloves garlic, minced
2 stalks celery, chopped
¼ cup fresh rosemary leaves
2 cups white wine

Lightly flour the veal shanks. Heat the olive oil in a large skillet and cook the veal, sprinkled with salt and pepper, for 15 minutes, until it begins to color. Remove the shanks. Add more oil to the skillet if necessary. Cook the onions, garlic and celery until they begin to color. Add the rosemary and wine. Bring the wine to a boil and return the veal shanks to the skillet. Cover the skillet and cook the veal until tender, about 2 hours.

Remove the veal to a deep platter. If you prefer a thicker sauce, boil the sauce to reduce. Taste for salt and pepper. Pour the sauce over the veal and serve. This dish is delicious served with rice to soak up some of the wonderful juices.

SAUSAGE AND BEANS
Butifarra amb mongetes

Although we use Castilian for the names of recipes throughout this book, we make an exception here. This is not just *Butifarra con judías*, sausages and beans. It is a very special Catalan eating experience. Spanish-style sausages are available in many Latin markets in the US, but if you can't find them, substitute a mild Italian sausage.

SERVES 6
1 pound dry Great Northern beans
1 small onion studded with 8 whole cloves
2 bay leaves
1 teaspoon salt
Six ¼ pound sausages
2 Tablespoons olive oil
Salt and pepper to taste

1 cup *allioli* (page 201)
2 Tablespoons parsley, finely minced

Begin preparation the day before, by soaking the beans in water overnight. The next day, drain the beans and put them into a pot, cover with cold water to 2 inches above the beans, and add the clove-studded onion and bay leaves. Bring to a boil. Skim off the foam. Reduce the heat and cook the beans, uncovered, for 45 minutes. Add the teaspoon of salt to the beans and continue to cook until tender. When done, remove the cloved onion and bay leaves. Partially drain the beans, leaving just a small amount of liquid.

Prick the sausages in several places. Grill or pan fry until done. Meanwhile, heat the olive oil and sauté the beans, seasoning to taste with salt and pepper. Divide the beans among 6 plates, put a sausage to the side and a dollop of allioli on the top. Sprinkle with the parsley and serve at once.

WHITE BEANS WITH SAUSAGE AND CHARD
Alubias estofadas

The paradores of Spain cannot only be counted on for a comfortable bed, often in a spectacular setting, but they offer typical local dishes as well. Sometimes, in an effort to cater to the tastes of tourists, these get a bit bland or over-refined. But, if your travel schedule is limited, it is possible to explore local cuisines in this way with some gusto. The parador in Mérida has an excellent reputation for local dishes. This wholesome, full-flavored bean and sausage stew, the perfect companion for a cold and rainy night, is a good example.

Note: Having your butcher crack the ham hocks will release rich flavors from the bone into the meat.

SERVES 6
1 pound dry Great Northern beans
1 pound ham hocks, cracked by your butcher
1 whole medium onion, plus 2 medium onions, minced
2 bay leaves

3 Tablespoons olive oil
3 cloves garlic, minced
½ pound chorizo
½ pound linguiça, Italian or blood sausages
3 large tomatoes, peeled, seeded and chopped
1 small bunch red chard, washed well and chopped
1 teaspoon salt
½ teaspoon freshly ground black pepper

Begin preparation 24 hours ahead by soaking the beans overnight in water. The next day drain the soaked beans and put into a large pot with the ham hocks, the whole onion and bay leaves, and cover with cold water to 3 inches above the beans. Bring to a boil. Reduce heat to moderate and cook the beans, uncovered, until tender. This may take as much as 2 hours. Season the beans during the last half hour of cooking with 1 or 2 teaspoons of salt. Don't season them at the beginning or they will be tough no matter how long you cook them.

Remove the ham hocks, onion and bay leaf from the beans. Discard the onion and bay leaf. Cut the tough outer skin from the ham hocks and discard it. Tear the ham meat into small pieces and set aside. Discard the bones.

Heat the oil, preferably in a ceramic casserole, and cook the garlic and minced onions until soft. Cut the sausages into rounds and add. (If they are the kind of sausages that will fall apart if cut into pieces when raw, cut into rounds after they have firmed during cooking.) Cook for about 5 minutes.

Stir in the tomatoes and cook for another 5 minutes but not to a paste. The tomatoes should still be juicy. Stir in the chard. Cook until the chard has wilted. Season with salt and pepper.

Add the cooked beans and any of their liquid, and the ham hock meat, and cook for another 30 minutes for all the flavors to mingle. Add water if the beans begin to dry or increase the heat if the beans are too soupy. Serve in flat soup plates.

Sweets and Desserts

CATALAN CHOCOLATE AND ALMOND CANDY
Catanias

Catanias are a specialty of Vilafranca del Penedés just south of Barcelona. There you will find them as individual almonds, caramelized and coated in white chocolate, then rolled in ground chocolate. For lazy cooks like us who don't want to hand dip each of the almonds, we came up with this version. They taste the same, just easier to achieve.

This candy makes an attractive gift. Wrap the whole circle of candy in clear or colored cellophane and tie it with a bow.

MAKES ABOUT 1½ POUNDS
½ pound whole almonds, with skins
½ pound sugar
½ pound white chocolate, in small pieces
2 Tablespoons ground sweetened chocolate

Have ready a buttered 12-inch pizza pan.

Heat a heavy skillet. Add the almonds and cook for 1 minute. Pour in the sugar. Stir and cook the almonds in the sugar as it melts. The almonds will start to pop and crack. Keep stirring and cooking over medium heat for about 3 to 5 minutes. You don't want the caramel to burn but it should get a very deep amber color.

Pour the almonds and caramel onto the prepared pizza pan and spread evenly. Allow to rest and set for 5 minutes.

Sprinkle the white chocolate pieces over the almonds, and as they melt, spread the chocolate smoothly with a spatula. When the chocolate has set, dust the top with the ground chocolate.

Break into pieces to serve. Keep tightly covered in a tin.

CHOCOLATE FLAN WITH MINT SAUCE
Toffe de chocolate con crema de menta

This specialty of the restaurant Ampurdán in Figueres is a chocolate lover's dream. A dense combination of chocolates that is part custard, part rich cake and part the best chocolate candy you've ever tasted.

Flan:
- 12 ounces bittersweet chocolate
- 1 cup sugar
- 12 ounces sweet butter
- 6 eggs
- 1 teaspoon cinnamon
- 2 Tablespoons dark rum

Sauce:
- 2 Tablespoon sugar
- ¼ cup *creme de menthe*
- 1 cup *creme fraiche*

Preheat oven to 375°. To prepare the *flan:* Melt the chocolate and cool slightly. In a separate bowl, cream together the sugar and butter. Add the eggs and mix well. Stir in the chocolate, cinnamon and rum.

Line a 9-inch round pan with a removable rim with buttered baking paper and cover the outside bottom and sides of the pan with foil so that there is no chance of water from the water bath seeping into it. Pour in the chocolate mixture. Cover the top of the pan lightly with foil.

Put the mold into a larger ovenproof container and pour boiling water half way up the sides of the mold. Bake for 30 minutes. Remove the foil top and bake for 10 minutes longer or until the top of the cake is fairly firm. (The top should not poof up, however.) Remove *flan* from the oven. Remove the mold from the water and let cool to room temperature. When cool, refrigerate for several hours or overnight.

To prepare the sauce: Dissolve the sugar in the *creme de menthe* and then stir into the creme fraiche. Allow the flavors to mingle several hours or overnight.

To serve, unmold the *flan* and slice into ½-inch thick wedges. Put slices on individual serving plates and pour a little of the sauce over or around the *flan*.

CRISP SPANISH PASTRIES
Churros

One morning we were walking across a plaza in Toledo during a local festival. The churro makers were doing a lively business. You could buy the churros individually, or they would string several on a long willow reed for you to carry home.

Churros, served with thick cups of hot chocolate, are also a common Spanish breakfast, especially after a long night, or an afternoon snack.

SERVES 1 TO 5
Rind of 1 lemon
1 cup water
1 cup all-purpose flour
1 teaspoon salt
1 egg
Oil for deep frying
Powdered sugar

Grate the lemon rind and combine with the water in a medium sauce pan. Bring to a boil and stir in the flour and salt. Stir while cooking over a medium heat until the mixture pulls away from the sides of the pan. Remove from the heat and stir in the egg, mixing until smooth.

Heat the oil in a deep fryer or skillet until it is about 360°. Put the churro mixture into a pastry bag fitted with a medium-wide fluted tip. Hold the bag over the hot oil and force the pastry out. As it flows out, cut with a sharp knife into 4-inch lengths—longer if your pan will hold them. Or you can curl the pastry so the ends come together to create circles.

Fry until golden. Remove from the oil and drain on paper towels. Dust with the powdered sugar and serve immediately.

CUSTARD WITH BURNT SUGAR TOPPING
Crema catalana

The Catalan version of the popular Spanish *flan* takes this dessert to a new level. In traditional Catalan restaurants, the striking aroma of burning sugar coming from the kitchen inspires diners to order this simple, rich custard with its caramelized surface. It is so much fun to use your spoon to break through the crust into the creaminess below.

SERVES 6
Rind of 1 lemon
1 cinnamon stick
4 cups milk
8 egg yolks
½ cup sugar
2 Tablespoons cornstarch
Granulated sugar

Combine lemon rind, cinnamon and milk in a heavy-bottomed sauce pan. Bring to a boil. Remove from the heat and let rest for 30 minutes.

Meanwhile beat together the egg yolks, sugar and corn starch. Strain the milk, discarding the lemon peel and cinnamon stick, and add one cup of the milk to the eggs and beat. Return the rest of the milk to the sauce pan. Add the egg mixture to the milk in the sauce pan and cook slowly over low heat, stirring until thickened. The custard should coat a spoon. Pour into individual, heat-proof serving bowls and allow to cool, then refrigerate.

To caramelize the top: In Spain there is a special branding iron for making *Crema catalana*—a round iron disk at the end of a long handle. These are available in some kitchen shops in the US. To use them, sprinkle the top of each bowl of custard generously and evenly with granulated sugar. Heat the *crema* iron over the gas or electric burner of your stove, or over a fire, until red hot. Press the iron gently against the sugar. The sugar will smoke dramatically while caramelizing the custard's surface.

If you can't find a *crema* iron, here are three options:

Option 1. First, sprinkle the top of each bowl of custard generously and evenly with granulated sugar. Then place each bowl close under a broiler to brown the top.

Option 2. This method is often used in American restaurants: First, sprinkle the top of each bowl of custard generously and evenly with granulated sugar. Then, using a small, hand-held propane flame, quickly scorch the surface of each serving.

Option 3. Do not sprinkle the sugar over the custard. Cover a baking sheet with wax paper. Roughly measure the surface of the custard servings and draw this shape onto the wax paper, 1 outline for each serving. Heat 1 cup of sugar with 1 Tablespoon water in a heavy pan and cook until a medium dark caramel is formed. Using a fork, lift caramel from the pan and quickly make a delicate lattice work of the caramel within the circles on the wax paper. When the caramel has cooled and firmed, peel away the paper and place a caramel on the surface of each custard just before serving.

Note: This recipe also makes a delicious *crema catalana* ice cream. Simply follow the instructions for the custard, and freeze it to ice cream according to your ice-cream machine's instructions.

FRESH SQUEEZED ORANGE JUICE WITH FRUIT
Zumo de naranja con frutas frescas

A balloon glass half-filled with sliced fresh kiwi, or tiny wild strawberries, or red ripe raspberries, floating in freshly squeezed orange juice is one of the most welcome and refreshing desserts you can offer. A dramatic presentation makes it even more inviting.

> Sliced kiwi, sliced strawberries, fresh raspberries,
>   sliced figs, blueberries or any good combination
>   of fresh fruits in season
> Freshly squeezed orange juice

Slice or otherwise prepare the fresh fruits and divide among individual glasses or bowls. Cover with the orange juice and serve immediately. Don't let the fruit stand in the juice any length of time or it will begin to wilt. In Spain a bowl of granulated sugar is served with this dessert for each guest to add to his or her taste.

MUSICIAN'S TART
Tarta de músico

The Spanish love music and recognize the worth of musicians. In the past, if a household was very poor, they might not be able to give street musicians any money, or perhaps little food. But there was usually some dried fruit and nuts around and the musicians would be served a bowl to share. In time, this became an informal dessert for casual meals and was known as *postre de músico*, or musician's dessert. This tart is a modern development, using the ingredients of the traditional *músico*. It is proper to eat it with your fingers just as you would the original *postre de músico*.

SERVES 8

Pastry:
    1½ cups flour
    2 Tablespoons sugar
    ½ cup sweet butter, cut in pieces
    1 egg, separated
    3 Tablespoons ice water

Filling:
    1 cup sugar
    ½ cup sweet butter
    ½ cup whipping cream
    ½ cup pine nuts
    ½ cup sliced almonds
    ¼ cup dried mission figs, minced
    ¼ cup pitted prunes, minced
    ½ cup raisins
    1 Tablespoon brandy
    1 teaspoon almond extract

To prepare the pastry: Combine the flour and sugar in the food processor. Cut the butter into the flour with a few pulses of the food processor motor. Add the egg yolk and quickly mix. Add the water, one Tablespoon at a time, pulsing, until the mixture holds together.

Turn the pastry out onto a flat surface and gather into a ball. Flatten and roll into a circle to fit a 9-inch tart pan with a removable rim. Put the rolled dough into the tart pan. When forming the rim of the tart, fold back the dough to create a double-thick rim. Refrigerate the pastry for 30 minutes.

Preheat oven to 350°. Line the pastry shell with waxed paper and fill it with dried beans or pie weights. Bake for 15 minutes. Remove the waxed paper and beans. Brush the baked shell with beaten egg white. Bake for 10 minutes more. Remove from the oven.

To prepare the filling: Increase oven temperature to 375°. Cook sugar and butter in a heavy bottomed pan, stirring until sugar dissolves and begins to caramelize. Cook to a dark golden. Pour in the whipping cream and mix well. Stir in the nuts, fruits, brandy and almond extract. Remove from the heat.

Pour filling into the tart shell and smooth the top. Put into the oven and cook for 20 minutes. Remove from the oven. Allow the tart to rest for about 2 hours until firm. Remove the rim and serve.

GALICIAN ALMOND TART
Tarta de Santiago

We first encountered this type of dessert in Madrid, where several restaurants serve a *Tarta de Santiago* that is actually a dense cake or torte. When we later visited Santiago de Compostela, we again tried *Tarta de Santiago*, and this time it was a wonderful tart, as given here. A thin slice of this tart, accompanied by fresh fruit, makes a perfect dessert.

SERVES 8

1 recipe *Tarta de músico* pastry (page 303) with ½ teaspoon almond extract added
⅓ pound whole almonds
4 large eggs
1 cup granulated sugar
½ teaspoon cinnamon
Grated zest of 1 lemon
½ cup thinly sliced almonds
Powdered sugar

Preheat oven to 350°. Prepare the tart crust following the *Tarta de músico* pastry recipe, adding ½ teaspoon almond extract to the ice water.

Increase oven temperature to 425°. Grind the whole almonds very finely in a food processor or mortar. Beat the eggs, granulated sugar, cinnamon and lemon zest until thick. Stir in the ground almonds. Pour the filling into the prepared tart shell and scatter the sliced almonds over the top.

Bake for 25 minutes or until the crust is uniformly golden. A toothpick should test clean when inserted in the middle of the tart. Allow to cool for 15 minutes, then sprinkle lavishly with powdered sugar. Serve warm or at room temperature.

GYPSY'S ARM
Brazo de Gitano

The top of this rolled cake is sometimes covered with cream and put under the broiler to brown the top, suggesting the browned arm of the Gypsy. Fillings vary from thick pastry creams to flavored whipped creams.

SERVES 8

Pastry:
- 5 eggs, separated
- ¾ cup sugar
- Grated zest of one lemon
- ½ teaspoon baking powder
- Salt
- ¾ cup cake flour
- Powdered sugar

Filling:
- 1 ⅓ cups cream
- 1 cup semi-sweet chocolate chips
- 1 Tablespoon brandy
- 1 Tablespoon Spanish anise, or other anise liqueur
- 2 Tablespoons powdered sugar
- 1 Tablespoon cocoa

Preheat oven to 375°. Beat the whites of 5 eggs until they form stiff peaks. Set aside. Beat the egg yolks with the sugar, lemon zest, baking powder and a small pinch of salt until thick and lemon colored.

Fold egg whites gently into the yolk mixture. Fold in the flour a third at a time. Do not overmix or you will loose the volume you have created in the eggs. Pour dough into an ungreased, paper-lined 10 x 15-inch pan with a 1-inch rim. Bake for 10 to 12 minutes or until the cake is golden and has begun to pull away from the sides of the pan.

Have ready a clean towel lightly sprinkled with powdered sugar. Take the cake from the oven and immediately turn it out onto the towel and remove the paper. Roll the cake in the towel to form a 15-inch long roll. The towel will be inside the rolled cake. Let cool.

Meanwhile prepare the filling. Warm ⅓ cup of the cream in a small pan. Gently melt the chocolate chips in the cream. Pour in the brandy and anise liqueur and let cool.

Whip the remaining cream until stiff. Fold the cooled chocolate mixture into the whipped cream. Refrigerate for 30 minutes until the mixture begins to firm.

Unroll the cake and spread the chocolate cream over the surface keeping a 1-inch wide uncovered border all around. Carefully roll the cake and put onto a platter. Combine 2 Tablespoons of powdered sugar with the Tablespoon of cocoa power and sprinkle over the cake. Chill, covered, until serving. The cake is firm enough to cut after 1 hour.

PEAR TART WITH WALNUTS AND CHEESE
Tarta de peras, nueces y queso

'The best pears in Spain come from Lérida,' we were told. This rustic, not-too-sweet pear, cheese and walnut-covered tart convinced us.

SERVES 8

Pastry:　　　　2 cups all-purpose flour
　　　　　　　1 cup sweet butter
　　　　　　　Salt
　　　　　　　3 to 5 Tablespoons of ice water
　　　　　　　1 Tablespoon granulated sugar

Filling: 5 large pears, about 3 pounds, peeled,
                            cored and cut into ½-inch cubes
                    1 cup of walnut pieces, coarsely chopped
                    ½ cup sugar
                    ½ cup grated sharp cheese (aged manchego,
                            asiago or parmesan)
                    Grated zest of one lemon

Put the flour into the food processor work bowl. Cut the butter into pieces. Add the butter to the flour with a pinch of salt and pulse a few times to distribute and cut the butter finer. Add the cold water a Tablespoon at a time, pulsing, until the butter is in tiny pieces and the dough is dampened.

Remove dough from the food processor, gather it into 2 balls and wrap them in plastic wrap. Flatten the dough. Refrigerate for 1 hour.

Uncover one of the dough flats and roll out on a floured surface. Roll into a 12-inch circle. Carefully transfer the dough to a 10-inch tart pan with a removable rim and form the pie shell.

Preheat the oven to 400°. Combine all the ingredients for the filling and pour into the prepared shell.

Roll out the remaining dough flat into a 12-inch circle. Cover the filling with the dough. Pinch the bottom and top dough overhangs together and tuck under attractively. Slit the top of the tart with a sharp knife in 2 or 3 places. Sprinkle the top of the tart with the Tablespoon of sugar.

Put the tart on a pizza pan so if any juices run over they don't go all over your oven. Put the tart in the oven and bake for 15 minutes. Reduce the heat to 350° and bake for about 45 minutes more, or until the tart is golden and the fruit is tender. Serve warm without cream.

PEARS POACHED IN WINE
Peras al vino

This is a favorite dessert in Spain. The addition of the star anise is our innovation. We like to serve a whole pear in a pool of syrup with a few pink peppercorns sprinkled over the top and a sprig of mint on the side.

SERVES 6

2 cups Port, red wine, or a sweet muscat wine

1 cup sugar

2 sticks cinnamon

6 star anise

6 ripe pears, Bosc, Comice or Anjou, depending on the season

Combine the wine, sugar, cinnamon and the star anise in a non-reactive pan. Bring to a boil, reduce heat and cook for 20 minutes.

Peel the pears, leaving the stems attached. Core the pears from the bottom, but not all the way through, being careful to leave the top and stem intact. Add the pears to the cooking liquid and cook for about 30 minutes, turning the pears carefully from time to time so all sides have absorbed color and flavor from the liquid.

Remove the pears from the liquid when they feel tender when pierced with a fork. Arrange the pears on a deep serving platter. It may be necessary to cut a slice from the bottom of the pear so that it will sit upright.

Remove the cinnamon sticks and star anise from the liquid and reserve. Boil the sauce to thicken, carefully, so as not to burn it. Pour the syrup over the pears and garnish with the cinnamon and star anise. Serve at once, or cool and serve at room temperature. Can be refrigerated to serve later, but bring to room temperature before serving.

QUINCE PASTE
Mermelada de membrillo

Each fall we get a windfall of quince from the trees of friends. The Spanish make this quince paste into a delicious dessert—quince paste with white cheese and walnuts. So simple and a perfect ending to a meal.

3 pounds quince, unpeeled
3$\frac{1}{3}$ cups granulated sugar

Cut the unpeeled quince into sixths and remove cores. Put into a heavy pot, cover with water and cook until tender, about 1 hour. Drain the quince, reserving the water.

In a blender or food processor, puree the quince and put through a fine sieve. Return to the pot, stir in the sugar, and $\frac{1}{3}$ cup of the reserved cooking liquid. Cook over a medium low heat, stirring continuously, until the mixture thickens and turns a deep amber in color.

Pour into a shallow, 9 x 9-inch glass dessert mold and spread evenly. Cool, then cover tightly and refrigerate. Allow to set until firm. Cut into thin pieces at serving time.

RICE PUDDING
Arroz con leche

One wet June evening we trudged several blocks through the streets of Madrid, propelled by new friends who had appointed themselves our guides. We were headed toward what they insisted was the best rice pudding in Madrid, and in all of Spain. Alas, there were far too many little bars to slip into for other research and we arrived after our destination had closed. We returned the next day to Bar Neru and tasted the *arroz con leche*, which was, indeed, excellent. A very nurturing kind of dish in any language.

SERVES 8

1 cup short-grain rice
²/₃ cup water
1 cinnamon stick
Peel of one lemon, in one piece if possible
½ cup sugar
Pinch of salt
6 cups of milk
Ground cinnamon

Put the rice, water, the cinnamon stick, lemon peel, sugar and salt in a pan and bring to a boil. Cover and simmer over low heat for about 10 minutes or until most of the water has been absorbed. Add the milk and continue to cook over low heat, stirring occasionally until most of the milk—but not all— is absorbed and the rice is very tender. This should take about 1 hour. Remove and discard the cinnamon and lemon peel.

Pour into a glass bowl, cool to room temperature, and refrigerate. Serve in pretty bowls very lightly sprinkled with cinnamon. Too much cinnamon on top of the pudding dulls it.

Spanish Wine Grapes

The international wine market is increasingly dominated by a handful of what are called the 'classic' wine grapes. What that means to most is the grapes associated with French wine. Chardonnay, Sauvignon Blanc, Cabernet Sauvignon, Pinot Noir, Merlot and, to a lesser degree Chenin Blanc, are all grapes that have been grown for centuries in France. Along with the German varietals, Gewurztraminer and Riesling, these grapes constitute for most the entire world of wine grapes.

That is a pity, for there are delightful wines made from dozens of other grapes. The wine grapes found in Spain belong to that class of grape that some have called meridional, or southern. The southern French wine growers in the Rhone and Provence share many grape varietals with the Spanish, sometimes under other names.

The entire question of nomenclature for Spanish grapes is a cloudy area. However, the following is a brief summary of the Spanish wine grapes, where they are grown and some synonyms.

RED WINE GRAPES

Bobal is grown in the Levante and can be made into a refreshing red wine for early consumption. It is also often made as a rosé.

Cariñena is widely planted in Aragon and Catalonia where it produces highly-tannic wines, very rich in color and high in alcohol. It is known in Rioja as the Mazuelo, where it is used as a blending grape with lighter Riojas.

Garnacha is grown all over Spain and well up into southern France. It is sometimes called Garnacha Tinta to avoid confusion with the Garnacha Blanca. It is occasionally spelled Garnacho, undergoing a mysterious sex change for no apparent purpose. When properly made, Garnacha can produce fruity, very attractive, young red wines and rosés. It is an important blending element in the Rioja red wines.

Graciano is planted almost entirely in Rioja and is important in the blend for Rioja reds. It has a delicate, perfumy aroma and is very flavorful.

Monastrell is widely planted over most of Spain, probably exceeded only by Garnacha. It is especially important in the area of Valencia, in

Catalonia and in Aragon. It is used chiefly as a blending grape, contributing alcohol and body.

Tempranillo is Spain's most important—from the standpoint of wine quality—red wine grape. It is planted in Rioja, Navarre and in some limited areas of Catalonia, where it is called *Ull de Llebre*. In La Mancha it is called *Cencibel*. It produces an elegant, perfumy wine with many of the aroma and flavor characteristics of the Pinot Noir of Burgundy and California.

WHITE WINE GRAPES

Airén is grown chiefly in La Mancha-Castilla, in Extremadura and to a limited degree in Valencia. Always regarded as a blending grape, vintners are discovering that, properly made, it can produce pleasant, fruity wines for early consumption.

Albarino is a low-yielding grape grown mostly in Galacia and Portugal. It yields a delightful, refreshing wine sharing characteristics with Riesling and Viognier. Albarino has become a trendy—and pricey—restaurant wine in the US.

Malvasia is a mystery grape. There are grapes grown all over Spain called Malvasia, and it is one of the most important grapes in the light, fruity white wines of the Canary Islands. It was once an important part of the oak-aged whites of Rioja, but is seldom used there now.

Moscatel is planted along the Mediterranean coast and used in dessert wines, especially around Tarragona, and further south around Valencia and Málaga. It is probably the same grape known elsewhere as Muscat of Alexandria.

Palomino is the chief grape of Jerez for sherry production. It is grown in small quantities elsewhere in Spain, producing unremarkable wines.

Parellada is an important grape in Catalonia, where it produces light, rather delicate table wines and is an important part of the *cava* sparkling wine blend.

Pedro Ximénez is widely grown in southern Spain where it is used in sweet sherry and other dessert wines. Some believe it is a distant cousin of Riesling.

Torrontés is grown in Galacia where it is used to make a fairly neutral white wine with a nutty tone. It is also an important grape in Argentina.

Verdejo is increasingly important as a quality white wine grape. Verdejo from Rueda in particular is a fresh tasting wine with apple and pear aromas.

Viura is fast becoming the most important white table wine grape of Spain. It is grown in Rioja where it produces crisp, refreshing, fruity white wines for early drinking. It is being planted around Valencia, in Navarre and Aragon, as well as in Catalonia where it is called *Macabeo*.

Xarel-lo is important in Catalonia as part of the *cava* blend. It is pronounced Char-el-o.

Bibliography

Andrews, Coleman. *Catalan Cuisine*. New York: Atheneum, 1988.

Asher, Gerald. *On Wine*. New York: Random House, 1982.

Atkinson, William C. *A History of Spain and Portugal*. London: Penguin, 1960.

Begg, Desmond, ed. *Wine Buyers' Guide to Spain*. London: Wine Buyers Guides, Ltd., 1988.

———. *Travelers' Wine Guide: Spain*. New York: Sterling, 1990.

Braker, Flo. *The Simple Art of Perfect Baking*. New York: William Morrow, 1985.

Brown, Edward Espe. *Tassajara Bread Book*, Berkeley: Shambala, 1970.

Burns, Tom. *Spain: Everything Under the Sun*. Madrid: Passport Books, 1988.

Busquets, Jordi. *Sardinas*. Barcelona: Ediciones Baussán, 1983.

Casas, Penelope. *Delicioso: The Regional Cooking of Spain*. New York: Alfred A Knopf, 1996.

———. *Discovering Spain: An Uncommon Guide*. New York: Alfred A Knopf, 1992.

———. *Tapas*. New York: Alfred A Knopf, 1986.

Cervantes, Miguel de. *Don Quixote*, trans. Peter Motteux. New York: Modern Library Edition, 1950.

Crow, John A. *Spain: The Root and the Flower*. Berkeley: University of California Press, 1985.

David, Elizabeth. *Italian Food*. London: Penguin, 1954.

Del Conte, Anna. *Gastronomy of Italy*. New York: Prentice-Hall, 1987.

Delgado, Carlos. *Diccionario de Gastronomía*. Madrid: Alianza Editorial, 1985.

Domingo, Xavier and Hussenot, Pierre. *The Taste of Spain*. Paris: Flammarion, 1992.

Duijker, Hubrecht. *The Wines of Rioja*. London: Mitchell Beazley, 1985.

Dumas, Alexandre. *From Paris to Cádiz*, trans. A.E. Murch. London: Peter Owen Ltd., 1958.

Edwards, John. *The Roman Cookery of Apicius*. Point Roberts, WA.: Hartley & Marks, 1984.

Freeling, Nicolas. *The Cook Book*. Boston: David R. Godine, 1972

Gray, Patience. *Honey From a Weed*. New York: Harper & Row, 1986.

Greene, Graham. *Monsignor Quixote*. New York, Simon & Schuster, 1982.

Grunfeld, Frederic, V. *Wild Spain*. New York: Prentice Hall, 1988.

Hooper, John. *The Spaniards*. London: Penguin Books, 1986.

Hornedo, Christina. *Come y Calla*. Madrid: Ediciones Akal, S.A., 1984.

Isusi, José María Busca. *Traditional Basque Cooking*. Reno: University of Nevada Press, 1987.

Jeffs, Julian. *Sherry*. London: Faber & Faber, 1982.

Lang, Jennifer Harvey, ed. *Larousse Gastronomique*. New York: Crown, 1988.

Lichine, Alexis. *New Encyclopedia of Wines & Spirits*. New York: Alfred A. Knopf, 1985.

Livesey, Herbert Bailey. *The American Express Pocket Guide to Spain*. New York: Prentice-Hall, 1988.

Lladonosa, Josep. *I Giro el Libro de la Cocina Catalana*. Madrid: Alianza Editorial, 1988.

Luján, Néstor and Tin. *La Cucina Moderna a Catalunya*. Madrid: Espasa-Calpe, S.A., 1985.

Luján, Néstor, et al. *Allegro Vivace*. San Sadurni de Noya: Freixenet, n.d.

McConnell, Carol and Malcolm. *The Mediterranean Diet: Wine, Pasta, Olive Oil and a Long, Healthy Life*. New York: W.W. Norton, 1987.

Mey, Wim. *Sherry*. The Netherlands: Asjoburo Press, 1988.

Morton, H. V. *A Stranger in Spain*. New York: Dodd, Mead & Co., 1955.

O'Brien, Kate. *Farewell Spain*. London: Virago Press, 1987.

Pritchett, V.S. *Marching Spain*. London: Hogarth Press, 1988.

Ranxets: La Cuina a Torredembarra. (No author listed) Tarragona: Edicions El Medol, 1990.

Read, Jan. *The Wines of Spain*. London: Faber & Faber, 1982.

Read, Jan and Manjón, Maite. *The Wine and Food of Spain*. Boston: Little, Brown, 1987.

Root, Waverly. *Food*. New York: Simon & Schuster: Fireside Books, 1980.

Sagarriga, Cristina Cebrian. *El Vino Albariño: Hijo Legítimo del Valle del Salnes*. Madrid: Self-published, 1988.

Scarlett, Elizabeth, ed. *Let's Go: The Budget Guide to Spain, Portugal & Morocco*. New York: Harvard Student Agencies, Inc., 1995.

Stamm, James R. *A Short History of Spanish Literature*. New York: Anchor, 1967.

Tannahill, Reay. *Food in History*. New York: Crown Publishers, 1988.

Torres, Marimar. *The Catalan Country Kitchen*. Berkeley: Aris, 1992.

———. *The Spanish Table*. New York: Doubleday, 1986.

Torres, Miguel A. *The Distinctive Wines of Catalonia*. Barcelona: Servicios Editoriales, S.A., 1986.

———*Wines and Vineyards of Spain*. Barcelona: Editorial Blume, 1982; San Francisco Wine Appreciation Guild, 1985.

Vélez, Carmen. *El Libro de los Pescados*. Madrid: Alianza Editorial, 1987.

Walker, Ted. *In Spain*. London: Secker & Warburg, 1987.

Recipe Index